SWEDISH CONTRIBUTIONS
TO MODERN THEOLOGY

Swedish Contributions to Modern Theology

With Special Reference to Lundensian Thought

Nels F. S. Ferré

with a new chapter,
"Developments in Swedish Theology, 1939–1966"
by WILLIAM A. JOHNSON

HARPER TORCHBOOKS
Harper & Row, Publishers
New York, Evanston, and London

To the memory of my father, the Reverend Frans Ferré, for fifty years a minister to Swedish people.

SWEDISH CONTRIBUTIONS TO MODERN THEOLOGY
Copyright © 1967 by Nels F. S. Ferré.
Chapter VI copyright © 1967 by William A. Johnson.
Preface to the Torchbook edition copyright © 1967 by Nels F. S. Ferré.
Printed in the United States of America.

This book was originally published in 1939 by Harper & Brothers.

All rights reserved. No part of this book may be used or reproduced in any manner whatsoever without written permission except in the case of brief quotations embodied in critical articles and reviews. For information address Harper & Row, Publishers, Incorporated, New York, N.Y. 10016.

First HARPER TORCHBOOK edition published 1967 by Harper & Row, Publishers, Incorporated, 49 East 33rd Street, New York, N.Y. 10016.

CONTENTS

PREFACE TO THE TORCHBOOK EDITION, 1967   vii

I. TOWARD AN UNDERSTANDING OF MODERN SWEDISH THEOLOGY   1

II. THEOLOGICAL METHODOLOGY   34
Introduction, 34

   I. *The Task and Scope of the Philosophy of Religion*, 37
      A. The Transcendental Method in Relation to Theology, 38
      B. The Transcendental Deduction of Religion, 41

   II. *The Task and Scope of Theology*, 46
      A. Theology and Science, 47
      B. Theology and Psychology, 51
      C. Theology and History, 54
      D. Theology and Knowledge, 69

   III. *The Methodological Relation of Philosophical to Theological Ethics*, 75
      Conclusion, 89

III. THE RELATION OF GOD TO MAN   95

   I. *The Idea of God*, 95
      A. God as the Subject of Faith, 95
      B. The Centrality of the Christ-deed, 99
      C. The Regions beyond the Rational, 102
      D. God as *Agape*, 104
      E. The Meaning of Holiness, 130
      F. The Problem of Evil in the Light of Faith, 132
      G. The Relation of Revelation to Nature and to History, 136
      H. Faith's Dynamic Synthesis, 138

   II. *The Idea of Man*, 141
      A. *Coram deo*, 143
         1. The Nature of Man before God, 143
         2. The Function of the Law, 150
         3. The Religious View of the Atonement, 153
         4. The New Interest in Eschatology, 165
         5. Immortality or Resurrection, 172
      B. *Coram hominibus*, 175
         1. Religion and Ethics, 175
      C. The Church and Culture, 189
         1. The Church as the Continuity of the Christian Consciousness, 189
         2. The Church and the Crises of Culture, 191

IV. Suggestions Toward a Philosophic Critique	198
V. Some Problems Connected with Christianity as *Agape*	219
VI. Developments in Swedish Theology, 1939—1966	242

Introduction, 242

   I. Constructive Developments in Contemporary Swedish Theology, 247
      A. Luther Studies (and Motif Research), 248
      B. Methodological Questions, 260
      C. Gustaf Wingren's Systematic Theology, 270
      D. Biblical Studies, 284
         1. Biblical Criticism, 286
         2. The Theory of Divine Kingship, 287

   II. Additional Developments in Swedish Theology, 288
      A. Special Scandinavian Theologico-Historical Problems, 289
      B. Continued Research on Luther, 290
      C. Continued Trend toward Less Theological Parochialism, 291
      D. Roman Catholic-Lutheran Conversations, 292
      E. Greater Appreciation of the Role of Søren Kierkegaard in Scandinavian Theology and Church Life, 292
      F. Renewed Discussion of Methodological Questions, 293

Bibliography, 296
Index, 303

PREFACE TO THE TORCHBOOK EDITION, 1967

At the time of the original publication of *Swedish Contributions to Modern Theology* I had no idea that interest in the subject would accumulate to the point that *agape* would be common currency in theological commerce. Accordingly, there has been a steady clamor for a new edition. My alert publishers, with their ears tuned to theological need, frequently suggested that I bring the volume up to date. When I finally considered doing so it occurred to me that Professor William Johnson of Drew University, having earned his doctorate in Lund, would be conversant with the modern situation in the kind of detail that would take me a long time to acquire. He readily agreed to write a chapter that would cover theological trends to the present. For me that meant principally an adequate dealing with the powerful works of Gustaf Wingren and with the Swedish Biblical scholarship that has excited Old Testament scholars especially for years.

I knew Professor Wingren as a young instructor when I was working on my own doctoral dissertation at the University of Lund. He was then considered to be the heir apparent to Anders Nygren, which indeed he turned out to be. In theological chairs the German and Swedish tradition is for the new occupant to demolish his predecessor's argument. Wingren, the vigorous theological taurus, has met his great trainer in the open arena for the decisive conflict. Now is the perfect time to republish this book, just when the struggle to the theological death is coming to a consummation—a struggle which will involve maximum encounter not only of the two chief combatants but also of the filled stadium of fans who will rush into the field to join in the free-for-all. Nygren in his method used mostly Kant's critical philosophy for a historic basis, and the logico-empirical method of the then reigning Axel Hägerström for the modern setting. (Hägerström is only now being translated and written about in English!) Existentialism was also abroad in Sweden, but its contribution was absorbed mostly by the Lundensians' insistence that concrete contents of faith could be only decisions of faith in actual history. Thus Nygren, concisely and fortuitously, incorporated three main philosophic strains in his theological method: he used philosophy to verify the form of religion as a necessary dimension of human experience; existential faith to make religion supreme in its own domain; and theology as rigorous descriptive discipline, a "science" at the end of the process.

This formidable combination Wingren challenged, even making philosophy an alien and not a servant in the house of God. Mighty were the blows he struck in the spirit of his Lutheran heritage and even of modern philosophy. Nygren, however, with great breadth of interest and scholarship and without forsaking his original redoubt, is returning to the defense of his position, after many years of preoccupation with ecumenical matters, with the aid of no less a philosophy of modernity than that of Ludwig Wittgenstein himself. Those of us who have had a foretaste of the depth and reach of Nygren's new work and theological method know that the forthcoming engagement will be at the very center of both human and theological interest.

Professor Johnson devotedly takes the side of Wingren. From working with Professor Wingren at close range over many years on the World Council of Churches' Commission on Christ and his Church, I consider Wingren, along with Edmund Schlinck and Thomas Torrance, to be one of the most profound and patient (if not downright stubborn) of thinkers and I foresee mighty rejoinders in the ongoing battle of the giants. Professor Nygren will need no help; he was the Chairman of our Commission! But neither will Wingren.

If I were to write critiques once again for the new edition they would be basically unchanged. The original edifice of Lundensian theology, method and content, stands the same today strong and steady, buttressed by volumes of Biblical commentaries to support the structure. What Nygren, Aulén, and Bring say to me basically with their philosophical method is that man cannot escape the dimension of the ultimate. Philosophy can show what man must ask concerning the meaning of life as a whole. The Kantian system asked questions concerning theoretical, practical and aesthetic knowledge, *a priori* and *sui generis*. Kant, of course, never fully deduced the categories, particularly not the last two, but whatever different kinds of answers we give to these aspects of life and knowledge, the meaning of it all remains man's inescapable burden. The Lundensians hold that this presuppositional question cannot be answered by knowledge, and cannot be controlled by reason or experience. Thus they attack metaphysics as a false faith that cannot substitute for religious decision. In his freedom man must answer by faith. Most of his answers have come in the terms of the great religions of the world, finding their faith, for instance, in the motif of the karmic law of deed and consequence, in the motif of the law or torah of the Hebrew faith, or in the motif of *agape* in the Christian faith. Theology neither produces nor proves faith, but rather describes the actual historic faiths.

Does philosophy have a needed place in this scheme? Nygren cries yes; Wingren, no. The question is, first, whether man needs to justify the integrity of his choice of faith by his most creative and critical thinking or whether even his choice must remain completely justified by faith; and, second, whether man has a responsibility to remove for others needless intellectual roadblocks to the faith they need. Can there be a *warranted* faith, which, remaining faith, can make man whole, or must faith as faith remain beyond the reach of reason? Does faith require man's whole response including his integral use of reason, or does faith itself afford man the only possible whole response? Do I believe in order to know, do I know in order to believe, or do I believe and therefore know? Or is there, as I personally believe, some still fuller answer to this basic question? *Swedish Contributions to Modern Theology* presented the Lundensian theologians' mighty approach to the problem; Professor Wingren has given a resounding answer. Now the encounter begins afresh and at a deeper level still!

Please permit me here to call attention to my careful critique of Nygren's interpretation of *agape*. Most writers on the subject have failed to differentiate our positions. I appreciate profoundly what

Nygren has done in setting forth the meaning and history of *agape* in *Agape and Eros,* and yet I feel he has by no means taken full advantage of his own position. When *The Theology of Anders Nygren* is published, in the near future (in the *Library of Living Theology*), both my immense appreciation and my basic suggestions for further use will be more fully revealed, but both are already available in the present volume. I am of course delighted that material which has proved of such widespread and lasting value will once more become generally available, enriched in the context of what has happened since the original publication and of what is now about to take place. I am deeply indebted to Professor Johnson for his help, to Mrs. Johnson for the typing of his chapter, and to Mrs. Paul Read, my secretary, for the final typing. To the Religious Books Department of Harper and Row I remain personally thankful for their every courtesy and for their continued confidence and support. For any contribution I am allowed to make I am most thankful to God whom, after a lifetime of critical thinking I still find far from dead!

N. F. S. F.
Scholar-in-residence

Parsons College
February 10, 1966

CHAPTER I

TOWARD AN UNDERSTANDING OF MODERN
SWEDISH THEOLOGY

Historically, Sweden is a land of theological conservatism. It is a land of religious seriousness. The Swedish people, to a great extent self-examining and conscientious often to the point of anxiety, as a rule either reject traditional religion with painful indifference or pugnacious radicalism, or, according to their degree of understanding and ability, worry and watch over its every aspect with a deep personal concern. Sweden is a land where theological literature is read both intensively and extensively. This conservatism is strongest, on the whole, in priestly circles, but has deep roots in the piety of the common people, until recently catechetically trained to orthodoxy throughout the entire compulsory educational system. As a whole, progressive theological thought, or thought diverging from the general viewpoint of the Lutheran Church, has been met either by heated opposition or by deliberate isolation. The emotional climate, religiously speaking, has been of the nature common to all communities bred in an absolutistic doctrinal authoritarianism. The dominating theological tendency, whether in the State Church or in the comparatively small, though active, free churches, has been continually in line with Lutheran orthodoxy, or, at least, in line with traditionalistic supernaturalism. Among all religious circles, except for a few emancipated thinkers, the Biblical world-view, seen through a Pauline-Lutheran evangelicalism, has formed the dominating religious background. In the sense of a traditional conservatism, unopened to the main currents of liberal thought, Sweden can claim, rightfully as well as literally, a true apostolic succession.

In view of the world-famous scholars which Sweden has produced in practically every branch of the natural sciences, the paucity of outstanding theologians, or, for that matter, of independent philosophers, is glaringly apparent. Although the reasons for this dearth of leading thinkers in the theoretical field may be far too deep and complex, socially, racially, geographically, and historically, to admit of analytic solution, a few relevant suggestions may help to elucidate the theological situation in Sweden. Perhaps the struggle with nature and the lack of leisure, the concrete seriousness of national life, have turned the energies of the Swedish people into more immediately practical channels. It is a suggestive idea, too, that a very large portion of Scandinavian literature also reflects a definitely strained imagination, a robust simplicity of thought. The same is true as well of its charming rural culture and is witnessed to by the austerity of its native architecture.

In the theological field, moreover, Sweden has been historically dependent, to a large extent, on Germany, the homeland of both historic Lutheranism and theological construction. Even today, some Swedish theologians, as far as the present conditions will allow, have intimate connections with German thinkers and reflect their tendencies. The recent dealings with the Anglican Church, moreover, have been unable to supplant these natural connections with Germany and are not so much questions of doctrine as of church policy and liturgy. The ecumenical movement, however, and the recent European confusion, along with the rising confidence, wholly justified, in Swedish cultural contributions to the world, are making for that present comprehensive and constructive movement of theology which is a significant sign of an increasingly positive theological era.

Another reason for this scarcity of independent thinking in theology until recently may be the close relation between the Church and the universities. The professors are, as a rule, anxious to become bishops, and, in general, the ablest are prevented from theological production by such appointments. Among the present bishops the majority have been taken from positions in the universities, and in some cases, away from promising beginnings as constructive theologians. The cases of Bishops Billing, Aulén, Bohlin, Andrae, and Runestam are amply illustrative. No wonder that prominent Swedish thinkers attribute Sweden's theological meagerness to an unholy ambition on the part of talented theologians to wear the bishop's robes. This feeling is obviously both one-sided and short-sighted since the Church, in this way, nearly always receives as its leaders its deepest seers so that the truth of the quiet study is concretely tested and applied to actual situations. On the other hand, no one can deny that theological creativity has thereby been seriously impeded.

A further restraining influence on restless theological thought may be the conservatism of the Church itself. This springs from a deep-running emotional appreciation of the values of religion and from the consequent dread of losing the best that life offers. The historic forms are not infrequently confused with the eternal reality which gave them life. The opposition to new forms of thought is that common to institutionalism, inclusive of both merit and demerit. With a people bred in an absolutistic authoritarianism issuing from a traditional concept of God, the element of fear of violating the sacred territory of the supernatural power must also, and always, form a strong psychological motivation for careful conservatism. The authoritarianism of the Church exerts its influence by an imponderable, unanalyzable, almost imperceptible pressure on the individual, by an intangible *status quo*; it forms a warming shelter of approval for the obedient, but a freezing isolation for the one recalcitrant to its biddings. Between obedience to advancing truth and the desire to be accepted by a Church which they deeply cherish, liberals, from the more moderate Söderblom to the more definitely liberal Linderholm and Segerstedt, have been inwardly torn, only to experience outwardly either the chills of isolation or the blasts of bitterness. Without the understanding of this deep-seated conservatism, issuing from the cherishing of the religious realm with its comfort and cheer, with its challenge and its power, it is impossible to comprehend either the theological situation or the forces which have gone into the making of modern Swedish theology, especially that originated and centered at Lund University which for convenience we may call Lundensian.

Inasmuch, however, as Lundensian thought represents not only an endeavor to preserve for the Church the deepest values in historic Christianity but also a vigorous theological advance challenging every emaciated liberalism, it is helpful, before proceeding to the immediate origins of Lundensian theology, to look for a moment at the liberal forces which in the early part of this century bade fair to take possession even of Swedish theology. From time to time in the past there had been, of course, isolated progressive thinkers usually inspired by foreign contacts, but the liberal currents had been only occasional, short-lived, and not of lasting depth. Around the turn of the century, however, several tendencies conspired to turn Swedish thought in a liberal direction; a steadily increasing liberal trend was, nevertheless, soon to meet the far stronger currents of post-war reaction, out of which, however, one of the most constructive systems of theology, an effective synthesis of conservative and liberal fundamentals, came to be born.

In the middle of the nineteenth century Sweden was won philosophically for idealism by the thorough, systematic work of its greatest philosopher, Christopher Jakob Boström. Through his disciples, Carl Yngve Sahlin and Pontus Wikner, idealism dominated Sweden's philosophical thought until the birth of the twentieth century. But in spite of the religious, even Christo-centric, nature of much of this philosophy, and in spite of friendly approaches from the side of the philosophers, the theologians spent their efforts in furious battle against this undermining of strict traditionalism.

When, with the dawn of a new century, the idealistic domination began to wane in philosophy, it found a home in theology. Theology, beset by problems of psychologism and historicism, and finding educational circles under the glamorous spell of the scientific method, began to become isolated and highly suspect as a respectable field of learning. Although late in arriving, naturalism commenced through literary, social, and philosophical channels to grip the thought of Sweden. The objective existence of a transcendent realm was challenged and ridiculed. With momentous powers the streams swelled and rose which were to obtain the philosophic field in the form of Axel Hägerström's scientific, logical positivism which resolutely limited all reality to phenomena. The young theologians could not remain indifferent to the rapidly changing mood. And to some able religious thinkers idealism became the refuge from the antireligious storms and offered a willing alliance in a time of isolation. The crisis of historicism needs no elaboration, inasmuch as the devastating effect on traditionalism of Biblical scholarship, and genetic research into the history of religions is obvious and well known. Most grippingly Einar Billing, later professor of theology in Uppsala, tells of his soul's despair after the reading of Wellhausen's *Prolegomena zur Geschichte Israel.* To him the experience was "an earthquake."[1] It is no wonder that a personalistic idealism seemed to many to form, in the thought of N. J. Göransson, later a professor of theology at Uppsala, the last line of intellectual defense for Christianity.[2] Traditionalism in crisis and idealistic philosophy—these condition the works of Söderblom and Billing, and form, to some extent, the background of Lundensian theology.

Another liberal source which fed into Swedish thought was the literary-historical. In the first half of the nineteenth century, Sweden produced one of its greatest literary geniuses, the optimistic, culture-affirming, personalistic idealist, Erik Gustaf Geijer. His spirit was incarnated in the next half of the century in the great

[1] Cf. Billing, *Herdabref till prästerskapet i Wästerås stift,* p. 33 ff.
[2] J. A. Eklund, one of these young theologians, has said that the only teachers of theology at this time were the philosophers. Cf. Olle Nystedt, *Från Studentkorståget till Sigtunastiftelsen,* p. 20.

literary mystic, Sweden's beloved Viktor Rydberg, the gifted personalistic idealist who championed liberalism at two great Swedish centers of thought, Stockholm and Göteborg, with all the pulsing power of his nature. The indirect, and direct, effect of these men on the despairing theological youth is difficult to estimate. But Swedish theological thought during its flow toward liberalism reflects considerable influence from this source, and, since then, this tradition has been a much-gnawed bone of contention in theological circles. Similarly, the great-spirited and able historian, Harald Hjärne, by accepting unreservedly the canons of historical criticism, recognizing fact as fact, and yet daring to live in a moral faith stronger than any external lean-to, became a shelter to many a young theologian in a weary land. Hjärne, a secular historian and a man of the Church, had the courage of the prophet who sees but in part and yet dares to hope. In a similar spirit, Erik Stave began to interpret the Old Testament in terms of religious development, much to the general horror of the Swedish Church, and, as is a frequent consequence, to feel himself a prophet in the wilderness.

A third force strengthened the liberal trend, Sweden's very dependence theologically on Germany. Even though the older and unworried theologians were unbelievably ignorant of the rapidly rising number of liberal scholars in the German "scientific" approach to religion,[3] the young theological students neither could nor would escape the intellectual pull of men like Wellhausen, Bousset, Ritschl, Herrmann, Eucken, Troeltsch, and Harnack.

[3] When Söderblom first studied at Uppsala, Wellhausen's *Prolegomena zur Geschichte Israel* was an unknown book. Cf. Andrae, *Nathan Söderblom*, p. 105.

Swedish traditionalism was threatened. Pehr Eklund in Lund, F. Fehr, Samuel Fries, and others began to import liberal ideas, especially from Ritschl. The Ritschlian appeal to history was to have a strong influence on Swedish thought, but not without admixtures of metaphysics and mysticism received from the philosophic and literary sources of Swedish liberalism. Today practically every Swedish theologian has been compelled to take a definite position with respect to Ritschl or Herrmann, and however battered these may have become by unsympathetic interpretation in the many books dealing with their theology or ethics, a great many of their thoughts survive in altered forms and moods.[4]

Against this background of institutional conservatism in an intellectual yet emotionally powerful crisis, with a swelling tide of liberal thought confronting it, a tide which was itself pulled by great historical and naturalistic forces hostile to all religions claiming the absolute authority of transcendent truth, we find the young liberals at the turn of the century, anxious to defend religion with weapons obtained from any accessible arsenal. By the very nature of the situation their works tended to be apologetic, eclectic, not widely constructive nor matured into an organic synthesis.[5] In relation to Lundensian thought, Söderblom and Billing are by far the most important.

Because of these varied streams of thought, interwoven into a personal but not intellectual system of ideas, both

[4] Eucken's influence is particularly strong in the idealistic philosophy of Sweden's deep and courageous contender with modern problems during the first two decades of this century, Vitalis Norström.

[5] In a personal conversation Mrs. Nathan Söderblom humbly disavowed that her husband ever tried to produce a system, saying that those who knew the tenseness of the situation realized that all they could do was to keep their heads above water. "All they could do was to keep going" (*knoga på*).

Söderblom and Billing lend themselves with greatest difficulty to theological description. Söderblom was of conservative nature and felt the priceless value in the faith of the fathers, but he was also possessed of the liberal mind which, trained and touched by all the winds of the earth, was unable to keep back the rays of new truth, however distressing. He loved religion and he loved truth; deep in his soul he was convinced that both belong together, and that the values of religion were best defended by the fuller light of truth.

Söderblom's was the generous mind that is unafraid to be inconsistent with past utterances, yet willing to be the servant of a few large ideas. For our present purposes a brief sketch of these will be sufficient. The most basic idea was perhaps that of a special revelation, qualitatively distinct, and absolutely realized in Jesus Christ. This special revelation is of a personal nature continuously disclosed through prophetism. There is also a general, or cultural, revelation of the divine, qualitatively incapable of disclosing the fullness of truth. Prophetism, whether in prophets, geniuses, or artists, leads through a mounting personal revelation to monotheism. The cultural revelation leads through thought to absolute identity. Prophetism with Söderblom was sufficiently wide to include, according to the bent of his thought, the joint creating artists of voluntaristic metaphysics, the gradual expressions of purposeful life of Bergsonian teleology, or the "sports," to him, mental, moral, and religious, of biological evolutionism. Prophetism is God's way to man independent of man's efforts; cultural revelation is man's restless search for the divine. This thought underlies Söderblom's distinction between the mysticism of personality and the mysticism of everlastingness, and between spontaneous and practiced mysticism. Prophetism is faith's daring solution *quand même*; cultural revelation discloses to man's efforts an external view of reality filled either with the contradictions or with the false simplifications of thought. In most moods, and increasingly with the years, Söderblom despaired of the power of human reason except to systematize God's revelation as objectively disclosed in history. Moral and rational endowments have their legitimate functions to fill, but religion is to be known religiously. Prophetism proclaims a dualism according to which history is an objective drama, a conflict of forces good and evil;[6] cultural religion is balked by the meaninglessness of historic repetition.

With every right the Lundensian theologians claim Söderblom as a source of the Lundensian system. The stress on the uniqueness of the special revelation, the typological approach to religions, the skepticism about reason in the primary matters of religion, the emphasis on dualism, holiness, eschatology, the accentuation on revelation as a divine gift independent of man's efforts—these are definitely Lundensian characteristics. And yet, Söderblom is far from Lundensian. Widely he differs by the inclusiveness of his thoughts and by the generosity, some would say generality, of his attitude. His Ritschlian stress on ethics as conditioning God's grace, his idealistic concept of revelation as illumination, as norms to be imitated, his activistic idea according to which individual religious insight is conditioned by moral rectitude, his

[6] Söderblom's thorough study of Zoroastrianism at the Sorbonne undoubtedly increased this tendency toward dualism. Zoroastrianism, along with the descendants of Judaism, was included in prophetism, although Söderblom's real interest was in the absolute revelation in Christ and its continuation through personalities.

teleological vision of the one unknown Will strugglingly realizing its purpose, his belief in the soul in animistic terms as a distinct entity enduring through life and death in forms unknown—these notions, among others, definitely preclude Söderblom's ideological inclusion in the Lundensian roster. Deeper than by any ideas, however, he differs by means of his cosmopolitan attitude which craved alliances, not isolation, constructive, comprehensive synthesis, not intellectual distinctness. Thus Söderblom must be understood both as the conservative churchman, in which sense and in surprisingly many respects, he is ideologically close to Lundensian thought, and as the restless, partially emancipated liberal, in which position he stands closer to other trends in contemporary Swedish thought. The distance between Söderblom's position and the drasticness of the Lundensian methodological isolation of the Christian revelation is well illustrated by what were almost his last words on his deathbed; "I know that God lives. I can prove it by the history of religions."[7]

A less dramatic personality than Söderblom, Einar Billing, formerly professor of theology at Uppsala and now the aging Bishop of Västerås, by his sterling honesty, depth of spirit, and profundity of thought, has greatly influenced Swedish theological thought. Much effort has been spent in the endeavor to prove the genetic significance of Billing's theology on the development of Lundensian thought. Even Billing's more direct disciples, like K. B. Westman and Gunnar Dahlquist, recognize Lundensians like Aulén and Bring, in a very great measure, as also followers of their master.[8] Unfortunately for

[7] Andrae, *Nathan Söderblom*, p. 328.
[8] Cf. K. B. Westman, "Billing," in *Nordisk familjebok*, 1935. In a private conversation, Dahlquist made the same affirmation.

his promising career as a theologian, Billing was promoted to a bishopric. Without question, he still remains, by means of his one work alone, *De etiska tankarna i urkristendomen i deras samband med dess religiösa tro* ("The Ethical Thoughts in Early Christianity in Relation to its Religious Faith"), especially in its improved and extended second edition of 1936, by far both the deepest and the broadest[9] of Swedish theological thinkers. In Billing as in Söderblom, a complete, organic system is lacking, and ideas often spill over their forms, but there are certain definite, basic ideas which characterize his thinking.

With the reading of Wellhausen, Billing's literalistic traditionalism received its deathblow, but from him he later received the leading idea of his theology: God's dramatic, immediate, prophetic revelation in history. Not in true ideas, but in historic, dramatic conflict with evil does God make himself known, in the demand made on the prophetic consciousness for concrete action in the present. Lessing's famous assertion that no eternal truths can be founded on finite facts, Billing discovers to be based on the false metaphysical assumption that the infinite is in a state of perpetual rest. The real, God's dramatic will, is continuously and actively creative. This will is the unity of history, the genetic synthesis of both miracle and regularity. Historic regularity is a stability of function, a purposed evenness in the pattern of process. The dialectical point of modern thought has been the notion of law, of formal regularity. Billing definitely dismisses laws as metaphysical entities. Severed from a

[9] "Broad" here refers not to the horizon of interest and information in the sense of learning, but to a spiritual and intellectual wideness in his approach to the fundamental problems of theological metaphysics.

creative will they become, whether as religious, moral, or natural laws, reflectively produced obstacles to the effective realization of dynamic history in terms of God's ever concrete, presently applicable will. Empiricism, by uncritically taking over the metaphysically colored word "law" has received a religious flavor. Miracle and law are both expressions of one living, concerned will; becoming and being are equally related to historic purpose. By reflection, however, man tends to sever the two aspects and make the laws independently real. In the Old Testament it was moral laws which tended to crowd between God and the soul; in Greece it was intellectual laws, formal consistency on the plane of being; today, it is the notion of natural law, regularity in the cosmic process, which tends to push itself between God and his immediate revelation in history. The basic fault is, however, invariably the same, man's pitiful deception by his own intellectual abstractions.

With this thought as a background, Billing attempts historical constructions. The prophetic, personal revelation is qualitatively distinct, fully disclosed in Christ, as the immediate recognition of God's concrete will with the present. The Hellenic religion, self-examining, reflective, built around the discovery of the concept, finds history to be only a repetitive, finally meaningless cycle. The Hebrew ethics, continued in Christianity, is built on the personal, vivid reality of a concrete will, on the consciousness of a challenging, immediate necessity. The Hellenic ideal is built on the concept of formal right, on reflectively produced, lifeless norms. The prophet's message is no true idea; it is a history within history, the very content of history; the idea is itself a bit of "condensed history."[10] The Hellenic teaching comprises intellectual abstractions from history dignified into norms for a process which in its living fullness can never be the servant of its past course. Prophetic religion is the immediate knowledge of God's present will; man-made religions express man's groping attempt to live by the light of the past, by the smoky candle of his own reflected abstractions from this concrete, living will. Both religions give light, but one alone possesses the adequate fullness for competent guidance; and one alone can give the living meaningfulness of divine immediacy.

From here on Billing's thought is less clear. At times this monistic stress on the one will is definitely broken by a cosmic, perhaps metaphysical, dualism where the dramatic struggle is with evil powers. Billing has also felt a divergence within the utterances of this will; the religious aspect of it is then called the history of election and, being identical with prophetism, is itself a historic continuity. But there is also a natural history which crosses the history of election and which is, in a sense, included within it. With a beautiful intellectual humility, fairness, and frankness, Billing admits his inconclusiveness at this point.

To judge the influence of Billing on the Lundensian school of thought is nearly impossible. Ideologically there are, naturally and undeniably, genetic relations. But the spirit, the approach, are decidedly different. The typological approach to the study of religions, the interest in the distinctive features of each, the lifting of a historic continuity of organic thought into an objective entity independent of genetic relations—this emphasis with Billing is truly Lundensian. But he has not only a

[10] Cf. Billing, *De etiska tankarna*, etc., p. 85.

"historical-systematic," but also a "systematic-methodical" interest, which he defines as a testing of historic truth pragmatically, i.e., with a view to its present value or applicability. Nothing could be more un-Lundensian. Billing is, furthermore, deeply concerned with the reality problem of theological dogma. Science and theology, reason and faith, must refer to the same system of truth. The objective value and truth of religion cannot, in the long run, be affirmed contrary to the result of man's patient, impartial investigation. The divorce of the disclosures of faith from those of empirical knowledge may be a temporary expedient, but never satisfactory as a continued state of mutual isolation. Methodologically, Billing, as well as Söderblom, has also a strong activistic trend entirely contrary to Lundensian thought. Revelation is conditioned by man's effort. The deepest finder must be the honest, persistent seeker. Moral rectitude is the password to the hall of truth.

With respect to the content of his thought, Billing differs equally widely from the position taken by the Lundensian school. Man's concept of nature has enriched his concept of God. Metaphysical monism in terms of God's all-embracing will is, at least, a basic motif which underlies much of his concept of prophetism, history, and nature. Moral obedience conditions man's relation with God. God's grace is ever primary, but inseparable from it is man's obedience. God's Covenant with Israel was a spontaneous act of electing grace, but upon Israel depended its duration. Election is moralized by the Covenant. Grace is not arbitrary goodness, but guided by righteousness. Billing also differs from Lundensian theological construction by his repeated, emphatic stress on the value of man, his conception of the soul as man's constant possession of God's image, his thought of life after death as the duration of personality.

To enter into details is for our purpose obviously impossible. Certain thoughts, as for instance the typological approach to the history of religions, the stress on the distinctive, organic unity of each, the view of history as drama, have undeniably left their indelible imprint on Lundensian thought, but, as a whole, Billing differs from Lundensian theology not only by differences in method and ideas, but by his entire philosophical, spiritual attitude, by his receptive, untraditional, undogmatic, humble yet unperturbed, liberal approach.

Before turning to other trends which have directly conditioned the birth of Lundensian theology, it is well to obtain a general idea, at least, of other Swedish tendencies in theology which have been, and are, the constant environment of the predominant tendency in modern Swedish theology. Farthest on the left stands Sweden's "radical," Emanuel Linderholm, a church historian with a deep interest in the Church. His Reform League comprises a small group of the clergy, mostly aging liberals, and a number of intellectual laymen. His published challenge to reform, *Från dogmat till evangeliet* ("From Dogma to Gospel"), has had a wide circulation. In the Church as a whole, however, he is not taken seriously, and is usually dismissed from conversation as a relic of a superannuated liberalism. By some, however, he has been belabored with criticism which to him, undoubtedly an over-sensitive soul, appears haughty and uncontrolled to the point of abuse. To what extent is he radical? He has dared to attack the worship of Christ as God, to stress ethical monotheism, to advocate the honest and fearless acceptance of the results of Biblical scholarship, to polemize against an uncritical bowing to an external, supernatural revelation, to denounce what to him is the teaching of a shameful anthropology based on a pious myth, to hold a scientific view of creation consistent with religious faith, to fight for the revision of the liturgy so as to exclude medieval remnants repulsive to modern thought, to cleanse the teachings about the sacraments from all magical intrusions, to reform religious education in line with the highest and best in modern thought. He is frequently accused of reducing the gospel to the doctrines of God, virtue, and immortality, of being theologically negative. To some extent this may be true but Linderholm is the ethical prophet, the searching conscience of a new day, a religious man whose constructive works in thought and liturgy reveal a grasp not only of moral but also of religious essentials. Perhaps, however, the stripping away from religion of the pictorial concreteness amply possessed by traditionalism makes religion inaccessible to most lives. Perhaps man is at present so constituted that he cannot live by truth alone, but also by every expression in myth which makes truth aesthetically appealing, imaginatively compelling, dramatically real. The emotional depth of traditionalism, its religious power, cannot be denied. Difficult it is, indeed, not to believe that there is a positive, concrete relation between this religious power and the simplicity, or perhaps the unvisioned complexity of truth. Whether this power springs from man's fear of the possible negativity of truth, from his desire to be left alone in an acclimated emotional environment, true or false, from his sense of the doom of truth, or from his grasp of truth through these accustomed media, it is most difficult to say. The nature of this chapter forbids such an investigation. In any case, Linderholm's passion for the practical application of truth is almost completely misunderstood in the Sweden of today. As a theological figure he stands quite alone, isolated, forlorn.

Possibly next to Linderholm in their independence of theological traditionalism stand two thinkers, N. J. Göransson and J. A. Eklund, whose intellectual background is furnished mostly by personalistic idealism and ethical liberalism. The former, now an old man but still a true successor to the Boström-Wikner line of thought, is the quiet protagonist of a religious, voluntaristic-psychological idealism. Innocuous to the Church because of the theoretical, intellectualistic nature of his investigations, and sheltered under the great names of his predecessors, this able scholar, more a philosopher than a theologian, is usually considered the noble representative of a distinguished but dying dynasty. Close to Göransson stands Eklund, a personalistic idealist, an ethical liberal, of impetuous, vigorous, creative nature. Eklund is a difficult man to describe: a writer of stirring psalms, a reviver of interest in the Church at its low tide, a thoroughly learned man with an unclouded view to essentials, a tense spiritual warrior, yet with a wide tolerance. The type of liberalism for which he stands, the fulfillment of the deepest continuity of traditionalism in creative life, not in oppressive dogma, is in Sweden, it must be admitted, even among the intellectuals, definitely on the wane.

A social outgrowth of liberalism, on the one hand, and to some extent an apologetic movement, on the other, is the Young Church Movement whose valiant co-founder and leader is Manfred Björkquist. For theological purposes this group is naturally difficult to classify, its interest being practical, religiously, socially, and ecumenically, best illustrated by the far-reaching work of *Sigtunastiftelsen* (the Sigtuna Foundation), but in the conservative circles of the Lutheran fold it is definitely suspect, in spite of its apologetic, educational service to the Church, as a sociological remains of a secularized liberalism.

Balancing between its liberal impulses and its traditional tendencies, stands the so-called Uppsala theology, an indefinite viewpoint trying to uphold the spirit and method of Söderblom and Billing, yet to a great extent characterized by its opposition to what is deemed the theological extremes of Lundensian thought. As we have seen, neither Söderblom nor Billing could free himself, in spite of a liberal education and spirit, from the creedal power of a traditional theology; their disciples continue their struggle for an adequate, realistic approach to systematic theology. But the disciples sail against, not with, the theological winds which most strongly affect Sweden. Of the three outstanding disciples, Torsten Bohlin, Arvid Runestam, and Tor Andrae, the first is the thinker most freed from traditional dogma. His systematic work on theology is as yet unpublished, but his interests as well as writings are extensive. An able biographer of religious geniuses, a recognized expert on the writings of Kierkegaard, a systematic critic of Dialectic Theology, an exponent of Luther, a defender in a voluminous work of a transcendent religious norm for ethics, a philosopher of religion in both systematic and fictional form, Bohlin is most deeply interested in real people, real problems, in the relation of theories to actual life, in their claim for truth, their practical possibility, their significance for culture and social fellowship.

Arvid Runestam, the former professor of practical theology in Uppsala, a conscientious, self-examining member of the Oxford Group, took over from Billing an interest in Scheler and a definitely voluntaristic trend of thought. Runestam's main interest has been the adjusting of Christian ethics, in the light of psychology, to reality. One of his latest books deals with the ethics of marriage. In a previous work he attempted to adjust the absoluteness of the ethics of Jesus to the necessary relativities of practical life. Most of his efforts, however, have been devoted to his works on Luther as the great psychologist and knower of man. With every personal admiration for Professor Runestam, one always feels, nevertheless, that his knowledge of reality is considerably conditioned by his knowledge of Lutheran theology. Runestam is best classified as a traditionalist, sterlingly honest, with deep desires to break the circle and really see the world in the light of a new day.

Since neither Bohlin nor Runestam has a definite dogmatic system, and since the currents of modern theological interest flow elsewhere, they have been unable to rally a large number of followers, but there are a few able young men in Uppsala who may in the future considerably influence Swedish thought.

The last outstanding figure among the Uppsala theologians, Bishop Tor Andrae, really by profession and training a historian of religion, has also been classified as an adherent of the Lundensian system. This fact reveals how indefinite a phenomenon the so-called Uppsala theology is, and how traditional much of its thought can be. Inasmuch as Andrae stands on the borderline of the two schools, and is, nevertheless, definitely excluded from all consideration in the later part of this work, a very brief indication of his theological position is highly desirable. Both Bohlin and Andrae are disciples of Söderblom. The former, on the whole, took over more of the liberal, the latter, of the conservative side of the master. Methodologically, however, Andrae has great appreciation for the liberal approach. This liberal attitude, plus a few minor un-Lundensian inclusions and a refusal to accept the systematic constructions of Aulén, Nygren, and Bring in their entirety, is practically the only justification for his own characterization, in a private conversation, of his inclusion among the Lundensian theologians as "somewhat hasty." His main ideas are, however, definitely Lundensian. The belief in the soul as a continuous entity surviving death is the result of thought, not faith, and contrary to the oldest and purest Christian tradition which clings to resurrection by the grace of God at the end of time. In the resurrection of Christ faith finds its only and immediate assurance. To this, thought cannot add. Faith and thought are categories entirely distinct and sovereign in their own spheres. "The more daring the report of faith, the more sure it is of being true; the more paradoxical, the more protected from the insidious contradictions of thought."[11] "In conscious spite, it seems, it wishes *not* to see. . . . Judged by radical psychology the way of faith is purely that of wishful thinking."[12] Science can in no way prove nor disprove faith's absolute assurance. Every admission of reason into the realm of faith is an evil. "This is the eternal task of Christian thought; continually to delimit the field of faith from the field of

[11] Andrae, *Det osynligas värld*, p. 58.
[12] *Ibid.*, p. 45.

knowledge."[13] The same anti-idealistic interest characterizes his historical investigations. A Swedish writer has truly observed that in Mohammedanism he selects the aspects which would appeal to an orthodox Lutheran clergyman: the unconditional demand for obedience of the Almighty, and the absolute assurance which this entails of an election which triumphs over man's fear of death. In selecting his material he occupies his attention with confessional creeds, not with explanations of the world, with concrete miracles, not with logical systems. His thesis is that no religion tries to give theories about reality, that no magic is rational technique, that even in the primitive stage knowledge gained through experience and reason is carefully kept apart from faith, which, detesting investigation, prefers rather to take a chance that its objects are but figments of the mind, while it also has the chance that they are the miracle which alone can render supernatural aid.[14] This radical separation of the field of faith from the realm of knowledge, this stress on the Resurrection as a miracle of grace, this interest in creeds, this daring assertion of the truth of faith which in its deeper understanding of reality can resolutely defy the reports of empirical knowledge—all this is thoroughly Lundensian in background, in motivation, and in apologetic purpose.

Before introducing the Lundensian system, it seems best, however, to mention a school of thought, small, to be sure, which in relation to traditionalism goes beyond the Lundensian position and stands at the very extreme of theological conservativism, the so-called Rosendal movement. Another deeply conservative tradition is the

[13] *Ibid.*, p. 279.
[14] Cf. Harrie, *Tjugotalet in memoriam*, p. 138 ff.

older Schartau movement in southwestern Sweden. But while this is pietistic, the Rosendal movement is high-churchly. Gunnar Rosendal has larger influence than he has following. For a definitely creedal Church claiming itself to be based on supernatural revelation, his theological position is strong and consistent. With burning zeal for his Church, he promises it renaissance on certain conditions: the Church must be reformed along four lines, the creedal, the sacramental, the hierarchical, and the liturgic. The stress must be on the Sacrament and the Word. When all liberal, social, rational, and practical compromises are surrendered, and when the priests once more honor the Holy Sacrament, the Church will be restored to its power and effectiveness.

Between this high-churchly trend and the so-called Uppsala theology stands the most powerful theological tendency in present-day Sweden, the Lundensian. It exerts considerable influence through two, and to some extent, three out of four professorships in theology and, through the theological quarterly publication, has a tremendous following among the young clergy, and seems to be growing in power. Lundensian theology is best understood as the resurgence of historic Christianity, as a reaction to the indefiniteness of a confused liberalism which never won much more than the minds of its converts, and that only partially, as an affirmation of the absolute assurance of religion in the face of a bewildered relativism. It is difficult to worship a God with a question mark before him. Undoubtedly the dominance in Sweden of Lundensian thought indicates an emotional deepening of religion. But this system also appeals to the mind, for it possesses a definite, strong, plausible methodology. Reason and faith have distinct fields, functions, and capacities. The disclosures of faith, barricaded behind a suggestive philosophical construction, are inaccessible to the criticism of reason. But reason is free to plow unimpeded the field of fact. In the realm of theology, reason has imposed upon it the historical task of discovering the objective, organic unities of faith obtainable synthetically from the field of history itself, and without special prerequisites on the part of the historian. These unities, moreover, can be grasped only intuitively in the form of basic motifs. The historic-systematic approach, furthermore, discovered a new light on historic thought, in which all past and present utterances must be viewed. No matter if to the uninitiated liberal these appear like the results of the modern *Lutherforschung* heavily spiced with Barthian thought; here was rest for the soul and work for the mind. Into a description of this trend of thought we cannot enter until the following two chapters, but we must understand before then a few of the influences which have helped to mold Lundensian theology into an anti-liberal, anti-idealistic system.

The general relation between Söderblom and Billing and the Lundensian system has already been sketched. For a historian to distinguish between direct and indirect influences is a genetic task difficult to the point of impossibility. The stress in Uppsala on eschatology and holiness was indicative of the general trends of the time. Directly, as well as indirectly, Ritschlian ideas were received into the stream of thought: the stress on history, the Christocentric approach, the distinction between the realm of fact and that of value, the interest in Luther, the bias against metaphysics. On the last point Uppsala theologians were really uncertain, but not the dominant philosopher, Axel Hägerström. This indication is sufficient to reveal the scope of the problem, and to exclude certainty in suggestions as to possible genetic relations. Perhaps the most certain, specific influences from the older Uppsala theology were Söderblom's stress on dualism and on the religious approach to the study of religion, the stress of both Söderblom and Billing on the distinctiveness of Christianity, the typological approach to the history of religions, the emphasis on the organic unity and uniqueness of each religion, and their view of history as a continuous, dramatic revelation.

We have seen, in our longer presentation, how Söderblom and, to some extent, Billing, were, in certain respects, conservative traditionalists. To be theologically traditional in Sweden is to accept as unquestionable the Pauline-Lutheran fundamentals. Luther, it is generally admitted, never freed himself from what to a liberal is the supernaturalistic, dogmatic continuity of the Catholic Church. In certain respects, however, he was astonishingly liberal and made steps toward the rationalistic-humanistic revolt. He was a complex, far-reaching thinker, an emotional polemicist, a religious genius whose basic ideas to a great extent embody the conceptions of his time. Söderblom, in his early struggle for more liberal thought, hid behind Luther's more liberal statements. But Luther's influence, in the long run, is toward conservatism, especially when he is considered not as a historical reaction and cleansing influence, but as a contemporaneously valid theological norm. Practically every Swedish theologian recognizes Luther as a final authority. Most theology is expounded with the works of Luther as a medium. Swedish conservatism owes much to Lutheran authoritarianism. This has been true through the centuries, is one reason for the conservative side of Söderblom and Billing, and is increasingly true of Lundensian thought.

The reasons for this last statement are many. One of the strongest movements, if not by far the strongest, in recent Swedish thought, is the new Lutheranism. Ritschl in his historical interest pointed to Luther. The effect in Sweden was immeasurable. Interest in Luther, always strong, became an intense passion. Every theologian was swept into an enthusiastic rediscovery of Luther as the refuge from bewilderment. The hand of Luther rested heavily on the ancestors of Lundensian thought. But much more, the young theologians themselves who were to found the school under consideration became imbued with this Lutheran enthusiasm for its authority and became from their early youth saturated with his thoughts. Gustaf Aulén, whose imprint on Lundensian ideology is in certain aspects the heaviest, likes to think of the movement as the rediscovery of Luther. This is a most important observation, for Luther, as he came to be interpreted, became increasingly conservative and supernaturalistic. Liberalism's, especially Ritschlianism's, view of Luther was considered a falsification, a modernizing of the Great Theologian. Ritschl's system was built on the two irreconcilable systems of Kant and Luther. What had a rational moralism to do with a religion of grace? Increasingly raged the battle between Kant and Luther. A historic stream of thought, at least an anti-idealistic, anti-rational, anti-liberal passion, was taking possession of the modern *Lutherforschung*. To a great extent this was merely the rediscovery of correct perspectives. Came Stange, Holl, and Hirsch. From the earliest beginning Luther had been misinterpreted. Through Melanchthon came in Hellenism's dangerous speculation. Orthodoxy succumbed to the rational and the moralistic temptation. Away with all irreligious alliances! Restore the purity of Luther's thought. Return to a theocentric religion devoid of false anthropologies, theodicies, blasphemies against the Unknown, the Irrational, the Holy, the Free-willed. Stress the reality of grace, but not its ways—an intellectualistic delusion—and make low and unworthy, yes, raze to the ground, man's Tower of Babel, that the incomprehensible light of grace may be revealed against its true background. More or less sharp, more or less radical, more or less systematically consistent were the protagonists of the *Lutherforschung*, but as a whole the total attitude of the movement has greatly affected the Lundensian theology. In the struggle between Luther and Kant it stands unquestionably *"fest auf Seiten Luthers."*[15]

From Söderblom and Billing the more conservative aspects were selected, the irrational, the dualistic, the eschatological, the transcendent, along with such more liberal anti-Ritschlian ideas as the intimate immediacy of faith. The new *Lutherforschung*, moreover, became to some extent a channel for the resurgence of traditionalism, with a Barthian flavor. The relation between Barthianism and Lundensianism is, once again, a difficult subject for appraisal. Sweden shared in the general German disillusionment after the war, although, naturally, in a milder measure. When the Lundensian theologians claim relative independence of Barth, Brunner, and Gogarten, the truth in the claim may be the fact that the anti-liberal, anti-idealist forces of which Fascism,

[15] Siegmund-Schultze, *Ekklesia* II, *Die Kirche in Schweden*, p. 10.

Marxism, and Dialectic Theology are all expressions, came also to Sweden in other than theological forms. That Lundensian theology is part of the crisis psychology, perhaps of the orientation of a new epoch, is certain. That the Lundensian theologians read the writings of the theologians of the dialectic movement is equally certain. That Lundensian thought is definitely Barthian in much of its approach and feeling is clear and undeniable. That ideological dependence is difficult to detect in oneself is not an uncommon occurrence. That Sweden has always tended theologically to shift along with the German moods is a historic fact. That Gustaf Aulén veered toward the dialectic position following his moving from Uppsala to Lund is evident from his writings. The claimed differences between the Barthian and the Lundensian positions: that the former is still oriented along philosophical lines, although negatively as a reaction, while the latter has altogether a religious approach; that the former isolates Christ, while the latter upholds a continuous revelation through history; that the former has a one-sided, temporal eschatology, while the latter has the double-phased, religious eschatology inclusive of both hoping and having, of both doom and grace, and of both present and future; that the former often comprises a moralistic stress on obedience, while the latter keeps salvation *sola gratia* in its religious purity—these differences sound impressive until the two systems are compared as a whole. Then, similarities of thought and spirit become easily apparent; but Lundensian theology is naturally a far more constructive and positively inclusive system than the more negative and confusing positions of Barthian writers.

Before turning to the genetic influences which helped

to bring forth Lundensian methodology, a word of psychological explanation of the system may be attempted. Theologically, Sweden's thought was and remains absolutistic. A supernatural revelation, an absolute authority, a total depravity, an absolute assurance of forgiveness—this was a psychology with a religious all-or-none theory. This was a burning, soteriologically oriented theology built on one of Stoicism's usual assumptions, that to fail partially is to fail totally, but without its scope of vision or capacity for adjustment to the ways of life. To one who has not himself heard the most preposterous statements as to the total evil of life and the absolute lack of all and every good in the world if Christ has not risen bodily, and that at one of the universities, this observation may not seem important. But for one who has himself read, heard, and felt this soul-gripping clinging to the absolute, the chaos introduced into Swedish conservatism by historical criticism is understandable. Lundensian theology is a return from all relativisms to the absolute assurance of religion, but not to the Biblical literalism of the past. In this respect the movement represents a compromise with traditionalism, and is suspect, in certain orthodox circles, as "radical to the point of stagnation." The movement is far rather intelligently traditional. Realizing the factual vulnerability of the old foundation as revealed by modern criticism, Biblical and historical, a new Biblicism was accepted, akin to that of Martin Kähler, who, in this respect, had considerable influence on Swedish thought. The new Biblicism interpreted the Bible in terms of basic truths, guiding motifs, rather than in results of exegetical confusion. This method considerably facilitated, as well, the interpretation of the New Testament in strict line with the modern interpretation of Luther. This "realistic" interpretation of the Bible is fervently championed by the late convert to Lundensian thought, the Norwegian exegete of the New Testament at Uppsala, Anton Fridricksen, and seems to mean an intuition of the Gospels as totalities and as the living Word of God, obedient to the tradition of the Church, in direct contrast to what seemed the deadly confusion and destructive analysis of formal and genetic criticism.[16] This was the way back to the desired power and assurance.

More help and comfort had come, and continued to come, from the brilliantly clear thinker and writer, Anders Nygren, professor of theology at Lund, who did for the methodology and ethical content what Gustaf Aulén had done and was doing for the content of theology. These are the two co-founders of the Lundensian system who in the early nineteen-twenties began to capture the theological thinking of Sweden. Aulén is the intuitive seer of possibilities, who, himself a historian as well as a theologian, set disciples to work on historical attestations of his theses. Nygren is the logical builder of a strong, philosophical defense for God's revelation in the history of Christian thought. The study of Kant, Husserl, and Troeltsch has stimulated his interest in the religious a priori. Kant had limited the field of knowledge to phenomena. But there were also transcendental categories, or pure forms of consciousness valid a priori, without which experience as a whole was impossible. Three such, Kant indicated, could be deduced. These categories made their established content transcendentally valid. A religious category Kant never discovered,

[16] Cf. Harrie, *op cit.*, p. 138.

to be sure, but, says Nygren, he had no real genius for religion.

This Nygren, however, sets out to discover and deduce. But if there is such a religious form of consciousness, there ought surely to be a religious content accessible to historical investigation. Theology is, therefore, freed from its misleading metaphysical tasks of explaining the world or proving the objective reality of its assertions. The object of theology is the content of religion findable in history. With Schleiermacher as a historical medium, Nygren then sets out to develop a definite, challenging, theological methodology. The task of theology is purely descriptive, strictly scientific. Nor can its objective truth be questioned by science, which is methodologically confined to phenomena. No knowledge can hurt the religious assurance.

But Nygren further strengthened his position by taking advantage of the forceful anti-idealistic stream in philosophy which dominated Sweden. The very writings of Axel Hägerström, Uppsala's vigorous empirico-logical positivist, became methodological ammunition. Sweden's leading philosopher held that all knowledge belongs to the realm of phenomena and is expressible only in logical categories. All value judgments are beyond the reach of objective knowledge and devoid of reality insofar as they claim to be objective truth. Value judgments are subjective and do not constitute valid objective knowledge. This idea that all knowledge is through and through descriptive in nature, that science is never normative, became an integral part of the Lundensian methodology, while the assertion that reality is strictly limited to the logical realm of factual relationships was ably shown by Lindroth, now professor of theology at

Uppsala and a disciple of Aulén, to be an illicit assumption on Hägerström's part totally at variance with his own philosophy. The thought that all knowledge is descriptive fitted, however, most conveniently into the Lundensian philosophical construction. If no science is ever normative, as Hägerström had spent almost his entire life to prove, then all facts, genetic or psychological, would from now on beat vainly, even if furiously, against the claims of religious validity. And still religion had its own untrespassable criterion of transcendental validity. It could gladly give up its claim to be able to prove its objective reality if it was admitted to possess a categorical certainty, a normativeness according to its own genius, without which experience as a whole would be impossible. Furthermore, theology had in this way gained the prestige of a science. Gladly it bartered its right to judge if, in turn, it could itself no longer be judged.

If, now, theology could unimpededly turn to history, was there in this field anything but a multitude of facts and thoughts devoid of definite organic relationship? Was not recourse to a philosophically fixed standard of judgment, a selective norm, necessary? No, said Nygren, for Christianity, as well as every ideologically distinct type, possesses an objective unity organically independent, accessible to any capable and impartial observer. This organic totality must, of course, be intuitively grasped in terms of basic motifs. The basic motif underlying Christianity became to Nygren, as well as to Aulén, a transcendent unmotivated love, the knowledge of which is through and through supernaturally disclosed. Perhaps a better characterization would be that the Lundensians rediscovered, in the light of their crisis theology, the purity of the Pauline-Lutheran theme: *sola gratia-sola fides*.

To say more would be to anticipate the exposition of the system. Aulén and Nygren did not long remain isolated in their effective collaboration of their theological construction, which, naturally, reveals many minor differences of opinion. They were soon joined by a thorough, clear-thinking, and vigorous disciple, Ragnar Bring, the successor to the professor's chair at Lund left vacant by Bishop Aulén. In both Aulén and Nygren there are liberal veins, as seen, for example, in their thought of God as *agape*, as spontaneous, unmotivated love creative of fellowship, and their indefiniteness as to eschatology, not to mention their attempts to make room for scientific scholarship within the field of Biblical exegesis, provided that the absoluteness of the religious truth in its entirety remain unimpaired—but Bring shows certain tendencies toward a further deepening of the system by delivering it, however partially, from its drastic distinctness. Other disciples there are, and many, but none who has mastered to the same extent as Bring the essentials of both methodology and content, and endeavored skilfully to complete the system or to remedy insufficiencies in its original structure.

CHAPTER II

THEOLOGICAL METHODOLOGY

Introduction

Theology was once the "Queen of the Sciences." Theology, in circles of learning, has become, not infrequently, a superannuated dowager cherished because of her venerable age, her influential connections, and her wealth of possessions. Among theologians as well as scientists there are few who ascribe scientific standing to this department of learning. The science that once ruled all others with harsh and heavy hand is today tottering from the vigorous onslaught of a logico-experimental method in the light of which its hesitant claims of revealed truth appear to be little more than wish-filled subjectivism, historical relativism, or metaphysical speculation. The theologian, moreover, who in his anxiety to be scientific reduces the content of theology to empirical psychology, positivistic history, and critical philosophy, is soon rebuked by an irate Church for having sacrificed adequacy of Christian truth for the sake of an inadequate and irrelevant scientific methodology. The compromiser who accepts the facts of science while reserving the right to interpret them in the light of religion, soon discovers himself disowned methodologically by most of his scientific colleagues because of his subjective extensions, and by many of his religious brethren because of the inadequate and often vague nature of the results.

In an age of upheaval, due to the disintegrating discoveries of historical research and psychological investigation, the theologian finds himself bewildered, inasmuch as he can no longer systematically expound an inherited body of knowledge, nor can his soul find peace in the meager relativities offered him by radical scholarship, nor yet can he turn to the philosophy of religion without finding it beset by the same difficulties, in addition to methodological problems of its own. It is, therefore, no small task that the Lundensian theologians have undertaken when they set out to prove that theology is not only as scientific in method as any science, but also that its content is fully distinctive and completely removed from the sphere of scientific criticism, that its field is historical but inaccessible to current methods of factual interpretation, that its object is tested as experience and yet cannot be comprehended in terms of psychological investigation, that its method is critically philosophic and that, nevertheless, philosophy has no jurisdiction over its definite disclosures.

Successfully to vindicate their contentions, the Lundensian theologians have labored industriously to establish the idea that theology is both strictly scientific and interpretatively adequate. Realizing that it is the method employed which makes or breaks theology, they have expended great efforts on the construction of a method which uninterruptedly must be objectively valid and unexceptionally capable of fixing and expressing with full adequacy that which is distinctively Christian. Theology, to be at its maximum strength, must, in the words of Aulén, "stand on its own feet."[1] Metaphysical speculation is banished, not only because of its vulner-

---

[1] Aulén, *Teologiska studier*, Vol. III, p. 162.

ability from scientific quarters, but also because of its inability to do justice to the characteristically Christian.[2] Turning away from all empirical and speculative methods by which to determine objective truth in the sense of ontological reality, this school of thought, in this instance represented by the former philosopher of religion, Anders Nygren, attempts to establish the objective validity of the content of theology by means of the transcendental deduction of religion. The deep insight underlying this approach, so emphatically stressed by Kant, is the truth that not all rational normativeness is theoretical in nature. Experience must be understood according to the demands of its several aspects; religion, and here Kant failed, is to be known according to the requirements of its own genius.

After the validity of the object of theology has been proved, the next challenge is to demonstrate how the valid religious experience can be scientifically treated, i.e., how this content of theology can be fully known in all its distinctiveness by the scientific theologian without any prejudicing prerequisites, and how that which by its very nature is atheoretical can be theoretically expressed. It is with this problem that Bring is particularly concerned. "The independent task of systematic theology must be fixed on a double front: in relation to the general sciences of religion and to a metaphysical point of view."[3] The method is definitely constructed to do full justice to the distinctively Christian, to let the voice of faith speak for itself in the objective deposit of Christian history, where the scientific theologian can find it and interpret it objectively, unconcerned with

[2] Nygren, *op. cit.*, p. 3.
[3] Bring, *Till fragan om den systematiska teologiens uppgift*, p. 5.

any questions as to its ultimate reality. Since an account of Lundensian theology, moreover, would in no way be complete without the inclusion of its Christian ethics, a short survey of ethical methodology will also be made. Though the brevity of the discussion may seem in direct contrast to the amount of care and effort expended on the problem by Professor Nygren, the reason for this is that the ethical methodology in general has the same approach as the theological, i.e., the same concern for the distinctively Christian on the subjective side, and for the strictly scientific on the objective. The general result is, thus, that the distinctively Christian is established as a validly given object, while this object is accessible to an unbroken chain of scientific methodology. "There is, thus, an unbroken chain of necessity from the vindication by the philosophy of religion of the necessity and unavoidability of religion, to the very last words on the periphery of dogmatics."[4] No wonder that Aulén, who is the systematic theologian par excellence of this school, speaks of the literalism and speculation of the past epochs and writes with confidence about the new era in theology.

I. The Task and Scope of the Philosophy of Religion

The characteristic methods of the pre-critical epochs prior to Kant or the adoption of his philosophic method, namely literalism, speculation, and the historical approach, suffered respectively from staticness, theoreticalness, and the last from both staticness and relativism. The main defect of theological methodology was that

---

[4] Nygren, "Till frågan om teologiens objektivitet," in *Teologiska studier, tillägnade Erik Stave,* p. 182.

of pre-critical philosophy in general, i.e., that it endeavored to deal with questions of objective reality. A metaphysical philosophy labored under the handicap of a psychological theory of knowledge which assumed a fundamental opposition between subject and object. In this way the object could be known only as part of the activity of the subject, or at least in the light of this activity, one side being active while the other remained passive. It follows, therefore, that the subject could not be known without being modified by the process of knowing. The very nature of metaphysics is consequently involved in the epistemological obfuscation which identifies reality with the concept of reality. Insofar as metaphysics is the postulating by space-thinking of a transcendent complement to sensuous reality, it follows that along with the subjectivistic-psychological theory of knowledge it must at last declare itself bankrupt by the admission that it cannot explain how these opposites can find each other, and that the correspondence between them is the secret of reality, for what it admits, in a roundabout way, is that it is unable to solve the very problem which it acknowledges to be its basic task. Trying to do the impossible, a metaphysically oriented philosophy was forced to resort to such assertive grounds of explanation as knowledge by recollection, innate ideas, or inexplicable psychological capacities. Those who could not accept such speculative explanations but who could not escape the subtlety of the original fallacy, landed in skepticism.

A. *The Transcendental Method in Relation to Theology.*

Against this background, the importance of Kant as the father of critical philosophy can be easily understood.

Realizing that since the deepest presuppositions for metaphysics are not to be found in experience, there can be no help from any empirical method, and that the rational-deductive method is useless insofar as it cannot prove its original premises by reference to any higher instance, he changed the entire approach of philosophy by abolishing rational metaphysics. Philosophy, to be critical, must disown the question of objective reality, and, confining itself within its sphere of competence, deal exclusively with the problem of objective validity. Kant's revolutionizing achievement is the construction of the transcendental method. Philosophy becomes definite and competent when it knows that its field of investigation is limited to the sphere of experience. Within this sphere, critical philosophy must make only one assumption. It must assume the principle of validity, i.e., that rational knowledge is possible. This assumption, however, is indispensable if there is to be any knowledge whatsoever, and not assumptive in the same sense as the rational-deductive systems which arbitrarily select their ultimate criteria. But if the first assumption is as inevitable as constructive thinking, every other aspect of the method is strictly critical, inasmuch as the principles of validity are defined as only those without which experience as a whole is impossible. Kant himself writes of this method as *"die Darstellung der reinen Verstandesbegriffe als Principien der Möglichkeit der Erfahrung."*[5] These principles of validity, or pure forms of experience, inasmuch as they are a priori not chronologically but logically, cannot be found empirically by psychological analysis, because a psychogenetic investigation

[5] Kant, *Gesammelte Schriften*, III, p. 129, as quoted by Nygren in "Söka och finna."

has no adequate basis for selecting such ultimate principles, nor metaphysically, because of the original disjunctive fallacy of metaphysics, namely the artificial separation of subject and object, but only by a logical analysis of experience as an abstracted totality. Universal validity and necessity are from this point of view tokens of experience a priori rather than essential criteria, for these tests lend themselves quite easily to methods of empirical analysis and may obscure the transcendental-logical approach. It can, therefore, be said, in summary, that the transcendental method is not concerned with the origin or the explanation of experience, but takes it as an abstracted totality for the sake of logically establishing categories a priori, or absolutely valid forms of experience.

The construction of this method potentially revolutionized theological methodology. The limits of philosophical competence are sharply drawn. Its competence ends with the testing of the religious experience as to its objective validity. The basic problem of the philosophy of religion must be the question as to the validity of the religious claim. "It is gradually becoming clear that the philosophy of religion has no right to exist except in the closest relation with critical philosophy, and that from this point of view its task can be no other than the investigation into the validity of religious experience as a whole."[6] More closely to fix the relation between philosophical and theological methodology at this point, it may be said that every field of investigation may be viewed from two angles, that of the special science, and that of the universal science, or philosophy. The task of the special science is genetic and systematic; that of

[6] Nygren, *Dogmatikens vetenskapliga grundläggning,* p. 52.

the universal science is to understand the field to be investigated from the synoptic point of view with reference to its claims for validity. Omitting, for the time being, the implications touching the general sciences of religion, it is clear that the tasks of philosophy and theology are distinct; philosophy establishes religion as valid experience *sui generis*; theology treats the field systematically, as will soon be seen, according to the organic unity of its object. To look at it from another point of view, philosophy validates the form of religion as the source of the theological content while theology then treats this content scientifically as a historical deposit.

B. The Transcendental Deduction of Religion.

If this application of Kant's philosophy is kept in mind, the task of the philosophy of religion is, obviously, to test the claims of religion to be an experience a priori. To ascertain whether or not religious experience is universally valid and necessary, the fairest and surest way is to listen to the testimony of religion in its factual historical form. Nygren immediately explains that the terms universal and necessary are to be interpreted not quantitatively but qualitatively, not extensively, but intensively, from the point of view of positive experience rather than the possible lack of it. With this, he rejects W. Herrmann's alternative that either religious experience is individual and therefore not valid for him who has not felt it, or else it is universally valid, but as such, logically demonstrable to anyone regardless of his experiential qualifications. The religious experience is universally valid because it is experienced as "something trans-subjectively and over-individually valid, something not arbitrary, but that commands with necessity and an intrinsic authority, something of which I am definitely certain that I, with every one else who has experienced it, must obey."[7] The experience is necessary, similarly, because it is experienced as binding and compelling. Its degree of necessity is absolute, not psychologically in the debatable realms of freedom and determinism, but transcendentally, in the light of which our whole existence would lose its significance if it were not for this religious point of view. According to the testimony of religion, the two tokens of an experience a priori have been fulfilled. Validity, however, can be subsumptive, and for this reason it remains to be seen whether religion can make good its claim to be an independent and unique form of experience. If so, can it also prove that it is the indispensable prerequisite for experience as a whole?

According to the Lundensian theologians, the religious experience claims to be an altogether independent form of experience that protests the violence it suffers when it is reduced to another form of experience. It refuses to be validated as an aspect of another form of the spirit, whether as ethics, knowledge, or aesthetics. For two distinct reasons, however, religion finds it much more difficult than the other forms of experience to prove its contention that it is an independent and unique form of consciousness. In the first place, the other forms of experience, the theoretical, the ethical, and the aesthetic, relate themselves most readily to the customary tripartite psychological division of consciousness into thinking, willing and feeling. Instead of modeling philosophical methodology according to the valid forms of the spirit, the tri-partite division of the philosophical

[7] Nygren, *Religiöst apriori*, p. 139.

investigation of consciousness has remained as an untoward residue of psychologism to raise an initial obstacle in the way of the recognition that religion is an independent and unique form of experience. In the second place, the other forms of consciousness have their objective counterparts in culture against which they can easily be checked. "The religious consciousness . . . in its original form is not actively productive but passively experiential."[8] Culture, by its very nature, is active and productive; religion, definitely passive. "Passivity is the characteristic nature of religion. In the grip of the religious experience man never feels himself to be active or giving, but always passive and receiving, never creative and productive, but invariably as the one in whom something is created and for whom something happens."[9] This explains, of course, why religion is not a form of culture, and also, what is more relevant, why the validity of the religious category is extremely difficult and indeed impossible to establish in the same manner as the other forms of experience a priori. Whatever is directly related to the cultural life of the community can be validated by the simple test that whosoever refuses to acknowledge the cultural values, automatically excludes himself from the life of the community. To deny the legitimacy of knowledge is to put oneself beyond the pale of disputing it. To deny moral validity is to cut oneself loose from the very moorings of civilization. Religion has no such ban, for it is possible to deny the basic value of religion, and still remain within the comforts of culture. To look at it another way, if the philosophy of religion could prove that without the

[8] *Ibid.*, p. 234.
[9] *Ibid.*, p. 175.

recognition of its basic value no religious experience were possible, this would in no way prove that religion itself as an experience *sui generis* is a valid category. Since, according to the Lundensian theologians, religion has no objective counterpart in culture, at least in no distinct and indispensable form, it must undertake to do what the other forms of experience ought theoretically to do, i.e., to prove that without it, experience as a whole is impossible. This religion endeavors to prove by showing that it is the prerequisite for all forms of experience insofar as these claim validity, but a validity which by its very nature is limited to time and place.

In this connection a few clear citations from Nygren seem helpful. "If all scientific, ethical, and aesthetic judgments are tested with reference to their content, it is impossible to discover the eternal point of view. These judgments presuppose the category of eternity as their source of validity, but do not *contain* it."[10] "While all other judgments to be valid must presuppose the category of eternity, but do not contain it, the characteristic fact of the content of the religious judgment is that it is a pronouncement about the eternal."[11] "If the transcendental method is to be used in the field of religion, we must show analogously, that a religious category is the basis for all experience without the recognition of which no experience would be possible, and that all validity would disappear if this category were invalid. All this is true of the category of eternity. . . . The basic category of religion is considered the inescapable presupposition for all non-religious experience. This is the *punctum saliens* of the transcendental proof that

[10] Nygren, "*Är evighetskategorien en religiös kategori?*" p. 236.
[11] *Ibid.*, p. 237.

every judgment—even the non-religious—must refer back to the category of eternity in order to be valid."[12] "The thing all forms of experience have in common is that every one in its way lays claim to validity. But the concept of validity contains a significant presupposition which points beyond the realm of sensuous experience. If a thing is called valid, this does not mean that it is valid in time and place, but without reference to time and place. That which is true today was also true yesterday, indeed, before anyone knew about it, and would be true even if no individual consciousness recognized it as such, even as it would remain true if all consciousness died out. . . . *But this presupposition on which all culture is founded, but which no single form of culture can found, nor which can be founded by all the forms of culture in their total unity, is religious in nature.* For it is the very claim of religion to lift human life above the givenness of this sensuous, finite sphere. . . . The category of eternity is the basic, transcendental category of religion."[13] These references have been given at length because of the importance that the transcendental method in its application to the field of theology has for the Lundensian theologians. For their methodology, religion must be an independent and unique form of experience transcendentally valid. The result of the transcendental deduction is that the category of eternity is the religious category which all others must presuppose in order to be separately valid. Eternity is defined negatively as that which is above time and space, and positively as absolute validity. The absolutistic

---

[12] *Ibid.*, p. 223.
[13] Nygren, *Religiöst apriori*, pp. 238, 239.

trait is important to note because of its significance in relation to the system as a whole.

Before leaving that aspect of methodology which is the task of the philosophy of religion, it is necessary to stress the notion that the religious category is pure form, a logical abstraction, and not to be considered synonymous with religion itself, or with a basically necessary potentiality inclusive of the minimum of psychological or rational content, or yet with an ideal norm by which to judge the actual religions. The philosophy of religion, therefore, accepting the self-testimony of religion that it is an independent and unique form of experience, establishes the validity of the form of religion by the transcendental deduction. But insofar as a pure form can give no indication as to the specific nature of its content, the content must be found in the historical religions themselves. Since, moreover, the form of religion being devoid of content can in nowise serve as a measuring rod for the different religions, it follows that the philosophy of religion is unable to deal with any specific or general content. The sphere of the philosophy of religion ends with the formal result reached through the critical method: there is valid religious content to be found in history. The task of theology begins at this point, and may be summarized as follows: how can this religious content be scientifically ascertained and systematically expressed?

II. The Task and Scope of Theology

Theology is a strictly scientific discipline with a logical-descriptive method. Its field is the object of faith which it finds in the positive religions. No special qualifications are necessary for the theologian except to treat the material objectively from its own organic point of view. Even though the material has its own principles of unity and validity which are atheoretical, it can be scientifically known and systematically expressed. These are the Lundensian propositions which must be more fully explained.

A. *Theology and Science.*

The Lundensian theologians are most anxious that theology be recognized as a science in good and regular standing. With science is meant the logico-descriptive method. This method has two aspects of investigation: the universal or philosophical sciences,[14] and the special sciences which investigate their specified fields either genetico-analytically, or synoptically, with reference to the organic unity imposed upon them by their several objects of investigation. The object of theology is the content of faith which it investigates scientifically, i.e., by means of the logico-descriptive method.

Theology cannot, of course, use the logico-experimental method which is proper to the natural sciences and equally inapplicable beyond the proper limits of its efficacy. Whenever the natural sciences arrogate to themselves their proper method as the only one, they have ceased to be sciences, i.e., descriptive, and have turned metaphysical in that they have identified their own field of investigation with reality. The truly scientific method is descriptive and does not define reality but busies itself with seeing it in all its aspects. Biology does not account for life, but accepts it as a working hypothesis, as a

[14] Cf. Nygren, "Hur är filosofi som vetenskap möjlig?" and *Filosofisk och kristen etik*, p. 13, where with H. Rickert Nygren differentiates between *das Gegebene* and *das Aufgegebene* as directive of the respective tasks of the philosophical and the special sciences.

phenomenon to be understood, not explained. For theology to attempt to prove the reality of its object would be to be neither philosophical nor scientific. The question of ultimate reality is and will remain insoluble, and can thus be solved by neither philosophy nor theology. The theological solution of this question consists simply in the affirmation that the claim to be transcendentally real is inseparable from religion. As a science theology accepts the content of faith as its field of investigation antecedently validated by critical philosophy. Metaphysics is, therefore, out of the question, for it is a bastard form of knowledge, unphilosophical because not critically confined to the sphere of immanence, and unscientific because not content to describe, but anxious to explain and test the conclusions of one field by the standards of another. To test the atheoretical content of faith by theoretical standards is to do violence to the field of investigation and to relinquish all claims to be scientific. Further to assume that as a science it can claim to supply information as to objective reality is simply to reveal a total ignorance as to the meaning of scientific method "Just as a scientific philosophy is the direct opposite of a metaphysical philosophy, scientific theology is in direct contrast to a metaphysical theology. No science, be it philosophy or theology, can contain any metaphysical ingredient without losing its scientific character."[15]

That to decry the metaphysical fallacy, or even vigorously to attack it, is not enough, is revealed by the bondage of Barthian theology to the metaphysical way of presenting the problem. In a suggestive chapter in *Till frågan om den systematiska teologiens uppgift* ("Concerning the Task of Systematic Theology"), Bring

[15] Bring, *op. cit.*, p. 74.

shows that in spite of his heated polemic against metaphysics, Brunner's theology is firmly bound up with it because of a negative relation. The fact that philosophical conclusions are to be avoided becomes the directive force in Brunner's early thought. He thus arrives at such metaphysical contradictions as the infinite and the finite, or time and eternity, and builds his system on them. The extreme eschatological transcendentalism of Barthianism is due to this metaphysical orientation which endeavors to be the direct contradiction of liberal idealism. Even such special theological categories as sin and forgiveness must therefore be conceived of in metaphysical terms. It even forces him into the basic fallacy of metaphysics, the psychologistic epistemology, so that Brunner must define scientific knowledge as that containing the contradictions of complete immanence, while the theologian by faith solves the contradictions. This, of course, is to strive for a general view of the world and to explain its problems. Because Brunner has neglected to be philosophically critical, and thus failed to see metaphysics for what it is, an absurd mixture of knowledge and speculation, he has himself become the prisoner of the enemy he means to have slain.

Theology must not only refuse to be identified with the cramped method of the natural sciences or with the vague speculation of metaphysics, but it must overcome all temptations to be normative. Science is never normative; theology is a science. For the Lundensian theologians there are two clear-cut activities in experience: theoretical judgments and value judgments. Faith and reason are independent functions. This is, of course, not a psychogenetic distinction, but a categorical division of experience. Although the relation between these two spheres must be more carefully explained in its proper setting, it is nevertheless interesting to notice at this point that the theological methodology as a whole is built on the supposition that the categorical distinction is absolute. Religion is an ideal; science, an interpretation of facts. Religion is an immediate value judgment; science, a judgment of value. Religion is a subjective commitment; science, an objective description. "There is science, and there is religion; there is also science of religion, but there is no scientific religion. Religion lies on an entirely different plane from science."[16] Nygren even wonders if a value judgment ought to be called a judgment at all, since it is not a definition of a formal relation, such as exists in theoretical judgments, but is, unexceptionally, a matter of personal commitment. To say, "This is good," is meaningless unless a personal commitment is involved; to say "God is almighty," is to have been religiously moved; but to say, "The table is round," is merely to express a theoretical truth, i.e., to define the form of the table. The same author even goes so far as to assert that "religion requires a free, individual decision, while science demands objective necessity, and (that) these two exclude each other with logical necessity."[17] The distinction between the categories of experience is complete when the possibility of having normative necessity serve as a bridge between the empirical necessity of the theoretical aspect of experience and the freedom of the religious experience is rejected. One necessity is fully as incompatible as the other with the assertion of religion that it must be a

---

[16] Aulén, "Kristendom och idealism," p. 31.
[17] Nygren, *Dogmatikens vetenskapliga grundläggning*, pp. 37-38.

question of free, individual commitment.[18] The construction of a theoretical ought is to condition, and thus to limit, freedom. There must be no dualism between the theoretical and the practical reason. Nygren, in definitely rejecting all theoretical conditioning of freedom, says, "There remains no freedom for him who has been thoroughly convinced. In such a case, it is not permissible to speak of the free commitment which is inseparable from the religious consciousness."[19] When, in the exposition of the content of the Lundensian theology and ethics, the words "spontaneous," "value-indifferent," "unmotivated" will occur with great frequency, it is important to view them against this complete separation of theoretical and value judgments. The content of theology, the form of which has already been validated by critical philosophy, is therefore filled by the faith judgment which can be scientifically understood but not tested. This aspect of methodology will be better understood in the light of a few explanations regarding the relation of theology to psychology and to history.

B. Theology and Psychology.

Even if the form of religion may be validated by the transcendental method, and the legitimacy of religion as a prerequisite for experience may thus be established, can theology prevent its becoming part and parcel of psychological subjectivism as soon as it begins to look for the content of religion which is to be found somewhere in the world of history? The Lundensian theologians strongly emphasize the fact that theology is in no way dependent upon psychological investigation.

[18] Ibid., p. 38.
[19] Ibid., p. 39.

The interest of psychology is the subject of faith; of theology, the object of faith. The content of faith as object for theological investigation is not a psychological reality but a scientific abstraction. Using the theological method of Schleiermacher as an illustration, Nygren writes approvingly: "On the contrary, we are now certain that *das christliche Selbstbewusstsein* denotes the Christian consciousness as a whole and is identical with the transcendental nature of religion. This insight is most significant in relation to the scientific validation of the statements of faith. This validation receives an entirely different meaning, depending upon whether the point of departure is the Christian self-consciousness in the sense of a psychological consciousness or in the sense of the nature of Christianity. Each interpretation requires an entirely different method."[20] If the point of departure is the psychological, theology becomes involved in all the problems of an experiential theology. Obviously the individual experience is inadequate as the basis of theology. Is it, then, the collective consciousness of the Church, or the least common denominator of the religious consciousness? If either is true, how can it be ascertained? If again, the individual consciousness is thus complemented by the collective experience, the presentation is very likely the expression of an objective system gradually induced into the individual interpreter. If, however, the point of departure is the Christian consciousness as a whole or the transcendental nature of Christian experience, theology receives a structure completely different from that of empirical psychology. The case may be viewed from another point of view. Psychology interests itself in the derivation and processes of the

[20] *Ibid.*, p. 158.

religious experience. Theology studies only the trans-subjective object of faith found in history by means of its own organic principle of unity. "When faith is the object of theological analysis it is not the phenomenon of the soul which is described, but faith is understood to mean a unique religious individuality, an organic connection among ideas with a definite center."[21] It is not so much faith as *the* faith. Insofar, moreover, as theology does not concern itself with any psychological endowment, it has no problem as to the actualization of religion. Inasmuch as it does not deal with any psychological explanations, it need not fear any damaging discoveries, uncertain and changing, in the field of psychology. Bring cites the illustration of Luther's suffering from fits of depression during which his writings were affected in such a way as to give them an organic unity of their own. Psychologically, these writings might be explained in terms of pathology as caused or at least conditioned by these moods of the spirit. Actually, however, they stand in harmonious relation with all his writings, and, as a matter of fact, express that which is most organically related to the very center of Christian faith. Theology is not concerned with the moods. It tests his writings with reference to the distinctiveness of Christianity as a system of historical truths. The same author gives another illustration when he shows how the content of thought produced by wrath may be quite independent of the feelings of wrath, and may be in itself objectively valid. Or, to turn to another field: "A systematic investigation of concrete ethical judgments will show that they are connected and capable of being understood by analysis entirely independent of any psychological anal-

[21] Bring, *Till frågan om den systematiska teologiens uppgift*, p. 215.

ysis of the individual valuing subject."[22] Not only do theology and psychology have different principles of investigation, but psychology as a science is completely impotent to judge the content of religion. Without anticipating too much, it is well to keep in mind that since the religious consciousness, according to Nygren, is passive, and since the content of faith is never theoretical, it is natural to claim that the content of religion, already validated by the philosophy of religion, is independent of the psychological channels of transmission, that the content of religion, religiously speaking, is revealed, not discovered, that God is the subject of faith, not its object. Even the Christian's love to others is primarily not his own love, but God's love in him; God's *agape*, the New Testament term for love, uses the Christian as its organ of expression. In all real struggle against evil, God is thus held to be the subject; he is both the subject of faith and the subject of love.

C. Theology and History.

We have seen that for the Lundensian theologians, theology is methodologically distinct and independent of metaphysics and psychology. But if the content of theology can be found neither rationally nor by the psychological approach, must it not be of such a nature as to make theology a purely historical discipline? This question comes close to the very heart of the Lundensian method, for in a certain meaningful way theology is understood to mean systematic history. Nevertheless, this systematic history is not to be confused with the positivistic method, for it interprets history in only one light, the organic unity of the object of theology.

[22] *Ibid.*, p. 100.

Theological Methodology

The factual and genetic interests are subordinated to the systematic expression through history of the basic Christian motifs.

Better to understand in what relation theology stands to the historical sciences, a negative definition of theology is helpful. First of all, theology is not the interpreter of a historic deposit in an exclusively static sense. "Every attempt to absolutize a certain piece of history and fence it off as a protected area is definitely doomed."[23] The legitimization of theology, therefore, cannot be Biblical. The birth of Lundensian theology took place while critical scholarship was undermining the confidence of historical theology. When, a few decades previously, the speculative approach had been found wanting, the theologians sought for refuge in the historical Jesus. This turn of thought stimulated further historical investigation, which, climaxing a century of strong historical activity, undermined the historical foundations of theology by the conclusions which it reached, and left the theologians more uncertain than ever. In this general uncertainty a new interest was taken in the possibilities for theology which were presented by the method of critical philosophy. The Lundensian theology is part of this flight from historical relativism into the absolute certainty of religion. Thus Nygren writes: "The reason that historical truths are insufficient as a foundation for faith is their relative degree of certainty. Even the facts most definitely ascertained possess but relative certainty, while the very nature of faith requires absolute certainty for its foundation. . . . Only the a priori has apodictic certainty."[24] The Lundensian theology will have nothing

---
[23] Aulén, *Teologiska studier*, Vol. II, p. 263.
[24] Nygren, *Religiöst apriori*, pp. 15-16.

to do with any historical criterion in static self-sufficiency. By endeavoring to avoid the very way of presenting the problem, it tries to escape the dilemma that either history is the foundation of theology or it is not. Since it is well known that this will lead either to relativism or to subjectivism, historical revelation in the Lundensian theology, as we shall see later, is not static but dynamic-dramatic.

Nor can it resort to any external tribunal of authority by which the historical can be interpreted and thus developed and renewed. All human institutions are relative. Aulén shows how both the legalistic theory of the Roman Catholic Church and the democratic theory which identifies *vox populi* with *vox dei* are inadequate. Lessing's words are often quoted by the Lundensian theologians: "It is impossible to found eternal truths on historical facts."[25]

If, however, systematic theology claims no definite historical deposit or organ of interpretation, how can it possibly escape becoming identified with the general science of religion? In being scientific, must it not concern itself with the facts of religion? And what facts are there besides the psychological and the historical? The distinction is definite. The general sciences deal with facts inductively without any specific, presupposed method of organization. These further seek to explain the facts positivistically according to their cultural connections or in terms of their source of derivation or development. They come, therefore, to no unified conclusion. They remain satisfied to deepen themselves in the thoughts of past ages but come to no independent

---

[25] Cf. for instance Aulén, *op. cit.*, p. 62, and Nygren, *Religiöst apriori*, p. 15, quoting Lessing's *Werke*, Vol. VII, p. 82:
"*Zufällige Geschichtswahrheiten können der Beweis von notwendigen Vernunftwahrheiten nie werden.*"

conclusions of their own. The historic-positivistic method has its place, but when it assumes that it has a monopoly on the scientific method and poses as the authority on the truth of religion, it has outlived its usefulness and destroyed itself through the barrenness of its results. Naturally a scientific theology can have no more to do with a speculative interpretation of history which forces the historic religions in all their abundant richness and variety into pre-made conceptual categories. Instead, it adopts the critical method, which avoids both the arbitrariness of the speculative method and the fault of the empirical, namely, the fact that the historical data are only a chaos of different religious conceptions, so that an investigation which lacks a point of orientation in the form of a definite idea fails to arrive at any synthetic-systematic conclusions. The critical method, on the other hand, combines the good features of both the a priori and the empirical methods, in that it has a point of orientation in the general category of religion, while it accepts the empirical religions as the data for its investigation. "With the religious category as its guide and organizing principle it approaches the historical religions; the chaotic multiplicity is thus overcome, while the transition from the formal to the factual territory is also made, inasmuch as its approach is by way of the historical givenness."[26] In order positively to illustrate this point of view and to fix the relation between theology and the general sciences, it may be well to quote at some length a passage from Bring: "The historic-genetic approach is no more concerned with the uniquely Christian than is empirical psychology, and no more is the kind of historic presentation which in the main limits itself

[26] Nygren, *Dogmatikens vetenskapliga grundläggning,* p. 133.

to the surface of Christianity. The characteristic thing about real theology, on the contrary, is its ability to present its problem in terms of the specifically, the uniquely Christian. A superficial judgment would declare such a point of view incompatible with a scientific investigation. But the Christian ideas belong to an organic unity which is just as truly given in history as are the separate data in the history of Christianity, or the separate ideas themselves, for these ideas are not forced into an arbitrary unity. On the contrary, they serve a special purpose, namely the presentation or the elucidation of different sides of the same thing. According to their position in this totality, the separate facts receive their significance. They are not given the status of self-sufficient concepts, but are pictures which reveal what is central and unique in faith. And to define this is just the task of systematic theology."[27]

It may now be clear what, according to the Lundensian theologians, is the object of theology. The object of theology is faith as an independent, organic continuity, unified by its possession of basic motifs. The symphonic theme of the Lundensian school of thought is "that religion is a completely independent and unique form of experience that develops according to its own autonomous principles and must be judged from its own center."[28] "*Und es ist die Aufgabe der Theologie, jedes Glaubensurteil im organischen Zusammenhang mit diesem Zentrum zu verstehen.*"[29] Theology is thus a special form of religious history with a special working hypothesis, according to which it accomplishes its sys-

[27] Bring, *op. cit.*, pp. 211-212.
[28] Nygren, *Religiöst apriori*, p. 12.
[29] Bring, "Die neuere schwedische Theologie," in *Die Kirche in Schweden*, p. 74.

tematic task, namely the discovery and the systematic exposition of each religion in accordance with its organic distinctiveness. *"Nicht die begriffliche Einheit, sondern die organische Ganzheit muss das Ziel der Darstellung sein."*[30] Theology is systematic history with a principle of interpretation received from its object. In the case of Christianity, it is Christian faith, a trans-subjective, empirical unity in, but not of, history, the limits of which are definitely drawn by its own uniqueness.

Since the relation of theological methodology to philosophy, psychology, and general history is now clear, it remains further to clarify its relation to the history of religions. The rapid growth of the latter science has of late caused Christian theology no little concern because of the material for earnest contemplation that its painstaking efforts have brought to light. We have already noted that even though religious experience is a form a priori, it is as such totally devoid of any content. There is, therefore, no way by which an ideal or "true religion" can be rationally constructed. Since, moreover, the religious category is no psychological endowment, it is equally impossible to expect an actualization of religion. Combining the transcendental method of deducing the religious category and the critical method of history, it appears obvious that religion must be realized, i.e., found in the given positive religions. Accepting the methodology of Schleiermacher in this respect, Nygren writes: "The religious category is entirely meaningless if it is isolated from the historical religions. If the method of the critical philosophy of religion is to be carried through to its logical conclusion, the historical religions must be considered to be the realization of the religious. . . .

[30] *Ibid.,* p. 10.

From the religious category it is impossible to determine according to what forms religion is to develop."[31] Instead of the actualization of religion according to which the differences in the historic religions are considered to be the uncouthness of growth which must be overcome by development in the "true religion," the realization of religion is the acceptance of cultural distinctiveness as the natural result of historical individualization. The one attempts to extract the unity out of the historic multiplicity, while the other believes that the nature of the form is to be filled by history with a profusely varied content.

All the positive-historical religions are, therefore, the realization of religion and the object for theological investigation. All the religions, moreover, are to be treated in the same manner, from the point of view of their own organic centers. Religion, in other words, has *centra* but no *centrum*. Since theology is a descriptive and not a normative science, it also follows that it can in no way judge among the religions either as to their truth in terms of objective reality, or as to the truth of any of their separate pronouncements, or even as to their comparative value. Each religion is a realization in its proper environment of the religious category. For that matter, as has been shown above, there is no way by which two ideals can be normatively compared. Science can compare descriptively, but is never normative; ideals are personal commitments, and, as such, are removed from the realm of theoretical comparisons. How can you ever, asks Nygren, compare heaven and nirvana either as to their objective reality or as to their comparative value? There is no science of objective reality, and that which

[31] Nygren, *Dogmatikens vetenskapliga grundläggning*, p. 131.

is most desired by the Christian is that which in the value judgment of a Buddhist is most to be avoided.

As a systematic discipline, theology is, accordingly, not concerned with problems of genesis, or with making obeisance to the unyielding supremacy of the individual fact, an attitude which invariably leads to an unreal spiritual atomism, or with the paralleling of individual doctrines such as karma and the idea of the Atonement. Such a comparison would be totally meaningless outside of the basic motifs of Hinduism (Buddhism, Jainism) and Christianity. The approach of theology must be typological, a non-normative analysis of the field of investigation with a view to the synoptic unity of the object. The basic motif, however, is only a working hypothesis to be increasingly verified. Naturally, both empathy and intuitive insight are required for the framing of this hypothesis. But no unnecessary subjective element has been injected into the investigation insofar as the hypothesis is tested by its adequacy of interpretation. This method is accessible to an objective test. Remove the basic motif, and the entire religion loses its unity and meaning. All the theologians of the Lundensian school further stress the idea that the basic motifs are only approximations and may even be a fundamental attitude or general notion rather than a clearly defined thought. Aulén, for this very reason, refuses to speak in terms of the "concept" of God, but speaks instead of the "picture" of God. If it is now said that interpretative history must also, to be meaningful, make use of illuminating intuitions, that it, too, must work with motifs as well as with facts, Nygren sees even here a decided difference: "Even the historic-genetic investigation concerns itself with motifs, but its primary interest is in their circulation, and the connections which history finds among similar motifs discovered in different places. . . . *Motivforskningen,* in the sense in which we are using it, is primarily interested in the content of the motifs."[32]

In a concrete work, *Den kristna kärlekstanken,* Nygren gives an illustration of the proposed method. Hellenism and Christianity are compared typologically. The basic motif of Hellenism as found in the Pythagorean-Neo-Platonic tradition is *eros,* the self-love which seeks the good, while the basic motif of Christianity is *agape,* the spontaneous, unmotivated, value-indifferent love creative of fellowship. Fundamentally, however, this typological differentiation is more than an ethical characterization, for it goes back to the foundational character of the religious experience, the category of eternity, which though devoid of content, is nevertheless one pole of interpretation, in the light of which the positively given religions must be viewed. It is easy to see how, then, the category of eternity in the Lundensian methodology is easily changed, although illegitimately, into the idea of God. The distinction now is expressed in terms of the divine. In the *eros* type, man is considered partially divine and capable of seeking God, while in the *agape* type, man is entirely the object of God's creative love. This descriptive comparison is legitimate for theology, but beyond it, it cannot go. If it ever appears normative, it is because of the ideal nature of the content which is treated, or because people have been so nurtured in the Christian tradition that a mere description seems to be other-criticism or self-praise.

In order to illustrate the importance of the basic

[32] *Ibid.,* p. 15.

motif, Aulén's characterization of the center of Christian faith as the picture of God received from his redemptive work in Christ, may be used. The thought of God is inseparably connected with the category of eternity, and Christianity as a positive religion can best be understood in this light of God in Christ. The formal demands made on the religious experience a priori, that it be definitely related to the category of eternity, are thus fulfilled, as well as the empirical requirements that the content be received from what is objectively given. Only now, however, does the great significance of the basic motif for systematic theology appear, for the uniqueness of each religion gives the systematic historian a principle of interpretation in the light of which the whole history can be viewed. The inadequacy of the *loci* method of interpretation is thus overcome, both in systematic theology and in the history of dogma. The all-inclusive law of interpretation is now that every bit of relevant material must be tested in the light of this uniqueness, this distinctive, organic principle. For the systematic task of Christian theology, the criterion must naturally be this: "Every statement of Christian faith must have an intrinsic relation with the center: the thought of God as revealed in the Christ-deed."[33] For the historic task of Christian theology, this must be the criterion: to analyze the history of Christian thought and test the separate data in regard to their compatibility with the principle of interpretation, the uniquely Christian. The question is, of course, not of the overt expressions but of the inner meaning. *"Die Dogmengeschichte will die innere Geschichte des Christentums verstehen. Es handelt sich also um die Eigenart des*

[33] Aulén, *Teologiska studier*, Vol. III, p. 384.

Christentums."[34] The mode of expression may hide the real significance of the underlying motif. The same motif may persist in almost totally different modes of expression, while the same mode of expression may persist, though giving utterance to an almost totally different motif. The task calls for great discrimination, and is impossible without the guiding presence of the basic motif. Nygren has very recently written an article on historical methodology, in which he illustrates how the identical expressions such as "God is creative love" differ in connotation in the writings of Thomas Aquinas and Luther because of the fundamental difference in their basic ideas.[35] In Aquinas God's creative love is thought of in terms of substance, while in Luther the fundamental notion of creativity is soteriological, the creation of a new fellowship between God and the sinner. This difference is understandable only in the light of the basic motifs in the thoughts of each writer. The synoptic method often reveals incompatible basic motifs struggling for supremacy within the history of Christian thought, as well as a continuous conflict between the basic motif and disharmonious minor motifs which are incapable of subsumption.

Not only has Nygren shown the intertwining of Christian and Hellenic motifs in *Den kristna kärlekstanken*, but Aulén has published two works devoted to the tracing of the basic motif in Christian thought. In the first, *Den kristna gudsbilden*, Aulén shows that the thought of God is the leading motif of Christian history, under which all others can be organically subsumed.

[34] Aulén, *Die Dogmengeschichte im Lichte der Lutherforschung*, p. 15.
[35] "Motivforskning som filosofiskt och historiskt problem," in *S.T.K.*, häft. 1, 1939.

The history of dogma has often strayed because it has been written from the point of view of a minor motif. This is especially true of Harnack's great work, *The History of Dogma,* in which the author's preoccupation with the doctrine of Christ led him to such a false conclusion as that the Christology of the early Church was a *"Hellenizierung des Christentums auf dem Boden des Evangeliums."* He did not sense, because of his Ritschlian dislike for metaphysics, that the early Church gospel *about* Christ was the very essence of Christianity; instead, he considered it a perversion of the simple gospel *of* Christ. If his point of reference had been the idea of God, he would have seen that the development of Christology was the greatest defense against Hellenism, as well as against Judaism, insofar as the God of the suffering Christ, the God of the cross and the empty tomb, must ever be but foolishness to the Hellenic ideal, concretely summarized as *eros.* The Christological motif is accordingly comprehended in radically different fashions, depending upon whether the point of view is rational knowledge or *das Eigenart des Christentums.* The other appropriate illustration appears in *Den kristna försoningstanken.* Most histories of the Atonement consider the early theories crudely mythological. What dealings can an enlightened conscience have with any proposal like a ransom paid to the devil? The Anselmian theology, say the liberal interpreters, at least tried to do away with a shameful mythology. Since Christ suffered *qua homo,* an attempt was also made to ethicize the concept of the Atonement. The views which require an objective change in God, they continue, are, nevertheless, destructive of the constancy of the love of God, and only an interpretation in terms of man's turning to God can do justice to both the concept of God and the moral requirements of the Atonement. This view Aulén claims to be mistaken, since the motifs do not have their genesis in the idea of God. If the historians of dogma had found the motif under the old ransom theories, they would have discovered that in all their crudeness they reflect the very heart of Christian faith. If they, further, had worked in the light of the uniquely Christian, history would have disclosed not two theories of the Atonement, the subjective and the objective, but three; for the classical motif is not a rational, but a religious explanation, which reveals God as both the subject and the object of the redemptive drama. The classical motif is consequently always God's way to man, while the other two are in the last analysis mostly man's way to God. The Atonement, according to the classical motif, is impossible of rational or psychological explanation, for it is an act of divine grace which is not confined within any rational or moral limits. The classical motif is further a dualistic-dramatic struggle with real forces of evil in which God is himself reconciled in that he reconciles the world with himself. In connection with methodology the theory itself is of little interest except as it illustrates the effect of a central idea on individual doctrines. If the heart of Christian faith is the mystery of God's spontaneous, unmotivated, creatively forgiving love, the classical motif, in spite of its crude modes of expression, reflects the distinctively Christian in all its fullness. Here the act of God in the Atonement is unbroken; in the Anselmian theory, on the other hand, the formally moral is unbroken, while God's way to man is interrupted. Similarly, scholasticism's *potentia ordinata* failed in Christian insight, which knows of no temporal *ordinata*, and, indeed, refuses to countenance any external limitation on God, holding rather to his unfathomable nature as revealed in the Christ-deed. Nominalism's valiant championing of God's unconditioned will as *potentia absoluta*, breaks the chain of the legal and the rational, only to be denied Christian standing, because in the Christian faith *deus absconditus* is also *deus revelatus*, through the mystery of the Christ-deed. The Reformation, again, was a return to the classical point of view, even though the form of expression was changed; while the Lutheran orthodoxy fought for the *sola gratia* principle without realizing that in taking over the Anselmian theory of the Atonement, no longer in form only, but in motif as well, it had put a most formal limitation on God and introduced a motif completely incompatible with its main principle. Liberalism's subjective theory of the Atonement is at once seen to be in direct opposition to the Christian idea of redemption as an uninterrupted work of God. The center of Christian faith is, therefore, a motif so basic that in its far-reaching light every historical proposition can be tested. The illustrations given show how the task of Christian theology is to analyze the historic forms with a view to their inner meaning, and then to test them as to their compatibility with the distinctiveness of Christian faith. This procedure may reduce quantitatively the content of theology, but the method has already given it a field both distinct and distinctive, as well as a principle of interpretation which does justice both to the uniqueness of Christian faith and to the scientific standing of theology.

In his most recent work on this subject to which reference has been made above, Nygren widens his concept of philosophy beyond the limits of transcendental deduction and conceptual analysis in order to arrive at a more adequate method of historical interpretation. History without any principles of organization is a mere ocean of factual chaos. To insist on a factual, punctual method of inquiry and to limit history to this is a procedure not only inadequate but impossible, for facts are known only in and through their relations. Emphasis and significance, furthermore, are philosophical terms involving valuation and therefore implying the presence of some unifying meaning. Motifs are unifying structures of meaningfulness apart from which a specific content of history is incapable of adequate understanding. These motifs are then a problem both for philosophy and for history. Historical investigation may start from the chaos of unorganized facts and work toward the synthetic interpretation of their meaningfulness or it may start by emphasizing the most distinctive features of a set of historical facts and work toward the systematic filling out of the historical picture presented by facts equally real and present but less distinctive in nature. Whether the road leads through manifoldness of fact to groups of facts organically related to each other in sets of meaningfulness or through the prior emphasis in obvious distinctness to general factual resemblance in and through this distinctness, the end is always the motifs through which the fullness of fact is alone understandable. Nygren illustrates this by a thought-provoking diagram with the giving of which this section must come to a close:

The Unifying Motif Through Which Facts Are Understood

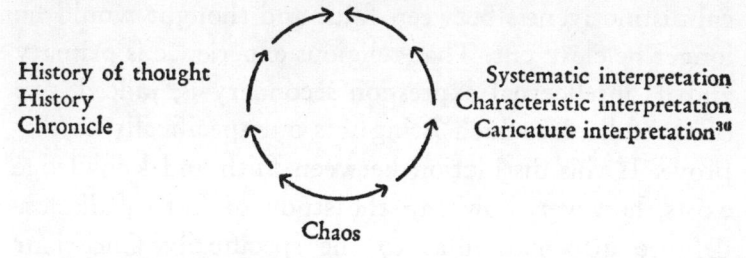

History of thought
History
Chronicle

Systematic interpretation
Characteristic interpretation
Caricature interpretation[36]

Chaos

D. Theology and Knowledge.

We have now explained at some length the first three propositions of the Lundensian theological methodology: that theology is a science with a logico-descriptive method, that its field is the content of faith as found in the historical religions, and that it is able to treat the material from its own objectively organic point of view without any unscientific presuppositions. There remains to consider only the atheoretical nature of faith and its capacity, in this respect, for scientific comprehension and systematic expression.

Bring, who deals at some length with this problem, takes as his original assumption the proposition which Nygren has labored to establish, that "faith and thought belong to separate areas of experience, and signify two different points of view."[37] Faith, as Nygren has pointed out, must be unconditionally free from theoretical compulsion. Faith is never theoretical knowledge. When this is insisted upon, however, another problem emerges. Faith as historically given is not a deep and dim emotional awareness beneath the superficial and inadequate expression of language. If it were so, theology would become associated with an experience a priori in the

[36] *Ibid.*, p. 14.
[37] Bring, *Till frågan om den systematiska teologiens uppgift*, p. 6.

form of a psychological endowment, and the categorical distinctiveness between faith and thought would no longer be clear-cut. That religious experience is primary and its intellectual expression secondary is, indeed, one of the fallacies which Bring sets out specifically to disprove. If this distinction between faith and knowledge exists, however, how can the study of history disclose definite information as to the specifically Christian? That this information is not knowledge is insisted upon: with knowledge is meant a theoretical act. Bring agrees with Hägerström that the value judgment can never claim to contain knowledge. Inasmuch as the content of faith cannot be logically tested, and insofar as Bring is unwilling to admit the existence of a dualism of knowledge which would reflect two realities, as, for instance, does Kant's distinction between the theoretical and the practical reason, it follows that knowledge must invariably mean theoretical knowledge, and to accept another kind of knowledge seems to be a contradiction. Discussing the general problem of the relation of a so-called practical reason to religious truth, the same author writes: "This would mean that religion is constituted as a special kind of comprehension; there must then be a question of two ways to knowledge, the logical and the religious. Religion must consequently be thought of as a special mediating organ of knowledge. But that thinking should be partly the organ of knowledge and partly the content of knowledge, or that religion should represent both the way to, or the organ of knowledge, and also the content of knowledge is obviously absurd."[38] From this it is evident that religion as faith is never knowledge, and that knowledge as theoretical thought is

[38] *Ibid.*, p. 93.

never religion. Theology is, therefore, in this respect, entirely distinct from religion, for theology as a logical discipline is knowledge.

The problem, however, is now all the more acute: how does history contain something which is not in itself knowledge and which nevertheless has a unity and a meaningfulness that is akin to the theoretical and can be grasped by it? Bring, to answer this question, differentiates between "the theology of faith" and the scientific theology. In "the theology of faith," the thought content is an intrinsic part of the faith-state. The faith-state is not an emotional act in distinction from the resulting ideation. "It is impossible to differentiate between faith and the content of faith."[39] The chasm between thought and faith is absolute. Whatever reflection this state may contain, even though it can be described as a groping, a struggle, it is not rational in the sense of theoretical activity or logical normativeness, but a direct consciousness of the contents, or an immediate realization of what is involved in the receiving of the divine. Experience and reflection are thus of one cloth. The faith-state is born with its content; the intellectual ingredient is part and parcel of faith's givenness. There can be no distinction between *fides qua* and *fides quae*. Nor must the intellectual content be called rational because it seems centered in the rational powers rather than in the affective or in the volitive, for the category of experience is determined not by psychological function, but by the nature of the source of stimulation to which the response is made. Theoretical thought employs the powers of reason according to logical laws, and the typical attitude of the theoretical function is detachment, while the intellectual content of the faith-

[39] *Ibid.*, pp. 196-197.

state is a direct response to a divine relation, and is thus included within the totality of the religious category. Again, it becomes clear that the logical has no jurisdiction over the content of faith, since this is received independent of any reference to logical demands. Nor can one category, such as the theoretical with its logical laws, demand that the others conform to its individual standards. Religion is alogical in nature; its attitude is immediate commitment and the immediacy of its insight is lost to detached observation. Religion is a value judgment and must be understood according to the normativeness of its own nature ascertainable objectively in the historical religions. The fact, moreover, that faith has paradoxes, insoluble from a logical or an empirical point of view, as for instance the common theme with Aulén that God is omnipotent while yet fighting against real powers of evil, or that God is both all-powerful and all-good, does not mean that faith is arbitrary or false, but rather that it has a religious unity, organically necessary, a system of connections with their own definite standard of truth, their own theocentric verification. Both empirical and logical tests are, therefore, beside the point. Faith speaks a language all its own beyond the scope of the logico-empirical realm. How this principle is an objective entity verifiable in history has already been explained.

Theology is now seen with increasing clarity to be the systematic exposition of the intellectual content of the original faith-states. Some of the confusions of theological methodology as treated above are easier to understand from this point of view. Some theologians endeavor to accept this original content and develop it outside the limits of its disclosures. It must be plain, however, that since theology is a descriptive science which receives and does not develop its content, it cannot arrive at an extension of its information except in and through the faith-states themselves. Religion limits the answers of theology. To go beyond this limit is to distort theology and end in unutterable confusion because of an uncritical mixing of the religious and the theoretical categories. Similar confusions result when the theologian attempts to accept the original content of faith and then to prove its objective reality by scientific means. The theologian who labors to prove the value of the disclosures of faith fares no better, for he has relinquished his scientific outlook and ventured into the realm of subjective commitments. The one and only task of systematic theology is scientifically to report the content of the faith-states according to the organic principle of interpretation which, along with the trans-subjective data themselves, is found in the givenness of history.

If the information derived from the original faith-states is not knowledge, if it is even categorically distinct from knowledge, the question still remains as to how it can become knowledge. How is it possible for that which by its very nature is alogical, atheoretical, to be logically known and theoretically expressed? Can science go beyond the limits of the material intrinsically its own, i.e., the logical, and give a scientific account of a category not its own, to grasp and express the intellectual content of the faith-states without attenuating or distorting it? Would it not be better to say that science is adequate within its own jurisdiction, namely the questions of historical genesis and psychological description?

This very problem has caused great differences of opinion in recent Swedish thought. Some who hold that there is a fundamental difference between faith and reason, between religion and science, claim that theology cannot be scientific in that it must leave the realms of cold scientific abstractions and enter into the light of life in order to know its deeper truth. The capacity of the theologian for truth is, therefore, commensurate with his depth of religious experience. Since language, moreover, is a hindrance to the expression of living truth, the theologian's capacity for expressing this truth is measured by his command of "words that laugh and cry." Theology is, then, not the prose of scientific fact, but the poetry of spiritual truth. Others with a more activistic-moralistic bent emphasize that theology is an organ in contagious words of ethical creativity. All these, however, have this in common, that they class theology with the original phenomenon of religion, rather than with the secondary discipline of science.

To the Lundensians, however, theology is a science, strictly, stringently a science. Bring, therefore, explains the relation between the theoretical and the atheoretical as follows: The faith-states are not devoid of intellectual content. Consequently, something is comprehended. But to speak of the incomprehensible's being comprehended is absurd. The atheoretical reflection receives an atheoretical content of information. This content is then not only felt but known. The forms of knowledge, to be sure, are logical, but it does not follow that the logical forms cannot transmit the alogical content from another sphere. Compare, Bring and Nygren frequently say in discussions, the description of a pain, an experience which is far from logical in nature. The content of faith is comprehended by the logical reason as an atheoretical body of knowledge with an atheoretical principle of validity. Since, therefore, it is comprehended as it is in all its atheoreticalness, it can also be expressed, for that which is truly comprehended is equally capable of expression. The field of expression, furthermore, is the logical. This again does not mean that the original content must receive a logical form, or that the fullness of dynamic life must somehow be caught and cramped in a net of logical abstraction, but merely that the alogical content receives a logical exposition in terms of its own alogical nature. To express logically, the author seems to say, is not to make logical but to describe objectively as well as accurately and systematically. The whole difficulty, as Bring devotes a good deal of space to explain, is what Nygren so often points out, that philosophy has long labored with an impossible theory of knowledge, in which the main problem has been how the subject knows the object, the very impossibility for solution lying in its way of presenting the problems in terms of irreconcilable opposites. Without repeating what has been previously dealt with, it is sufficient to say that Bring maintains that thought refers itself directly to its object, that it is not a mediating function, but the immediate representation of a factual reality. Without considering further analysis or demonstration necessary, he contents himself with saying that thought is thus capable of comprehending directly the content of the faith-states, and of adequately passing them into expression without essential modification or distortion.

III. The Methodological Relation of Philosophical to Theological Ethics

As previously stated in the introduction to this chapter, the ethical methodology in the Lundensian system of thought has an approach so similar to the theological that it seems unnecessary to treat it except summarily. It may, instead, be more profitable to give a general summary of Nygren's most important book on the subject, *Filosofisk och kristen etik,* and to complement this, wherever it seems to make the meaning more clear, by references to his later work in the same field, *Etiska grundfrågor* ("Basic Questions in Ethics").

The book starts with an observation as to the uncertain status of Christian ethics as a necessary and independent science. Several attempts at solution have been made. The most persistent of these have been from the side of philosophical ethics, where reasons have been advanced why Christian ethics cannot justifiably claim to be a scientific discipline. The first of these is the accusation that Christian ethics moves in a circle: the good is the divine, but the divine can be known only because it is the highest good. For its basic notions, therefore, Christian ethics is dependent on philosophical ethics. In the second place, Christian ethics is heteronomous in that it refers to God's will, while moral autonomy is the very birthright of ethics. It is claimed, again, that the rewards which seem an integral part of Christian ethics inevitably lead to eudaemonism and thus corrupt the basic idea of ethics, the primacy of the good will as such. By others, moreover, it is claimed that the orientation of Christian ethics is ascetic, whether supra- or intra-mundane, and that this orientation is too much of an evasion of actual problems to allow Christian ethics any independent and necessary place as a special science. It is at times also claimed that Christian ethics stresses love to a degree which crowds out other necessary aspects of an adequate ethics. As protagonists of philosophical ethics to the exclusion of the distinctively Christian are given such men as Schopenhauer, Höffding, von Hartmann, and Paulsen.

But the elimination of Christian ethics as a necessary and independent science is attempted also in the interest of theology. This interest is mostly apologetic. If the demands of ethics are universal and independent of specific religious presuppositions; if ethics, furthermore, leads every earnest seeker into conflicts which are insoluble apart from religion; if Christianity is needed as the only adequate power to realize the highest demands of a universal ethics; then Christianity has received an unshakable validation in the eyes of every honest and earnest man. If, on the other hand, ethics is to constitute this foundation for religion, it is also obvious that Christian ethics must yield to the universal demands of morality as such. By way of illustration, Nygren cites the works of two men who have championed this point of view: Herrmann and Mandel.

Not only have attempts been made to delete Christian ethics from the special sciences, but some, like Runestam and E. W. Mayer, have tried to eliminate philosophical ethics by proving that all ethics is religious, inasmuch as religion and ethics are inseparable to such a degree that only a religious ethics is able to do justice to the deepest demands of the moral life.

Others, again, have tried to produce complementary theories. Naumann and Troeltsch have worked hard to show that philosophical ethics has a legitimate and independent sphere in relation to this-worldly goals, whereas Christian ethics deals with the highest, the other-worldly objectives. A different complementary relation is proposed by Troeltsch and Süskind, who hold that philosophical ethics is motivated solely by scientific interests while Christian ethics has a motivation of more practical nature. The aim of philosophical ethics is truth; that of Christian ethics, the fostering of the Christian life. There are also attempts at methodological complementing of philosophical and Christian ethics where the former, to quote from a summary by Nygren himself, "is the general philosophy or ethics of culture, while the latter must express the willing and acting which flows from the Christian self-consciousness (Schleiermacher), or philosophical ethics may produce a formal, categorical scheme for the ethical life as a whole (Schleiermacher in *Grundlinien einer Kritik der bisherigen Sittenlehre*), or deal with the formal side of the will, while theological ethics has to set forth its real content (H. Rosén); or: philosophical ethics has to set forth the ethical a priori, the universally endowed ethical disposition which, nevertheless, can find its completion only in the ethics of Christian love (H. H. Wendt, H. Rosén, R. Jelke)."[40]

Having thus stated the problem, Nygren decides his own approach. To assume the necessity of one or both sciences is uncritical. The safest way is to pursue each independently according to its own nature. Should one prove superfluous, it eliminates itself. If both, on the other hand, prove to be indispensable in their own right, the question naturally must be answered as to what extent there can be a positive relation between philosophical and Christian ethics and in what way they may complement each other.

With this in view, Nygren sets out to investigate the nature of philosophical ethics. He soon discovers that

[40] Nygren, *Filosofisk och kristen etik*, p. 97.

the total field of ethical experience is already in the hands of special sciences, but this causes him no concern, inasmuch as philosophy, as a universal science investigating experience as a whole with a view to the validity of its several forms, confines itself to no limited field. On the other hand, ethics itself is dependent upon the validation of its form of experience, in that the validity of the particular ethical act, as ethical, stands or falls with the validity of the ethical category. This task, which is beyond the adequacy of any special science, is, therefore, necessitated both from the nature of critical philosophy and from the nature of ethical experience. It is clear, moreover, that only a critical philosophy, a philosophy with a transcendental method for testing claims of validity, can fulfil the demands laid upon it.

The next two chapters Nygren devotes to polemics against metaphysical and normative ethics. As seen in connection with theology, metaphysics is rejected insofar as it deals exclusively neither with *quaestio facti* nor *quaestio juris*, but endeavors to become a Weltanschauung. In a special article devoted to philosophy, "Hur är filosofi som vetenskap möjlig?"[41] ("How is Philosophy as a Science Possible?"), Nygren defines philosophy as a universal science in distinction from sciences of fact or experience. Metaphysics is here described as the dignifying of certain arbitrarily selected portions of experience with the incomparable prestige of reality. It is appropriate that in this article, appearing in a collection of writings in the honor of Hägerström, the ontological task of philosophy is repudiated, while the logical task of philosophy is stressed. The task of philosophy now becomes limited to a much smaller field

[41] In *Festskrift tillägnad Axel Hägerström*.

than that assigned it by Hägerström, however, and is reduced to the transcendental testing of the categories of experience. For this, it has at its disposal the negative method or the analysis of concepts, and the positive method or the transcendental. In *Filosofisk och kristen etik* philosophy is pictured as standing before three choices:[42] first, it can renounce its claim to universality and become a special science. This is, to be sure, impossible insofar as there is at its disposal no special science both adequate for philosophical interpretation, and still capable of retaining its objective methodology. This is true of even psychology, as its recent history has amply proved. Or, secondly, philosophy can renounce its scientific character and become metaphysics, claiming to obtain objectively, although with a smaller degree of scientific vigor, a unity within the multiplicity of facts produced by the special sciences. Deduction as a method has, of course, been discarded by the philosophers themselves. Strict rationalism, therefore, is impossible. But, says Nygren, the inductive method is not better, except in claim and appearance. All unity in a metaphysical system is the unity of preconception. For a certain number of facts which point one way in respect to a general interpretation of the world, there is an equal number pointing in a different direction. The metaphysician is caught in self-delusion. Nygren even goes so far as to write that metaphysics "obtains no objective, generally valid results, and does not even make attempts to do so. . . . The principle of selection is the personal, purely subjective attitude and, from the point of view of science, the irrational and the arbitrary."[43]

[42] P. 103 ff.
[43] *Ibid.*, p. 121.

The third possibility for philosophy is to have a new relation to experience other than the factual, i.e., to test its very presuppositions. The critical philosophy is the science of general principles, of logical validity, critical, scientific, universalistic, and true to experience, not in parts, but as a whole. At the same time, it does not in the least encroach on the field of the special sciences. The sphere of competence of philosophical ethics in relation to metaphysics or to the special science, descriptive ethics, is thus illustrated.[44]

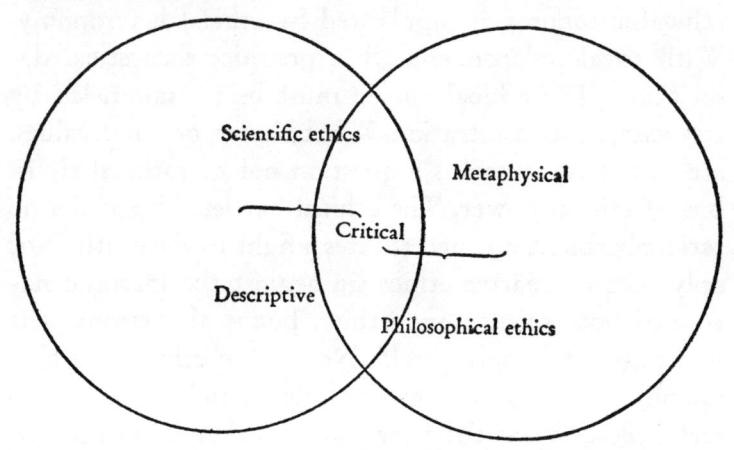

[Diagram: Two overlapping circles. Left circle labeled "Scientific ethics" and "Descriptive"; right circle labeled "Metaphysical"; overlap labeled "Critical" and "Philosophical ethics".]

Philosophical ethics as a critical discipline is thus distinguished from scientific ethics by the fact that it is philosophic; from metaphysical ethics, by the fact that it is scientific.

Inasmuch as the Lundensian rejection of the normative, in philosophy as well as in science, has been treated in connection with theological methodology proper, it seems unnecessary at this point to dwell on the topic at any length. Nygren attacks the normative idea of philosophical ethics by showing that it wrongs science inso-

[44] *Ibid.*, p. 116.

far as the latter deals with reflective judgments, whereas an ideal is in no way capable of rational construction or demonstration. A normative ethics also wrongs the ethical itself in that it logically leads to casuistry. If ideals are capable of rational tests, not only can general principles be provided for the individual, but specific rules of conduct can also be constructed, which from a rational point of view must have more weight and authority than the feeble judgment of the individual. But if norms, let alone specific rules, can be established, ethical autonomy is supplanted by ethical heteronomy. With royal independence, life precedes theoretical description. The ethical choice must be untrammeled by any external consideration. What choice, or what values, are finally to prevail is a question not of rational right, but of ethical power. The ethical battlefield permits no rational arbiter, but necessitates a fight to the death. Not only does normative ethics sin against the intrinsic nature of both science and ethics, but it also wrongs the nature of philosophy itself. Normative ethics *uses* philosophy. "Philosophy, on the other hand, ceases to be real philosophy at the very moment that it is degraded as a means to something else." "*Wer nicht um der Philosophie willen philosophiert, sondern die Philosophie als Mittel braucht, ist ein Sophist.*"[45] This brief summary of Nygren's rejection of normative ethics, together with its previous fuller rendering, will at least suggest his general approach to the problem.

Nygren next proceeds to the discussion of the validity of the ethical. This, like the religious, is divisible into form and content. The validity of the ethical judgment is naturally secondary to the primary ethical judging.

[45] *Ibid.,* p. 134.

The author uses a convenient analogy: in the judging "the sun warms the stone," the general law of cause and effect is primary to the special judgment. The form must be valid as such if its content is to receive any validation. In general, this can be summarized by saying that there is a logical validity which the forms of experience presuppose, and a derived validity which the content receives from the form. A careful distinction, therefore, must be made between the validity of the ethical, and ethical validity. Dismissing, after an analysis, both ethical scepticism and ethical heteronomy, the author proves that ethics has an autonomous, i.e., an independent and primary, validity. The ethical choice is never a means, but always its own end. Like the religious experience, the ethical judgment is felt as transsubjectively valid. Ethical necessity and universality, in other words, are no more extensive or quantitative concepts than the religious, but are equally intensive and qualitative.

Empirical or rational proofs for ethical validity are rejected, first, because the empirical tests its object by experience, whereas it is the ethical form of experience itself which is to be tested, and, secondly, because the rational test is an appeal to ultimate principles, whereas it is here a case of testing those very principles. Critical philosophy differs from both rationalism and empiricism by its use of the transcendent method, for in contrast to the rational method, it has its point of departure in experience, and in contrast to empirical methods, it rejects induction in favor of the analysis of concepts. As a matter of fact, only one indubitable ethical judgment is necessary, since if the ethical is at all valid, this validity must "be expressed clearly at every point of the ethical experience; in every ethical judgment this validity must be discernible and demonstrable."[46] If the validity of the independent form of the ethical experience is found to be the unconditional presupposition for experience as a whole, it follows that it has transcendental validity, i.e., that it is a form of experience *sui generis* and a priori. It also follows that whatever can be shown to be indisputably related to this form as its content, whatever, in other words, can be proved ethical, has the derived validity of the ethical content. "To prove anything ethical and to prove it valid are no longer two separate tasks. So far as anything is known as ethical it is also known as unconditionally valid."[47]

Nygren continues his investigation of philosophical ethics with a section dealing with "Endowment and Validity,"[48] in which he stresses the necessity of keeping the form pure and not hypostasizing it into a psychological or transcendental reality. The ethical a priori is a category and not a factual reality. In a footnote the author repeats that the a priori neither exists nor has reality, but is universally and necessarily valid. In *Etiska grundfrågor*, Nygren devotes an important section to "Kant and Christian Ethics,"[49] for the purpose of showing how Kant, even though the father of the critical method, vitiated his own results simply because of his inability to deny himself the psychological and the normative tendencies. Kant first analyzes the good as something unconditionally good, the good *ohne Einschränkung*, the good *an sich*. This can be only *ein guter Wille*. The will, again, can be characterized by nothing

[46] *Ibid.*, p. 147.
[47] *Ibid.*, p. 149.
[48] *Ibid.*, p. 152 ff.
[49] P. 98 ff.

external to itself, by nothing but the call of duty within the will itself. The rigorism goes so far as to insist that only when duty is contrary to inclination is the act of the will ethically good. Even though the analysis up to this point has revealed the sharpest of rigorism, Kant now gives up the problem of the transcendental deduction, subsumes it under the theoretical, extracts the ethical content from the ethical form, and constructs his practical postulates as presuppositions for the ethical. The reason for this, Nygren claims, is that Kant never clearly differentiated between the several meanings of the word "good," thus confusing the ethical category of critical ethics with the ethical ideal of the normative. After Kant had arrived at the category of duty as the highest principle, he was unable to stop at that, but asked for *its* content, i.e., "What, then, is our duty?" But this is, of course, to enter the field of normative ethics, and to construct the content from the form. Kant's mistake is, obviously, that he puts both investigations on the same plane and thus makes it appear that the ideal as empirical content can be obtained from the category. This is also the reason that Kant's ethics, especially in relation to ethical autonomy, can be so differently interpreted when approached from a purely critical or from a psychological point of view. If even Kant himself failed to be stringently critical, to be true to the highest efficacy or potentiality in his own method, critical philosophy, to be effective, must obviously take its task earnestly and keep itself in every way from using the pure form as though it has a content, or, for that matter, any factual existence or reality whatsoever.

In a chapter on teleological, legalistic, or dispositional ethics, Nygren rejects the first two inasmuch as they are inconsistent with the purity of the ethical category. The ethical must be an autonomous form of experience free from any external requirements or any factors which so condition it as to destroy its untrammeled independence. Only the good will has a primary ethical meaning, although both the action of the legalistic ethics and the ends of the teleological have a derived significance. The important thing, moreover, is that in dispositional ethics their relation with the will is purely causal. Every ethical disposition has a natural tendency to realize itself in action, and every action attempts as far as possible to accomplish its end. To give a concise indication of the reasoning on this point the final paragraph of the chapter which occurs in both books on the subject may be given: "the fact that a teleological ethics is incapable of doing justice to the ethical phenomenon as a whole, is partly due to the difficulty to put up objective ends of a specifically ethical character, partly to the fact that even if an ethical end is established and a certain disposition and action can receive a degree of validation through its teleological connection with this end, nevertheless there is no guarantee at all that this disposition and action is really ethical. Dispositional ethics is freed from this difficulty in that the relation of the three aspects is causal, not teleological, i.e., that it takes as its point of departure the disposition as an ethical spring, out of which, with inner necessity, flow ethical actions and goals. Provided that the point of departure itself is ethical, the whole process is ethical. Whenever the ethical disposition expresses itself, ethical actions necessarily follow, and these must also necessarily lead to a final ethical goal."[50]

[50] Nygren, *Etiska grundfrågor*, pp. 154, 155.

Nygren ends his investigation of philosophical ethics by indicating what he considers to be the ethical category, but with Kant he does not deduce it, although he promises to do so at a later time. His subsequent work on the subject barely mentions the problem, and even then not from the point of view of ethical methodology. The ethical category is the category of fellowship. The category of duty is also possible, and the question as to which is truly primary must at this time be left open. In any case, it seems most difficult to speak of duty aside from fellowship. Even Kant, who started with the primacy of duty, arrived at last at fellowship, even if this fellowship is located within the subject in its capacity as rational, law-making being, and in its capacity as a sensuous, obeying creature. Thus we always come back, in the last analysis, to the category of fellowship as the foundation for the ethical outlook. This category, nevertheless, must be a completely empty form, accessible to any truly ethical ideal. Empirically, for instance, the ethical ideal can be Nietzsche's ethics of might, or Kant's ethics of rights, or the Christian ethics of love. All are ethical; all, forms of fellowship, and no choice between them is possible from a rational point of view. The decision is always one of personal commitment.

A large part of both books is devoted to Christian ethics, but this must be reserved for our later discussion of the content of Lundensian theology. Methodologically, Christian ethics is shown to be dispositional, thus filling the demand made on a genuine ethics from the point of view of critical philosophy. Christian ethics knows "only a causal motivation: the action is judged good only when it springs from a good disposition; and vice versa: whatever result grows with inner necessity out of the good disposition must be recognized as good."[51] Christ and Luther, as always in the Lundensian theology, are the standards of Christian distinctiveness. "Every good tree beareth good fruit, but an evil tree beareth evil fruit."[52] *"Gute fromme Werke machen nimmermehr einen guten frommen Mann, sondern ein guter frommer Mann macht gute fromme Werke."*[53] Christian ethics is also proved to be a unique form of ethics by means of its specific ideal, the unmotivated, spontaneous, value-indifferent love which is known only through fellowship with God. In this way Christian ethics has presented excellent credentials as to its right to be ethical content.

After completing the structural analysis of philosophical and Christian ethics, Nygren returns to his original analysis of the relation between the two. Without an analysis of the nature of the two sciences, it was impossible to decide as to whether one of them was superfluous and should be eliminated, or whether they complemented each other. The structural analysis leaves as its result, on the one hand, a science dealing with the ethical form but totally devoid of any content, and on the other hand, a science dealing with genuine ethical content, but without any way of validating its basic principles. The solution, therefore, is begging to be accepted. The two sciences need each other. The form is empty and needs to obtain a content. "Philosophically," Nygren naturally maintains, "it is impossible to get further than 'the possibility'" (of such a content).[54] Nevertheless, "an objective historical investigation re-

---

[51] Nygren, *Filosofisk och kristen etik*, pp. 207-208.
[52] Matthew 7:17.
[53] Luther, *Von der Freiheit eines Christenmenschen*, 1520, §23, as quoted in Nygren, *Filosofisk och kristen etik*, p. 208.
[54] *Ibid.*, p. 325.

veals, apart from the worth of the ideal in other respects, that no ideal exists which can be compared with the Christian in regard to immediate power. Most of its rivals are more like deliberate rational constructions than immediate experience. This is especially true of the two main types other than Christianity, Kant's ethics of rights and Nietzsche's ethics of might."[55] No wonder that Christian ethics has a most important place to fill within the field of the ethical sciences. From the side of Christian ethics, moreover, it is equally clear that "there are two problems, one philosophical and the other theological. . . . The question of the validity of the ethical as such can be answered only philosophically. . . . Without this foundation in the general character and validity of the ethical experience, the purely theological problems of Christian ethics would be left in mid-air. . . . The relation between philosophical and Christian ethics is thus reciprocally positive. . . . Every possibility of conflict is eliminated. If philosophical ethics should attempt to delete Christian ethics, it would destroy itself as a critical discipline. If, on the other hand, Christian ethics should endeavor to eliminate the critical-philosophical discipline, it would at the same time be destroying its own scientific foundation."[56]

CONCLUSION

In the general summary it is necessary to stress the two all-inclusive poles of interest in the Lundensian construction of methodology: theology must do justice to the uniquely Christian, and theology must be a strictly

[55] *Ibid.*, p. 323.
[56] *Ibid.*, pp. 326, 327.

scientific discipline. This is accomplished, as we have seen, by the drawing of a rigid line of demarcation between the subjective nature of faith and the objective nature of science. The subjective nature of faith is respected in its claim to be an independent and unique category, trans-subjectively valid and necessary. It is further allowed to supply its self-originated material for theological investigation besides its own principle of interpretation. But this reverence for the givenness of a subject is the first principle of science. From this original scientific attitude down to the very last statement of faith there is no abatement. If the form of religious experience is found to be valid, it is by means of a critical-scientific philosophy. The object to be investigated is received objectively from history, and the principle of interpretation is the organic necessity dictated by the nature of the object itself. All attempts to be normative within or outside a given religion are resolutely rejected. Christianity is accepted only because it is the most relevant, and all other religions are allowed the same absolute claims as Christianity. All attempts to explain, extend, or verify the content in any terms except those dictated by its own object of investigation are refused a hearing. The atheoretical content of faith is left atheoretical for what it is worth. What method could be more thoroughly scientific?

In order to assure the greatest degree of objectivity, an article written by Nygren dealing with the method as a whole may be used as an appropriate summary. In "Till fragan om teologiens objektivitet" ("Concerning the Objectivity of Theology"), Nygren points out the necessity for Christian theology to accept Christianity as a historically given reality, to accept Christian faith and life as facts which can serve as points of departure for its investigation. He continues by observing how theology is frequently accused of lacking scientific objectivity. The accusation comes especially from three directions: (1) the philosophical positivism or illusionism, (2) the religious positivism or subjectivism, (3) the scientific objectivism.

The first does not deny the presence of religion, or that it may always continue as part of man's life, at least among certain people in low cultural or psychological conditions, but it does claim that theology has no object, that the content of theology is illusion, that its existence may be even a sign of pathological conditions. The fallacy of this school of thought, fortunately, has been revealed by critical philosophy. This has not remained satisfied by a mere counter-assertion, but has critically established the fact that the religious experience is not only as valid as any other form, but the very presupposition of all experience. Religion cannot be accused of illusionism without the destruction of all objective knowledge. The second objection, that of religious positivism or subjectivism, claims, on the other hand, that religion cannot be scientific. This assertion is in the interest of religion itself. The objectivity of science depends on its material which is demonstrable and subject to verifiably uniform laws. Religion, on the other hand, is personal experience, and by its very nature lacks scientific objectivity. Both the first two schools of thought, therefore, emphasize the subjectivity of religion. To one, subjectivity means illusionism; to the other, the irrefutable, immediate reality of the object of faith. Both schools equally deny theology scientific status. Both schools, further, fail to realize that it is not the philosophical status of the object, but the nature of the method employed which determines scientific objectivity. The object can be a subjectively conditioned reality and still be the object of scientific investigation. The third objection comes from the objectivism of the general sciences of religion.

This is, in short, that theology presupposes the truth of Christianity. Inasmuch as this is only subjectively valid, i.e., accepted only by those who share the Christion conviction, theology cannot be scientific, for if the presupposition were removed, theology could no longer be theology. On account of its nature, theology must inevitably forego the testing of Christianity's claim to be true; it must also forego all claims to objectivity. The general sciences of religion, on the contrary, start without any presuppositions to test all religious phenomena impartially in order to arrive at an objective appraisal of their truth. The fault of this method is, however, that it constructs a theoretical religion more unscientific than any given religion to take the place of what has been naturally individualized and concretely realized in historic forms, that, further, it speaks of an objective test by which to measure the religious phenomena, while every evaluation implies an ideal, and it is a contradiction in terms to establish an objective ideal. Furthermore, if this impersonal, objective way of judging the religions were possible, an irreparable injustice would be done to the justifiably subjective nature of religious truth, i.e., that religious experience is a personal commitment.

These three schools of thought reveal both the complexity of the subject and the impossibility of drawing inference from the nature of religion to the nature of theology or vice versa. Dismissing the charge of the first school because of its own self-destructiveness, Nygren shows how the second and the third start with right assumptions but arrive at wrong conclusions. The second correctly emphasizes the subjective nature of faith, while the third with justice stresses the objectivity of whatever method is to study religion scientifically; but respectively they draw the conclusions that theology cannot be an objective science because it is subjectively conditioned, and that religion is a matter of decision on scientific as well as personal grounds. The confusion on the whole subject is due to hazy thinking on the nature of subjectivity and objectivity. Critical thinking will show the need of a theology which will do justice to both the subjectively conditioned nature of religion and the objective nature of theology. Subjectivity and objectivity Nygren analyzes into the following pairs of opposites:

Subjectivity	Objectivity
1. content of consciousness	1. the thing in itself
2. the psychic	2. the physical
3. the value-colored	3. the value-indifferent
4. the arbitrary	4. the necessary

When theology is accused of subjectivity, the implication usually is that it is arbitrary, i.e., that it lacks scientific or logical necessity. The confusion, or the logical equivocation, is often made that the subjective nature of faith as value-colored is bracketed with the wrong opposite, so that the false conclusion follows: therefore, not scientifically necessary. This is quite as incorrect as to say, for instance, that a state is psychic and therefore value-indifferent. The psychic realm includes both pairs of opposites. Only the direct opposites are contradictories. Religion is value-colored, but not arbitrary; theology is value-indifferent and at the same time logically necessary even though its object is subjectively conditioned. Much material for scientific investigation is subjective. Only subjectivism in terms of arbitrariness deprives a methodology of scientific status. Since the method of theology is objective, theology is established as an objective science, but as a science with an ample capacity for the expression of the uniquely Christian.

CHAPTER III

THE RELATION OF GOD TO MAN

I. The Idea of God

A. *God as the Subject of Faith.*

By far the most important factor in the relation of God to man, as defined by Lundensian theology, is the idea of God. Religion is fellowship with God. This fellowship is by no means reciprocal, however, in the sense that anything is contributed to it by man. Every thought of a bi-polar relation is resolutely rejected. Religion "appears in two diametrically opposite forms: as theocentric, or as egocentric."[1] "Either the 'I' serves as a point of departure, in which case the road to religion is the expansion and sublimation of one's own interest, or the point of departure is God, and the road to religion, then, is through our being overpowered and compelled by him and thus surrendering our own."[2] "It is clear that the question about God is absolutely decisive for Christian thought. Christian faith is entirely faith in God."[3] "Faith is the outlook where God is central, where life is ruled by God alone. Faith is completely theocentric in nature.... God appears as entirely sovereign in the divine relation. As far as faith reaches, God is the ruler whose will is done. In this sense it is really fallacious to speak of God as the 'ob-

---
[1] Nygren, *Religiositet och kristendom*, p. 31.
[2] Nygren, *Urkristendom och reformation*, p. 101.
[3] Aulén, *Den kristna gudsbilden*, p. 6.

ject of faith,' for God is better depicted as subject in the world of faith."[4] In speaking of the inability of science to go beyond its methodological limits, Lindroth affirms that the transcendent realm, which, to critical philosophy, appears to be the negation of knowledge, in reality is God's positive revelation, the content of which is grasped through faith. Reality as such, the absolute, by its very nature cannot be *known* without immediately losing its absoluteness, but it can be *made known*. At the utmost limit of knowledge, as established by critical philosophy, there is no possibility of definitely knowing absolute reality, but only a question of God's making himself definitely known. Faith, as a medium of knowledge, is being gripped by God, the passive acceptance of revelation. This is the heart of Nygren's exceedingly forceful presentation, "Det religionsfilosofiska grundproblemet" ("The Basic Problem in the Philosophy of Religion"), in which he asserts an absolute dualism in matters of knowledge. Since the work of Kant, it has been perfectly clear that *das Ding an sich* is incomprehensible, that reality as the really real cannot be known by the theoretical reason. Religion has become intellectualized and philosophy mystical by man's vain attempt to know that which lies qualitatively beyond his ken.[5] God alone is the source of revelation. From this point of view Nygren can differentiate between egocentric religion as the "desired" and theocentric as the "compelled."[6] Aulén writes with an emphasis needing no italics: "Faith arises through our *compulsion by God*, and exists through his ruling us."[7] "This is to believe—

---
[4] Aulén, Den allmänneliga kristna tron, p. 35.
[5] In *Bibelforskaren*, 1919.
[6] Cf. Nygren, *Urkristendom och reformation*, p. 103.
[7] Aulén, *op. cit.*, p. 39.

to be compelled and ruled by God."[8] Using almost the same words, Nygren defines faith as being "compelled and overpowered by God."[9] This idea occurs with such frequency in Lundensian thought that it cannot be sufficiently stressed. The basic principles are those of the Reformation: *sola gratia, sola fides*. Religion is to them altogether theocentric. God is the subject of faith. God is the subject of love. In the religious world, God is all. Any deviation from this focus becomes entirely negligible by the force of the main emphasis. Even if Luther may have failed to be thoroughly consistent in his application of the *sola gratia-sola fides* principle, the Lundensian school is characterized by nothing so much as an extraordinary power of concentration on this one thesis. Discussing Luther's view on the subject, Bring tries to show that even synteresis, according to his best insight, is nothing apart from God's work in man, nothing at all apart from God's immediate presence in man.[10] In the relation of God to man, God is first, last, and foremost.

From this it naturally follows that God is the subject of revelation, the active source of all knowledge[11] of the eternal. This is, of course, the governing center of Lundensian theology. Revelation alone, not man's thought, gives light. Naturally Krook, in the first volume of his work, *Uppenbarelsebegreppet* ("The Concept of Revelation"), stresses that "everything must be related to the thought of revelation. This thought is

[8] Aulén, *Kristendomens själ*, p. 24.
[9] Nygren, *Filosofisk och kristen etik*, p. 307.
[10] Cf. Bring, "Ordet, samvetet, och den inre människan," in *Ordet och tron*, pp. 65-66.
[11] For the sake of convenience, the word "knowledge" will be used, since Lundensian theology has produced no word to express "the information contained in faith."

vital and basic to theology; this alone makes theology theology."[12] Krook polemizes sharply against the idea that faith as a conditioning factor for revelation is in any way man's work. "Revelation itself creates faith; faith is God's own work."[13] To seek for light outside of revelation is simply "meaningless."[14] On this point all Lundensian theologians, whether disciples or pioneers, are agreed. Most definitely Aulén writes: "If you would try to say what revelation may add to the knowledge of God reached through reason, you would be speaking of another God than the God of Christian faith. Certainly the Christian faith is conscious of having a true knowledge of God. But this knowledge does not mean only certain ideas or a certain doctrine about a being called God; it means a personal relation brought into existence through the action of God. And therefore if we are to use the word revelation in our Christian language, revelation must always be connected with *the activity of God*; it must signify the self-communication of God through his own activity."[15] In a sharp polemic against idealism, Aulén states that idealism is concerned with "a scientific motivation of religion," whereas Christianity is "a matter of faith and nothing but faith."[16] But "faith by itself is nothing—nothing aside from the revelation of God compelling man."[17] "The God that compels and governs us is the God that 'reveals himself' to us. . . . By means of his revelation God meets and compels us."[18] "Outside God faith has

---

[12] P. 21.
[13] *Ibid.*, p. 181.
[14] *Ibid.*, p. 187.
[15] In *Revelation*, ed. by Baillie and Martin, pp. 275-276.
[16] Aulén, "Kristendom och idealism," p. 31.
[17] Aulén, *Den allmänneliga kristna tron*, p. 97.
[18] *Ibid.*, p. 39.

relation to nothing. When it speaks of revelation, the question is only and ever of *God's* revelation, of God's way to man—this and nothing else."[19] "Faith alone discovers the revelation of God. Without faith there is no revelation. . . . We see religiousness but no divine revelation. Faith opens the eyes. . . . Revelation and faith are corresponding concepts: on the one hand, faith has its source and nourishment in revelation, and on the other, revelation is discovered and known only through the eye of faith."[20] This does not mean, however, that faith is man's activity without which God cannot reach him. When Lundensian theology mentions man's side of the relation, it is always and, as we shall see, quite naturally, from a forced point of view. From the point of view of faith, from the religious point of view, even man's receptivity is God's work. "We believe . . . . because we have met the revelation of a God whom we cannot escape. . . . In regard to the question of man's activity there is no curtailment of the fact that faith is altogether a work of God."[21] From the quotations given, which can be multiplied, it is clear that in the Lundensian view regarding the relation of God to man, the idea of God as self-revelation is of such importance that its general characteristics must be given.

B. *The Centrality of the Christ-deed.*

This self-revelation of God is definitely disclosed in Christ. "The content of faith must reflect uninterruptedly the picture of God which is given through the

[19] *Ibid.,* p. 70.
[20] *Ibid.,* pp. 40-41.
[21] *Ibid.,* p. 41.

Christ-deed."[22] "The motif .... which is basic for, and indeed constitutes the Christian relation with God, is the motif enfolded in the Christ-deed, and is thus constitutive of the Christian picture of God as it appears to the eye of faith. If God is everything in the world of faith, the all-governing center in the Christian content of faith must be the *nature* of the divine revelation in Christ. With inner necessity, all Christian reflections through faith are characterized and determined by the nature of this divine revelation, of this divine will."[23] Similarly, Nygren's rendering of the uniqueness of Christianity when understood in the light of religion as the category of eternity and interpreted positively with Christ as the standard of faith in regard to the four main questions characteristic of any religion, namely eternal revelation, judgment, atonement, and penetration, can be summarized in one sentence: "What God is like, what God most deeply wills, the Christian can understand only by looking at Jesus."[24] This means, not that God never reveals himself outside of Christ, but that all revelation, wherever found, is already to be found in Christ. He is the fulfilment of all revelation. All things are measured as Christian, or as important for Christian faith, in direct proportion to their vital connection with the Christ-deed. In this way, Judaism stands closer to Christianity than any other religion,[25] and the New Testament is foundational for Christian faith.[26] Both extensively and intensively all revelation is measured by the God revealed in the Christ-deed.

[22] *Ibid.*, p. 112.
[23] *Ibid.*, p. 102.
[24] Nygren, *op. cit.*, p. 239.
[25] Cf. Aulén, *Den allmänneliga kristna tron*, p. 49 ff.
[26] Cf. *ibid.*, p. 114 ff.

"Christ is not the only revelation of God . . . . but he is the fulfilment of the divine revelation: Christian faith knows no God with features different from those reflected in the face of Christ."[27] Nor can there be a question of revelation in the sense of the will or law of God apart from his nature, for if God is a personal spirit (which Lundensian theology naturally affirms, provided that the usage of the word "personality" does not imply limitations inconsistent with the God-hood),[28] there is "nothing more essential, nothing more constitutive of his nature, than his will, the disposition of his heart."[29]

This revelation of God through the Christ-deed must not be thought of, moreover, as only an isolated fact at a particular time in history, but also as God's continuous disclosing of himself. This disclosure must always be that of the God revealed in the Christ-deed, for this is the God disclosing himself. The revelation, thus, is not static, yet fixed. Nor can this revelation be static, for it is not words or law, but life. Revelation is, rather, God's dramatic struggle to make himself known against an opposition of forces of evil. Discussion of the question of evil must be postponed for the present, but it is well to mention that the important thought in this connection is the conception of revelation as the divine drama fighting to make itself known, a continuous, living, loving self-disclosure of the divine Father-heart. This thought of a dramatic-dynamic revelation of God was vigorously championed in Swedish theology by Einar Billing with intent to avoid the pitfalls of both

---

[27] Aulén and Rosén, *Den kristna tros- och livsåskådningen*, p. 23.
[28] Cf. Aulén, *Den allmänneliga kristna tron*, p. 189 ff.
[29] Aulén and Rosén, *op. cit.*, p. 67.

the static and the evolutionistic conceptions. Because of its monistic presuppositions, the evolutionistic did not do justice to the dualistic nature of life. "Evolutionism is succeeded by drama."[30] Billing thus defines the dynamic-dramatic revelation as "the action of God's will breaking itself through obstacles."[31] Revelation is, therefore, fixed. "Christ stands at the very center of the great drama."[32] But yet is it progressive, for it is the dynamic struggle of a living God. Withal, it is not an even, steady progress according to the nature of things, for it realistically recognizes the dualistic nature of existence against which the personal subject of revelation discloses God's will. Revelation is, therefore, dynamic-dramatic against a dualistic background.

C. *The Regions Beyond the Rational.*

Before proceeding to the content of this revelation in the Christ-deed, the fact must be heavily accentuated that this revelation is not capable of being rationally comprehended. As we shall see in a later connection, the God in Christ is not at all a picture from which can be gathered a rational world-view. "The Christian faith in God is something entirely different from a rational explanation of the world."[33] As early as 1915 Aulén had published a little book, *Syndernas förlåtelse* ("The Forgiveness of Sin"), in which his main thesis was the irrationality of the Atonement, namely that a holy God should approach a sinner. In this book, also, appears Aulén's basic idea of the religious paradox, or irrationality: that it is qualitatively different from man's knowl-

[30] Aulén, *Den kristna gudsbilden*, p. 360.
[31] *Ibid.*, p. 361; quoting Billing, *Herdabrev*, p. 40.
[32] Aulén, *I vilken riktning går nutidens teologiska tänkande?*
[33] Aulén, *Den allmänneliga kristna tron*, p. 25.

edge, so that the unknown grows in direct proportion to its being known. The clearer the thought, the clearer its irrational aspect, or the more incomprehensible the mystery. The mystery is by its very nature incomprehensible. "The more faith penetrates into the world of the divine revelation, the more it stands before the unsearchable."[34] Lundensian thought resolutely rejects all rationality in the world of faith, refusing, like Rudolph Otto, to speak of a rational and irrational side. The incomprehensible is not something besides the incomprehensible, but that which faith comprehends is by its very nature incomprehensible. It is not a question of a *deus absconditus* and a *deus revelatus*, but of a *deus absconditus* which paradoxically is revealed as such through *deus revelatus*. With consistency and vigor Ljunggren maintains that the paradox is the necessary medium of theological expression.[35] Similarly Bring a few years later in an article dealing with "The Idea of Paradox in Theology"[36] is particularly anxious that paradox or irrationality be interpreted from a religious and not a rational point of view. "Principially *ratio* may occur in two connections through which it receives two different meanings. *At times ratio* connotes our rational thought, our theoretical experience, our knowledge. *At times* it means a special form of religion, namely, the thought of salvation as arrived at through man's common manner of evaluation, through the 'natural' man's way of thinking."[37] If *ratio* is interpreted in the first sense, irrational naturally means theoretical contradiction. This is the absurdity into which much of Barthian

---

[34] Aulén, *Dèn allmänneliga kristna tron*, p. 125.
[35] Cf. Ljunggren, "Paradoxen som teologiskt uttrycksmedel," pp. 333 ff.
[36] Bring, "Paradoxtanken i teologien," p. 3 ff.
[37] *Ibid.*, p. 5.

thought has been driven by its opposition to rational speculation. Reason by its very nature, in that system, lands in insoluble antinomies graspable only through faith. In Lundensian theology, however, religion and knowledge are two separate areas of experience, but without the assertion of any such contradictory relation. Aulén calls this incomprehensibility of the comprehensible "the positive irrationalism"[38] of the divine love. Aulén's latest expression on the subject is equally clear: "It is important to see in what way God appears to faith as the Unfathomable. It does not mean only that the revelation of God has certain limits. It does not mean only that, as long as we live under the conditions of this life, there are questions that cannot be answered and riddles that cannot be explained. It does not mean only that faith in God cannot be transformed into a rational explanation of the world, which would make the divine government of the world transparently clear. It means also that precisely the revelation of God itself has the character of unfathomableness."[39] Between the world of reason and the world of faith the chasm is absolute. It cannot be bridged.

D. *God as* Agape.

We have seen that in the relation of God to man, God is by far the more important factor, that the picture of God is the governing center without which nothing can be understood, that only faith can know this God, and that faith itself is man's compulsion by God, that in the last analysis God and not man is the subject of faith. We have also seen that God is known

---

[38] Aulén, *Den kristna gudsbilden*, p. 30.
[39] In *Revelation*, p. 309.

to faith through the Christ-deed, which is not only a fixed fulfillment of revelation through a particular act at a particular time, but also the living presence of God at all times. That revelation is to be thought of as a dynamic-dramatic self-disclosure of God against a dualistic background. Last of all we have noticed that this revelation is entirely distinct from all human knowledge, that revelation is always and ever the revelation of the divine mystery, that even the picture of God as seen in the fact of Christ is the divine compulsion through faith. We now come to the very center of Lundensian thought, that God is definitely known through Christ. What, then, is meant by this definiteness which by its very nature cannot be theoretical definiteness? The sum and substance of this revelation is that God is spontaneous, unmotivated, value-indifferent love creative of fellowship. *God is agape.* To prove their main thesis from the history of Christian thought, Aulén and Nygren have written their most challenging books. In his book on general theology, Aulén accordingly writes as follows: "The highest and last word about the God of the Christ-deed is the word concerning God's *agape.* God's nature, as Luther says, is *'eitel Liebe.'* . . . Thus in the last analysis all the utterances of Christian faith gather around God's *agape* as its center. This *agape* breaks to pieces all legalistic or rationalistic frames. . . . Faith can never go deeper than to the divine *agape.*"[40] "Not the order of justice expresses God's deepest nature, but his spontaneous, free, sovereign love which gives because it is its nature to give."[41] "All statements that can be made about God are statements concerning his

[40] Aulén, *Den allmänneliga kristna tron,* p. 159.
[41] Aulén, *Den kristna gudsbilden,* pp. 186-187.

love."[42] God's power and holiness are nothing but descriptions of his love. Equally clear is Aulén's latest statement on the subject: "All that the Christian faith has to say about the revelation of God is summed up in God's Love; 'God is Love.' Faith cannot say anything about God that is not a statement about His Love. The Majesty of God is the Majesty of His Love. The Righteousness of God is the Righteousness of His Love. The Judgment of God is the Judgment of His Love."[43] God's love, which gives itself freely, unconditionally, sovereignly to the unworthy sinner—a love high as the heavens above thought or law—this is God's definite disclosure in the Christ-deed. Around this thought is centered all else.

In *Den kristna gudsbilden* ("The Christian Concept of God"), Aulén sets out to prove his definite thesis that there is only one way between man and God, and that this way is always God's way to man, the way of the divine *agape*. In the early Church, the author asserts, the leading motif was always the dualistic-dramatic in which God conquers death, sin, and the devil. The mythological language or figures used stand for the deepest insight in Christian revelation, namely that the Atonement is God's own, God's uninterrupted way to man. The main emphasis in this respect is naturally given to Paul, Marcion, and Augustine, though Aulén maintains with no little force that the Christian concept of God, the governing center of any religion, is qualitatively different from the Jewish concept, that Jesus broke through the juridical barrier of the law and the rational hindrance of the *Torah* and gave to the

[42] Aulén and Rosén, *Den kristna tros och livsåskådningen*, p. 29.
[43] In *Revelation*, p. 304.

world the picture of a God who loves the sinner and unreservedly gives himself in unmotivated love for him. This qualitatively unique picture of God, however, is gradually more obscured by the legalism of the Latin way of thinking. The very presence of the juridical concept immediately breaks God's uninterrupted way to man, destroys the depth and power of God's *agape*. The Reformation, again, was a return to the classical motif; *sola gratia-sola fides* are the definitions of God's *agape* seen respectively from the point of view of God or of man. When Luther, especially in *De servo arbitrio*, gave forceful expression to the dualistic-dramatic revelation of God's *agape*, he broke mightily with all the formal limitations which Latin thought had placed on God, whether Anselm's *nihil rationabilius* or scholasticism's *potentia ordinata*. Luther's gospel was the first liberty in God's *agape contra legem* and *contra rationem*. It was the tragedy of Lutheran orthodoxy of taking over the forms of its great founder without having sufficient depth to realize that often the motifs realizing themselves in Luther were inconsistent with the inherited forms. It did not keep sufficiently clear the purity of God's *agape*, God's free, spontaneous, unconditioned, unmotivated, value-indifferent love.

With the *Aufklärung* starts an entirely new period in Christian thought. The love of God is now made central, but has lost its tension because it has become part of a metaphysical monistic scheme. In this the causal order of the world is attributed to God. This destroys the acuteness of the sinful situation. The period is also marked by a new anthropology, a new optimism, which exists in the form of perfectibility in the eighteenth century and in the form of evolutionism in the nineteenth. The Atonement in these forms of thought is viewed in the light of Christ's significance as the ideal of humanity, as humanity's highest and best representative. The stress on reconciliation and redemption is mitigated, and the new stress is on development. The kingdom of God, moreover, becomes more and more an intra-mundane ethical ideal. God tends more and more to become the means toward man's self-realization or his establishment of the kingdom. The subjective emphasis wins more and more strength until finally man stands openly in the middle of the picture with God as the servant of his welfare, or even of his happiness. The author finally suggests that we stand before a new era in which such deeper motifs, stressed in modern theology, as God's holiness, the dualistic-dramatic, the eschatological, and the collective, tend to bring into prominence the basic motif of God's *agape*. The way this is done, naturally, is by emphasizing the qualitative difference between God and man, and man's rational and moral impotence before God. God alone can give, because it is his nature to give. Similar emphasis on *agape* as God's unmotivated love freely giving itself for the sinner, is given by Nygren in *Urkristendom och reformation*, and especially in the one book which is fully devoted to the theme, and which draws out the Lundensian thesis to the sharpness of a razor's edge: *Den kristna kärlekstanken* (title in English translation, *Agape and Eros*). *Agape* is God's way to man. *Eros* is man's way to God. *Agape* is unmotivated love. *Eros* is self-centered desire. The uniqueness of Christianity lies in its basic motif, in its new picture of God as *agape*. Jesus broke with Judaism qualitatively when he spoke of calling not the righteous but sinners, when he spoke of loving enemies, for then he spoke no longer of human love, but of God's *agape*. God's love for the sinner is the clearest expression for the new relation with God. "*The Christian way of fellowship with God depends wholly on the Divine Agape.* Thus the question how far those whom God loves deserve His love falls to the ground. To the question, Why does God love? there is only one right answer: Because it is His nature (*essentia*) to love."[44] In succinct sections, Nygren then defines *agape* as spontaneous, unmotivated, value-indifferent, creative, and productive of fellowship. *Agape* is entirely, unconditionally independent of the worth of its object. There is no relation whatsoever between *agape* and its object, except the free overflowing of a creative love, which by the power of its purity, is productive of the highest and most beautiful fellowship. The section as a whole is ended by the conclusion: "Hence in this respect also the advent of Agape implies a complete revolution. Hitherto the possibility of man's fellowship with God had been summed up in the question by what way man could attain unto God. But now, when the way of self-abasement and amendment is set on one side as decisively as the way of righteousness and merit, the conclusion follows that *there is no way, from man's side, by which he can attain to God.* If, then, there manifestly is such a thing as a fellowship of man with God, this can depend only on God's own action; God must Himself come to man to offer him fellowship with Himself. There is thus no way for man to God other than the way which God has made in coming to man: the way of the Divine Agape

[44] Nygren, *Agape and Eros*, p. 52.

and the Divine forgiveness. Agape is God's own way to man."[45]

With true insight as to its great importance, Nygren then takes up a theme which he has treated more extensively at an earlier time:[46] the meaning of Jesus' parables. In this he especially turns against A. Jülicher's monumental work on the subject: *Die Gleichnisreden Jesu*, since the latter author explains the parables demonstratively, i.e., as common incidents used in order to elicit an inevitable affirmative from the hearers, even in application to the spiritual realm. The strength of the parables lies, therefore, according to Jülicher, in their obviousness. The parables would thus be reasoning from the natural to the spiritual, from man to God. Nygren, on the other hand, endeavors to show that they are not demonstrative, but revelatory, that they deal not with general religious or ethical truths, obvious in nature if demonstratively revealed, but with relations directly contrary to human customs and ideas. The two parables which Nygren makes most use of are those of the Workers in the Vineyard and the Prodigal Son. Here the accepted order of justice is broken, and through it all a picture is drawn revealing God's *agape*, God's spontaneous, unmotivated, value-indifferent, creative love productive of fellowship.

Needless to say, Paul provides a great deal of material, although it must be stressed that, in Lundensian thought, no basic cleavage between the thought of Jesus and Paul is allowed. To Paul the Gospel is the news of the Cross, and the theology of the Cross is nothing but God's

[45] *Ibid.*, p. 56.
[46] Cf. *Svensk teologisk kvartalskrift*, 1928.

free, overwelling love giving itself to the absolutely unworthy, for whom, for the sake of driving home the lesson, Paul uses four different expressions: "weak, ungodly, sinners, enemies."[47] Paul himself, in that the persecutor became apostle, had experienced God's *agape*. In connection with Paul's famous hymn to love, Nygren differs sharply with the interpretations of both Harnack and Reitzenstein, who make it, respectively, love to neighbor and love to God, but who also respectively interpret it moralistically and as an expansion of *eros*. For Nygren, the hymn is a most definite statement of *agape*, for "the fact is that for Paul Agape has a meaning and a character all its own, independent of its object. He thinks of Agape as primarily God's own love."[48] Even though, according to its nature, it has overflowed into our hearts where it constrains and compels us, it is still God's *agape*, the divine love which has taken possession of the inner man. It is no longer we who live, but "Christ liveth" in us. Paul is definitely, whether or not conscious of it in these terms, breaking with the *gnosis* "which is in part," for this is the very expression of the Hellenistic *eros* motif. Here is, perhaps, the first historic clash between the two motifs. "If Reitzenstein is right in his conjectures that 'Faith, Hope, and Agape' is a formula set forth by Paul in direct opposition to a Hellenistic formula, 'Faith, Gnosis, Eros, and Hope,' this means that we have in this passage the first direct and formal opposition of Agape and Eros. But in any case, there is no doubt of the actual opposition of the two ideas in this passage; he here sets out in the clearest light the Christian meaning

---

[47] Nygren, *Agape and Eros*, p. 87.
[48] *Ibid.*, p. 104.

of Agape and its contrast with Eros."[49] Paul has so deeply impressed the meaning of *agape* on his gospel, that whenever Paulinism is renewed, whether in Marcion, Augustine, or Luther, the gospel is always connected with a revival of the *agape* motif. "By connecting the Divine Agape with the Cross of Christ, Paul gives to the Christian idea of Agape its highest expression, and in a true sense its final expression; and this gives the essential difference between Christianity and Jewish legal religion on the one hand and Greek Eros-religion on the other."[50]

The highest formal expression of *agape*, however, is given in the First Epistle of John. "Both in the Synoptic Gospels and in Paul the thought of God and the thought of Agape are brought so near together that they are virtually identified. Paul in particular hovers on the edge of the formal identification in such phrases as 'the God of Agape'; but though he has in fact fully grasped the essential idea, the phrase which clinches the matter is never uttered by him. The first Epistle of John takes the final step: 'God is Agape' (I John iv:8 and 16). God is Agape, *and Agape is God.*"[51] Nevertheless, the *agape* motif is nowhere nearly so purely expressed in John as in Paul, and that for three definite reasons: (1) The Johannine literature gives a metaphysical background to *agape* which has even a cosmic flavor. God's *agape* is schematized into a love flowing from God to Christ, then to the disciples, and finally, to the brethren. This scheme makes of *agape* a process of continuous self-impartation. The love of God for his Son, moreover, might have a definite motivation. John even lets Jesus

[49] *Ibid.*, p. 107.
[50] *Ibid.*, p. 106.
[51] *Ibid.*, p. 109.

speak of the Father's loving the disciples *because* they have loved the Son. (John 16:27) (2) The love of the disciples, furthermore, is particularistic, i.e., the love of "the brethren." For *agape* to be entirely unmotivated, however, it can in no way countenance any particularism. (3) Besides, the love of the world is specifically forbidden, and this involves selective reflection, i.e., some recognition of the worth of its object. John's significance in relation to the *agape* motif, therefore, can be looked at from two points of view. From the one, he gave the highest formal expression to the motif: God is *agape*. He also gave the immortal thought that "God so loved the world that he gave . . ." On the other hand, he weakened the force of the motif by introducing a particularism entirely inconsistent with its innermost nature.

In discussing the *eros* motif, Nygren centers his attention around Plato, Aristotle, and Neo-Platonism. He begins by showing that the origin of the idea of *eros* is the Zagreus myth. When Zeus created man from the Titanic ashes, containing among them the remains of Zagreus, man became both earthly and divine. The divine in him is, by its very nature, always yearning to be freed from its false relation with the earthly and the sensuous. "This conception of the double nature of man, of the Divine origin and quality of the soul, its liberation from the fetters of sense, and its ascent to its original Divine home, is the universal basis of the idea of Eros in every form in which it appears."[52]

Plato, it is well known, took over this myth, and the idea of *eros* forms no little part of his soteriological

[52] *Ibid.*, p. 122.

philosophy.[53] Nygren further maintains that the genuine Platonic system is so sharply dualistic that it allows for only *one* active relation between the world of ideas and the world of existence: namely an upward relation. "The authentic Platonic teaching knows only one direction of movement, that of ascent. Plato's forms are not real forces, and they cannot either directly or mediately exert their influence on the lower world; Plato sharpens the dualism between the Two Worlds to an extreme point."[54] Although the two worlds are distinct, man has a part in both, not so that he in any way bridges the two, but in such a way that he must ever desire to escape from the sensuous in order to find the ideal. "*Eros is man's conversion from the sensible to the super-sensible; it is the upward movement of the soul; it is a real force, driving the soul upwards to seek the world of the Forms.* If there were no such thing as Eros, there would be no interaction between the two worlds at all; they would simply remain at rest, side by side with one another."[55] From this point of view, "the Myth of Eros can be regarded as the chief of all Plato's myths, the myth which gives us the clearest view of the inner meaning of Plato's thought."[56] Thus we can understand Plato's doctrines of

---

[53] Cf. *Ibid.*, p. 124:
"It is important to remember, on the other hand, that in Plato we do not get philosophy in the modern sense of an abstract critical study, but a philosophy which is also a world-outlook, constructed largely on a religious basis; it might be said that it is a doctrine of salvation as much as a philosophy, for we constantly hear the exhortation to take thought for our soul's health. The ancient world drew no sharp line between religion and philosophy; both had a message to give concerning the attainment of the true and the blessed life."

[54] *Ibid.*, pp. 153-154.
Cf. also *Ibid.*, p. 126: "Nothing is more characteristic of Plato's outlook than the sharp dualism which he makes between the two worlds, the world of sense and the world of the Forms."

[55] *Ibid.*, pp. 127-128.
[56] *Ibid.*, p. 125.

recollection in the *Phaedrus*, and of Eros as the child of Penia and Poros in the *Symposion*. Even though *eros* in the nobler sense always desires the beautiful and the good, it is, nevertheless, always man's selfish yearning for what is above him. It is man's way to the divine; it is egocentric love. *Eros* desires to obtain and possess eternally. Its doctrine of immortality is merely selfish desire eternally prolonged.

Aristotle, on the other hand, is historically important in that he gave a cosmic scope to the *eros* motif. "The whole process of nature is represented by Aristotle as a movement or successive ascent from matter to form, from potentiality to actuality, from imperfection to perfection of being. The cause of this movement is to be found in the influence of form on matter, an influence which works in two ways: partly as an attraction, drawing matter into the likeness of the form, and partly as the actual change made by the form in the matter, so that the resulting thing itself becomes matter for the production of a higher form."[57] Even as in Plato the forms have the primacy, for they affect, but are in no way affected by, matter. The forms are ever and entirely unmoved, while moving matter or lower degrees of form according to the principle. The motion found in matter or in the incomplete form is caused by *eros*, and this motion is always in an ascending direction. "*In Aristotle we meet again the Platonic Eros, exalted to become the driving-force of the universe.* However wide be the gulf between them in other respects, in regard to Eros Aristotle is Plato's faithful disciple."[58] No wonder that the Catholic Church in the Middle Ages was

[57] *Ibid.*, pp. 141-142.
[58] *Ibid.*, p. 142.

unable to give expression to the basically Christian idea while working with this philosophy which, at its very foundations, directly opposed Christianity.

Similarly Neo-Platonism taught the *eros* doctrine, the way from man to God alone. This may, at first, seem to be an obvious mis-statement, since the Neo-Platonic philosophers plainly taught a downward as well as an upward movement. Nevertheless, whatever may be the other relations of Neo-Platonism with Gnosticism or Alexandrianism, as to *eros* its teachings are perfectly clear. Between the idea of descent in Platonic philosophy and the Christian *agape* there is no connection. The Neo-Platonic descent is invariably cosmological and caused by a philosophical desire to explain how the lower world, the world of evil matter, could proceed from the One. In short, the problem was ontological. Soteriologically, Neo-Platonism has only one way: from man to God. The descent, further, is really unreal. The One in its absoluteness still remains divinely elevated and never descends from its heavenly throne. Since the idea of *eros* in the Neo-Platonic system as well as in the Platonic is far from above controversial considerations, it seems best to let Nygren sum up his own position.

"It would be a complete mistake to infer . . . . that the teaching of Plotinus makes a real approach toward the Christian idea of Agape; there is no connection between the two. The differences may be tabulated thus: (i) When Plotinus speaks of a Descent, he is thinking of a cosmic process, corresponding to the creation of the world, the process by which the lower world proceeded forth from the One, and not at all of salvation; salvation is described by him exclusively in terms of the upward way. The union with God of which he speaks is attained, not at all through God in Agape coming down to man, but through man by Eros ascending to God. (ii) His language about the downward way does not at all mean that God in any true sense came down. The One, the Divine, remains ever in its exalted place; and in the same way reason and the world-soul and the individual souls which maintain their connection with the world-soul are never thought of as descending from their royal thrones; for when the higher cares for the lower and 'sets it in order and adorns it,' it is regarded as remaining in its exalted place while it exercises this influence. It never enters in under the conditions of the lower level of life; it acts altogether by 'passive rule' . . . It is fundamental to Plotinus' thought that the Divine is self-sufficient, and cannot be thought of as leaving its exalted repose. The idea of a spontaneous coming-down is to him inconceivable. (iii) In so far as the downward way means a real Descent, *it means not a Divine 'coming down,' but a fall—the fall of the soul into sin and guilt.* That which descends to a lower level does so involuntarily; its fall is the result of weakness and inability to retain its exalted place. Therefore it is impossible for the Divine Being ever really to descend.

"It is clear, therefore, that the likeness between the downward way in Plotinus and the Christian idea of Agape is purely superficial; the two conceptions have nothing to do with one another. Zeller sums the matter up thus: 'The one speaks of a Descent of the Godhead to the lowest depths of human weakness; the other calls for an ascent of man to superhuman divinity.' "[59]

Even when Plotinus identifies God with *eros*, the love

[59] *Ibid.*, pp. 154-155.

which God is, or has, is from and for himself. God in himself is beautiful, lovely, and by his very nature can love nothing but himself. God, to be sure, is *eros*, but *eros* desiring himself. Thus we see that *eros* and *agape* are completely distinct, qualitatively different. *Agape* is the Christian motif depicting a loving God who freely, unreservedly gives himself without any thought as to the worth of the object of his love. *Eros* is always the desiring, craving, self-centered love so thoroughly characteristic of the motif that even when God is called *eros* it is meaningless unless understood in the sense of self-satisfaction. "The idea of Eros does not really apply to God, and if it can, by a *tour de force*, be used of Him, its character as love of desire and egocentric love forces the consequence that it can only mean a love centering wholly in Himself and enjoying His own perfection. 'God is Eros' is meaningless unless Eros is interpreted as αὐτοῦ ἔρως. But it would be pure nonsense to speak of Agape as self-love."[60]

Agape, on the other hand, is the transvaluation of all values. "*Agape is a slap in the face to the Jewish piety of the law as well as to the Hellenistic piety of eros.*"[61] *Agape* is the direct contradictory of *nomos* and as such destroys the entire foundation of the Jewish world of values. *Agape* is also the direct opposite of Greek wisdom: God loves not the wise, as Aristotle said, but the foolish, in order to confound the wise. In the Christian motif the chasm between God and man is absolute. Man cannot by work or by wisdom find God. God alone can bridge the gap. Truly and ever *agape* is a stumbling block to the Jews, and to the Greeks, foolishness. *Agape* is the

[60] *Ibid.*, pp. 156-157.
[61] Nygren, *Den kristna kärlekstanken*, p. 162.

value-indifferent love of God, who simply loves by his own nature, unconditionally, unreservedly.

In contrast with *eros, agape* can be effectively illustrated by Nygren's own tabulation of opposite descriptive terms:

"Eros is a desire of good for the self.

Agape is self-giving.

Eros is man's effort to ascend.

Agape comes down from above.

Eros is man's way to God.

Agape is God's way to man.

Eros is man's achievement, the endeavor of man to achieve salvation.

Agape is a free gift, a salvation which is the work of Divine love.

Eros is ego-centric love, a form of self-assertion of the highest, noblest, sublimest kind.

Agape is unselfish love, which 'seeketh not its own,' and freely spends itself.

Eros seeks to gain its life, a life Divine, immortal.

Agape lives by God's life, and therefore dares to 'lose it.'

Eros is a will to have and to possess, resting on a sense of need.

Agape freely gives and spends, for it rests on God's own richness and fullness.

Eros is primarily human love, and God is the object of Eros.

Agape is primarily God's own love, for God is Agape.

Eros, when it is applied to God, is a love fashioned after the pattern of human love.

Agape, when it appears in man, is a love that takes its form from God's own love.

Eros is determined by and dependent on the quality of its object, its beauty and value; hence it is not spontaneous, but 'caused,' called forth by the value of its object.

Agape is sovereign and independent with regard to its object, and is poured out on 'the evil and the good'; hence it is spontaneous, 'uncaused,' and bestows itself on those who are not worthy of it.

| Eros recognizes value in its object, and therefore loves it. | Agape loves, and creates value in its object."[62] |

The two motifs may be compared systematically: "Love expresses a relation between a subject who loves and an object that is loved. We have, then, three 'relations' of love, according to its possible subjects and objects: (i) God's love for man; (ii) man's love for God; (iii) man's love for his fellow-men. To these, however, we must add (iv) man's self-love; for though this is not properly a relation, since the subject and the object are the same, human self-love has held so important a part in the history of the idea of love, that it is necessary to include it in our scheme.

"We must now see what different forms these four relations of love take in the contexts of Eros and of Agape respectively, and how they illustrate the opposition of the two ideas."[63]

God's love as *eros* is entirely meaningless. If *eros* is desiring love, and if God needs nothing, but remains in untroubled bliss, God's *eros* is, naturally, non-existent except as it can be interpreted by a *tour de force* as self-love or self-affirmation. In the *agape* motif, however, God is in the very center. God is the source of all *agape*. *God is agape*. Love to God must be central in the *eros* system, however, since God represents the acme of the values which egocentric love desires. In the *agape* motif, on the other hand, it is difficult to speak of *agape* to God, partly because of the fact that since God only is by his nature love, man has no real independence and spontaneity in relation with God, and partly because

[62] Nygren, *Agape and Eros*, p. 165.
[63] *Ibid.*, p. 166.

man's love to God is only gratitude for belonging to him. This love is a "reflex" of God's love, and might better be termed faith. It is purely theocentric, and man has no choice in the matter. "Man's love to God cannot, except in a limited sense, be the love of desire; for God is too high, too great, to be simply the object of man's desiring. He is not the Highest Good, in the sense that He surpasses all other objects of desire, but he stands above and beyond the things that man can desire.[64] Man's love to God, in the Christian sense, must be a purely theocentric love, in which all human choice is excluded: 'ye did not choose Me, but I chose you.' (John xv:16) Here lies the deep truth of predestination. Man is to love God, not because he finds fuller and completer satisfaction of his need in God than in any other object of desire, but because God's 'uncaused' love has overpowered him and constrained him, so that he can do nothing else than love God."[65]

In the love of man for his neighbor the two ideas are equally distinct. *Eros* is man's love of neighbor for the sake of reaching God, for the sake of selfish achievement and advancement. It is, then, not the love of neighbor for his own sake, a free, happy, overflowing love, but the selfish love of the divine in the neighbor. *Agape,* however, is God's free love flowing through man over to his neighbor. "The use of the term Agape to describe the love of the Christian for men means that *in this case also Agape denotes God's own love.* It is not

---

[64] This sentence, in *Agape and Eros*, reads: "He is the Highest Good, not in the sense that He surpasses all other objects of desire, but that he stands above and beyond . . ." When Professor Nygren's attention was called to the inconsistency of this with his position as a whole, the fault was found to be in the translation, and his authorization was given to change the sentence as above.

[65] *Ibid.,* p. 168.

that God's love for man and man's love for his neighbor are two different things; they are one thing. Agape is used to denote God's love, not human love; God's love present in the Christian heart."[66] The love of neighbor is, then, *agape's* free overwelling according to its nature. Man finds a freedom, a spontaneity through the gift of God which as sinful he could not have. In the love of neighbor, thus, God is not *causa finalis* but *causa efficiens*. Since "for God's sake" is not a teleological but exclusively a causal concept, the Christian *agape* has a love to neighbor which in the teleologically oriented Platonic *eros* is definitely impossible. *Eros,* moreover, is even formally self-love. Egocentricity is the basic form of the drive. *Agape,* on the other hand, is restlessly, exclusively outgoing love. The very nature of *agape,* once and for all, excludes even the consideration of self-love. These relations are summarized by Nygren verbally and diagrammatically:

"If now we attempt to summarize our consideration of the 'relations' of love, it is clear that the matter resolves itself into this, that Eros and Agape stand as direct opposites at every point. Eros begins with self-love, and lays great stress on love to God, as the final satisfaction of the needs of the self. On the other hand, Eros always has difficulty in finding room for love to man. It might be true to say that love to man was never really welcomed into an Eros-scheme till that scheme had been adopted into Christian theology and a compromise effected with the idea of Agape. In any case, Eros must always regard love to man as a love for the good in man and thus a step in the soul's ascent.

[66] *Ibid.*, p. 96.

But there is one form of love for which Eros has no place: God's own love.

"Agape is the precise opposite. God's own love is the ground of all love, and the pattern of all love; it consists in free self-giving, and it finds its continuation in man's love for man; for he who has received all for nothing, is thereby constrained to pass on to others that which he has received. Love to God is far from absent from the Agape-scheme, but its significance is wholly different from that of Eros-love to God; Agape-love to God lacks entirely the egocentric note, and is identical with the complete abandonment of self. And there is one form of love for which Agape has no place: self-love.

"This result may be represented diagrammatically in the following scheme:"[67]

Agape		The Relations of Love		Eros
Fundamental. Term freely used.	Downward movement ↓	God's own love. Man's love to man.	↑ Upward movement	Absent. Term used with reservations.
Term used with reservations. Absent.		Man's love to God. Man's love for himself.		Term freely used. Fundamental.

The comparison of these two ideas has been given a prominent place under the idea of God as love, because more and more this approach becomes the all-dominating, the all-governing center of Lundensian thought. The perusal of *Svensk teologisk kvartalskrift* since the publication of the first volume of this influential work reveals that most subsequent Lundensian thought reflects quite consciously this sharp division between *agape* and

[67] *Ibid.*, p. 171.

eros. This is the basis of Lundensian theology: God is *agape*, revealed in the Christ-deed. God loves freely, unreflectively, unconditionally, unreservedly. God loves sufferingly, redeemingly, victoriously. God loves, but this love cannot at all be understood or seen except through God's special revelation. This is the revelation unique in history, yet objectively discoverable in the Christ-deed. The God of Christian revelation, the God of faith, is the God of love, the God of the Christ-deed.

The second volume of *Den kristna kärlekstanken*, now available in English, adds little of principial importance to the first, but concerns itself with the interpretation of the history of Christian thought from the early Church through the Reformation in the light of the persistent conflict of the two motifs *agape* and *eros*. Merely to indicate the approach of this extensive work, it may be summarized as follows: The New Testament *agape* motif became exceedingly attenuated in the history of the Church until the Reformation, when it was revived and deepened. But it persisted. In the first period, that of the Ancient Church, the *agape* type was mostly broken by the prevailing *nomos* type among the Apostolic Fathers and the Apologetes, and the *eros* type among the Gnostics. But law and wisdom were both spurned by Marcion in the interest of God's *agape*. Even Marcion, however, could not free himself from the influence of *eros*, as can be seen not only in his ascetic teachings but in his divorcing the God of Jesus Christ from the universe, in his docetism, and in his conception of the immortality of the soul, ideas which testify to their origin in Greek intellectualism and Orphic animism. In the following period, the same motifs are struggling with each other, though naturally not in pure forms, with Tertullian representing the *nomos* type, the Alexandrian theologians, the *eros* motif, and Irenaeus, to a great extent, the *agape* line from God to man. Thereafter follow theologies which are eclectic compromises as found in Methodius of Olympia, Athanasius, and Gregory of Nyssa.

Augustine, however, effected a synthesis of the two motifs. Dismissing the realistic-institutional side of Augustine, and passing over as irrelevant to his subject the polemic-practical nature of most of Augustine's Christian writings, Nygren takes up the Pauline and Neo-Platonic, the so-called religious and philosophic, aspects of the great Catholic writer, with intent to show that both were synthesized into the *caritas* type. However eclectic Augustine may be in other respects, in regard to love, which is the center of his Christian system of thought, he has arrived at a unified position.[68] And in this position it is love to God, not God's love, which is central. The content of the synthesis achieved is characterized by Nygren as follows: "The Christian commandment of love gives the final answer to the questions put by ancient philosophy as to 'the highest good.' "[69] Dominated by the very way philosophy puts the question, the Christian motif is naturally the losing partner. Love in the Christian sense, moreover, is never a command, but always a gift. Augustine's real difficulty, however, lies in his acceptance of universal eudaemonism, of the egocentric point of view, according to which Christianity merely shows the way and provides the means to realize the Neo-Platonic truths. God becomes *man's* good. The love of God is also the highest

---

[68] Cf. Nygren, *Den kristna kärlekstanken*, Vol. II, pp. 252, 255 ff.
[69] *Ibid.*, p. 311.

form of self-love. Even the sharp distinction between *frui* and *uti*, between enjoying God for his own sake and using him as a means for man's happiness, cannot remove this fundamental difficulty. Even his emphasis on *sola gratia* or the Incarnation as the descent of God's love cannot redirect or outbalance his initial orientation, for the merit system finds a place within God's grace and the Incarnation is chiefly teleologically, not causally, motivated. Whether speaking of God's actually ordained means of salvation as inclusive of man's effort or of the Incarnation as an example in humility, Augustine has a distinct moralistic vein. Over and over again, these are seen to harmonize: God's grace and man's effort, or, as before, *amor Dei* and *amor sui*. Nygren has summarized Augustine's relation to the *agape* motif as follows: "1) From the point of view of *the object* Augustine's view of love is emphatically *theocentric*, in that no object can compete with *God* for our love, 2) but in relation to the nature of love it is equally egocentric, for even in God I seek *my* good."[70] This, then, is Augustine's synthesis of *eros* and *agape* into *caritas*: the universal eudaemonism and man's efforts to satisfy it, i.e., the human reference, are combined with God's way to man *sola gratia* in the Incarnation, while man's self-love is seen to be satisfiable only in his uncalculating love to God. This is the great *caritas* synthesis which has conquered and ruled Catholic thought.

In an interesting study Nygren then writes about Proclus and Dionysius the Areopagite, and reveals how almost unalloyed the *eros* type ran in this channel from Plotinus into Christianity. John Scotus Erigena is not treated at any length because his influence on the Chris-

[70] *Ibid.*, p. 357.

tian church was greatest through his translation of Pseudo-Dionysius. Surely the contemporary Catholic Church could find little to appreciate in his intellectualistic, pantheistic system of thought.

Almost dismissing the Middle Ages with a scant eighty-four pages, the author briefly relates how Thomas Aquinas, Dante, Bonaventura, and Bernard of Clairvaux belong among the theologians of *eros*, with its way from man to God, and how thoroughly possessed they are by Augustine's *caritas* synthesis. The three ladders to heaven are the *meritum* ladder of moralism, the analogic ladder of speculation, and the anagogic ladder of mysticism. In each case, the direction is clear, and the grace of God enables man to overcome his natural impotence and scale the ladders to his intended destination. Even where the problem of self-love is clearly seen, as in Thomas and Bernard of Clairvaux, the final solution is always its acceptance as Christian. Even Thomas' *amor amicitiae* and Bernard's *diligere pure Deum propter Ipsum* lead back at last to *bonum sui* or *diligere se propter Deum*. Mysticism's mortification of self, moreover, is "the most refined form of egocentric piety . . . . the highest triumph of the selfish will,"[71] in that it identifies the self with God. Occam's and Biel's insistence on *contritio* as against *attritio*, since it teaches man's capacity to love God with a pure motive, is the very acme of moralism. Not even Aelred of Rievaulx' God as *amicitia* could refrain from making friendship the best of heavenly ladders. No, the Middle Ages wanted fellowship on the basis of righteousness, whereas *agape* knows it possible only on the basis of sin. New forms of the love motif were introduced by the Minne piety and the pas-

[71] *Ibid.,* p. 468.

sion mysticism, but the former tended toward vulgar *eros*, and the second was precluded from grasping the full significance of the *agape* message because of its imitative idea.

The third division of the book is devoted to the "bursting of the synthesis." After a short discussion of Ficino to show how almost crassly the Renaissance accepted the *eros* motif in nearly its full strength, Nygren turns to Luther to indicate how the Reformation is the revival of the *agape* motif. Luther performs "the Copernican Revolution" in Christian thought. In him the *nomos* and the *eros* types are completely rejected. Fellowship with God is on the basis of sin. God is the subject of love and of faith. Man is nothing but the channel of God's grace. *Sola gratia, sola fides* reign supreme. To expound this, however, would be anticipatorially inappropriate, and would be almost to expound the whole of Lundensian theology, since the latter is identical with their exposition of Luther. It is a significant fact to ponder, however, that until recently the *agape* motif has been really strong only twice, in New Testament times and in Luther. Even Luther, moreover, was unconscious of the struggle from this point of view. No wonder that the Lundensian theologians can write with vigor and assurance, for, if they are right, and surely their thought is both religiously and historically suggestive, this is the greatest find in the history of Christian thought.

From a principial point of view, as we have said, the second volume adds little. *Agape* is now defined as "absolutely sovereign, spontaneous, and ungrounded," and secondly, as "free from all egocentric calculations."[72] All *agape* is of God. Nygren's summary, as one of his

[72] *Ibid.*, p. 539.

most recent statements on the subject, may be valuable for our consideration: "*Eros*, the central motif in Hellenistic soteriology, is in its nature desiring, egocentric. The idea of man dominates this view, both as the point of departure and as the goal. The point of departure for *eros* is man's need; the goal, its satisfaction. That man be lifted to the divine is characteristic of *eros*' way to salvation. Man is thought of as at innermost like God. It is necessary only to become conscious of one's highness and cease seeking satisfaction in shifting and perishable things. It is true wisdom to fly on the wings of the soul from the temporal to that higher world where the soul once had its abode before it became incarcerated in its bodily prison. . . . Through *eros* the soul ascends to heaven whether through cumbersome struggle, in rapt vision, or in intoxicated enjoyment. . . . In its most sublimated form *eros* maintains its egocentric aspect.

"*Agape*, Christian love, is entirely different. It has nothing to do with desire or selfish longing. 'It seeketh not its own'; it does not, like *eros*, seek privileges, but is, rather, self-offering and self-sacrifice. The reason for this nature of Christian love is that it is like God's. It is not a question now of lifting the human to the divine, but of the merciful descent to man of the divine. *Agape* is, first of all, God's love as unveiled most fully in the cross of Christ, in his self-sacrifice for sinners."[73]

One thought, however, is new. Nygren asserts *nomos* as the necessary background for *agape*. "It is as if it should always need this background in order not to lose any of its seriousness and depth. *Agape* is in its nature a re-evaluation. It is a conquering of *nomos*, and exists

[73] *Ibid.*, pp. 9-10.

only in this tension."[74] To magnify this thought, which occurs only once, for the sake of showing that Marcion's thought needed a structural background and that love is not formless, may be dangerous. This need of the law is used by the author in this connection as a defense of the Old Testament. But the indication is that Nygren has seen, at least in a flash, the probable need of finding a basic structure which somehow gives fullness and concreteness to the thought of *agape* as unmotivated and groundless love.

E. The Meaning of Holiness.

God's *agape* as the uninterrupted way of God to man is, as we have seen, the most important picture revealed in the Christ-deed, but this love must in no way be considered lax simply because it is unmotivated. As a matter of fact, Aulén specifically polemizes against the tendency in theology prevailing since before the Enlightenment, which, to him, is characterized by "the Mild Providence."[75] Even though in the third edition of *Den allmänneliga kristna tron* Aulén has changed the headings of the main sections from holiness to love, holiness remains as the indispensable background against which love is made manifest. "The Holy One is an expression synonymous with God. Holiness does not supply the content of the Christian picture of God, but it is the background without which the picture cannot appear: Everything that belongs to God and the divine sphere bears the stamp of holiness and is consequently seen to be entirely separate from everything human."[76]

---
[74] *Ibid.*, pp. 36-37.
[75] Cf. Aulén, *Den kristna gudsbilden*, pp. 274 ff., especially p. 288.
[76] Aulén, *Den allmänneliga kristna tron*, p. 149.

Holiness, in Aulén's thought, has a fourfold significance. In the first place, it affirms the purely religious nature of the picture of God, in sharp distinction from all moralisms or ethicisms. Holiness is not an aspect of God, not a metaphysical qualification, but a term especially denoted to exclude from Christian thought all judgments based on human morality. In the second place, holiness means God's unconditioned majesty. "Holiness guards against all eudaemonistic and anthropocentric interpretations of religion. Holiness is God's unconditioned majesty."[77] Religion rises in sovereign splendor above our wishes, desires, and needs. God's holiness denotes sovereign majesty, absolute independence. "He has us in his power, but he is not in ours. He is the unchallenged ruler in the world of faith."[78] In the third place, God's holiness signifies his incomprehensibility. This aspect has already been sufficiently stressed. Finally, holiness means God's qualitative distinction from man. The fault of mysticism as well as rationalism is the blurring of the absolute separation between the divine and the human. Mysticism's identity of God and man is in the last analysis man's basic sin, man's blasphemy, man's unholy pride in wishing to be like God. Against all such self-glorification stands sternly the holiness of God. By his holiness, God is God and not man. Holiness, therefore, is a term to denote the absolute distinction between God and man. In relation to *agape* it accentuates the *divine* nature of God's love. For this reason also holiness has no meaning except as the characterization of *agape*. With this view of holiness in mind, Aulén, in *Den kristna gudsbilden*, criticizes both the dialectical theologians and R. Otto for

[77] *Ibid.*, p. 152.
[78] *Ibid.*, p. 153.

their factual separation, respectively, of God's transcendence or wrath from his love, and of his rational love from his irrational holiness. So integrally is holiness a characterization of divine love that Nygren can write: "The Atonement is necessary not because God's love is holy, but simply because it is love."[79]

F. The Problem of Evil in the Light of Faith.

We have now seen how *agape* is revealed definitely yet continuously through Christ against the background of the dynamic-dramatic struggle of a loving God who is qualitatively above rational comprehension, who is spontaneous, unmotivated love, a holy love which eternally keeps distinct the divine from the human. Continuously through all these discussions, the thought of the evil against which God is struggling has been prominent. Dualism is also openly announced in the Lundensian system: "It is not only God's will that is to be found in history. There is also another will to be found there, which is more opposed to the will of God than the brightest brightness is to the darkest darkness. History is a drama, the arena of conflict between the will of God and this opposed will."[80] As a whole, this problem is less clearly cut than any other, but the general lines of affirmation are unmistakable. It is real evil that God is fighting: the love of God is overcoming real obstacles. Evil is to be taken seriously, as real, as vital, as in no way positively related to God. This goes so far as to reject the idea that God in any way or in any sense allows evil. "Nor can we escape by the common saying that even though God does not directly want evil, he nevertheless

---

[79] Nygren, *Försoningen*, p. 52.
[80] In *Revelation*, p. 288.

allows it."[81] God is definitely, unreservedly, ever and ever against evil, directly and indirectly. God is dramatically and with all his being engaged in the conquering of evil. The nature of evil must be explained in connection with man, but as seen above, evil is not entirely human perversion, not to be identified with human sin. Evil has also cosmic, if not metaphysical status (for the metaphysical point of view is banned). Cosmic evil, religiously speaking, means that there are objective powers of evil known by faith, or revealed objectively in the historical deposit of faith.

When all this is said, it in no way minimizes the fact that God can use evil. At times, Aulén even approaches Luther's idea that evil is part of God's wrath.[82] Evil is then nearly drawn within the scope of God's activity, but this thought is never strong. In the Atonement, where God by reconciling the world with himself is also reconciled, the idea is naturally quite tempting, but Aulén never formally accepts the implications involved. God has no relation with evil except to use it when present as a means to drive man to seek God's love. The wrath of God is the intensity with which the love of God affirms its own purity. In the last analysis, evil is in no way positively attributable to God's will. God is positively, unconditionally against evil. As we shall see, insofar as the universe is evil, it is separated from God. At times the thought approaches the logical sharpness of Marcion: the God of Christ and the God of the universe cannot be one.[83] The fault of idealism has been an at-

[81] Aulén, *Kristendomens själ,* p. 43.
[82] Cf., for instance, Aulén, *Den allmänneliga kristna tron,* p. 168.
[83] Bring and Nygren suggest that this distinction is a matter of religious approach rather than a content in faith. If the point of departure is nature, a rational dualism arises which is foreign to faith's fervent avowal that God is both all-loving and the creator and sustainer of all. Inasmuch as faith is

tempt to identify the God of nature with the God of the Christ-deed. God must, therefore, be resolutely cut from the universe where this is conceived of as a causal system. Man's faith in God, when identified with the God of the universe, has been rudely shaken by cosmic catastrophes. In one way, to be sure, even as Luther thought such phenomena a part of God's wrath, faith may see them as such, but even then it refuses to think of evil as positively caused by God in the sense that God's absolute opposition to evil should in any way be weakened.

The most important point in relation to the whole problem, however, is that evil cannot be solved rationally, but religiously, through the eye of faith. And the eye of faith is very trusting, as we shall soon see, and does not ask questions beyond its competency. Its solution is that of dynamic synthesis. Thus, to the eye of faith, dualism is legitimate so far as it affirms unreservedly God's opposition to evil, but illegitimate if it is interpreted to mean a limitation of God's power. Dualism is not a metaphysical category. The questions of genesis and theodicy faith leaves with the wisdom of God. It can affirm, and does affirm, that God's love is unconditionally opposed to evil, directly and indirectly irresponsible for its existence, but that, nevertheless, the sovereignty of God's love is in no way impaired. God's love is sovereign whether in judgment or in grace. In all religious solutions there is a tension, but the intrinsic tension of faith. To affirm that evil is cosmologically but not metaphysically real, a historical opposition finally to be overcome by God, is to pass beyond the limits of

---

not rational it finds, moreover, no difficulty in affirming with equal positiveness that evil is real and diametrically opposed to the will of God.

faith. Faith can affirm both that God unmitigatedly hates evil, and that the sovereignty of his love is uninterruptedly complete. But, as the methodology revealed, faith never arrives at rational conclusions.

God's relation with evil is, above all, positively characterized by the fact that his love overcomes it. The love of God is a sovereign love. The God of the Christ-deed can legitimately be described by the title of the English translation of *Den kristna försoningstanken: Christus Victor*. The picture of God as revealed in his redemptive work against the dualistic background is that of a love divinely sovereign. There is again, quite naturally, a tension between God's love and his power which cannot be rationally explained without losing the significant picture of the Christian God. Paradoxically, however, love is sovereign, not as the sovereignty according to which all that happens is caused by the divine love, but "as love's sovereignty in relation to everything that happens."[84] "In relation to evil, the divine power is seen from a double point of view: *as grace and as judgment*. In grace, evil is overcome and compelled to serve the interests of the divine will. In the condemning judgment, the unconquered evil confronts the divine sovereignty. The divine will, therefore, is thought of not as a power superior to all others, but as, in the deepest meaning of the word, the sovereign power in existence."[85] When faith sees love as tension, but yet as a complete victorious unity, what in rational language would mean that love is strong enough to win its object, it is clearly sovereign; but also when it cannot win, it is sovereign in its might to reject. Only paradox is able to

[84] Aulén, *op. cit.*, p. 173.
[85] *Ibid.*, p. 179.

write the following: "The divine love meets us as a 'lost love.' But only the love that sacrifices itself until it becomes a lost love, trampled under foot by selfishness, is also *omnipotent* love. In that the love of Christ on the cross became a lost love, the cross has become a *crux triumphans*."[86]

G. The Relation of Revelation to Nature and to History.

We have now seen the most important aspects of the idea of God as revealed, according to Lundensian thought, in the Christ-deed. God is seen through the Christ-deed as revealed fully, once for all, but yet as dynamically-dramatically continuing his revelation against a background of real evil which he sovereignly overcomes either by means of his spontaneous, unmotivated, value-indifferent love, creative of fellowship, or by means of his sovereign judgment. These ideas in the picture of God make clear his relation with man, but there are also three more relations, two indirect and one direct, which must be definitely included in order to see the proposed relation more clearly. God's relations with nature and history are important, both because through them God affects men, and because they have been of strategic importance in modern theological thought. In this, as practically always, Lundensian thought is strictly consistent with its own genius: God works in nature and more in history, but the measure of God's working in both nature and history is measured by the picture of God as revealed in the Christ-deed. The presence of evil both in nature and in history is far too great to speak of the God of nature. Only the name is common between the God which is viewed as the

[86] Nygren, *op. cit.*, p. 63.

causal source of nature or as the God ascertainable through teleological possibilities and the God of Christian faith. Creation is not a causal concept but a religious knowledge of the sovereignty of God, of man's continuous dependence on the Creator. Creation is neither a temporal nor a causal, but a religious concept, akin to the idea of God's logical priority to the created. It has nothing to do with idealistic attempts to bridge the absolute chasm between God and the natural, or with the metaphysical dualism which sees nature as evil. Religiously, creation means "existence seen as completely dependent on God, and the consequent view of life as good, given by the giver of all good gifts, inclusive of an unconditional responsibility on the part of the created."[87] If this is the causal connotation from the religious point of view, teleologically, nature implies no intra-mundane goal, but ever and only the realization of the divine will through continuous creation, on the one hand, and on the other, a new heaven and a new earth. Similarly, Providence does not mean a fatalistic attributing of what happens to God, but the religious assurance "that He means something with everything that happens, and that we can place everything in God's hands."[88] The extent of God's positive revelation in history, extensively and intensively, moreover, is measured by the Christ-deed. Aulén polemizes against all attempts to exclude God from history, on the one hand, whether by means of mysticism's pneumatic Christ or otherwise, and, on the other hand, against every attempt to identify God with history whether by theories of immanence or by recourse to "the historical Jesus." "The revelation of

---

[87] Aulén, *op. cit.*, p. 211.
[88] *Ibid.*, p. 219.

God to Christian faith is inseparably connected with history but without intermingling with the human."[89] Without using Lundensian terminology, the point of view can best be expressed by saying that God reveals himself in history, but not in all history; that he similarly discloses himself in nature, but to a lesser extent. The important point religiously, however, is that he makes himself known as God, not as man, i.e., by external manipulation however spiritually interpreted, and never by means of immanence in resident forces. Revelation is thus a new purpose inserted from above, continuously operating *in parte* but never *in toto*. Another solution by faith must also be mentioned. Theological thought has wavered between God's working by means or directly, mediately or immediately. Aulén finds that faith knows God to work both through means and immediately. This, moreover, is not thought consecutively, but simultaneously; not disjunctively, but conjunctively. In working through means, God works immediately. Faith, most fortunately, can be entirely unconcerned with the "wisdom of the wise," who might from this try to draw philosophical implications.

H. Faith's Dynamic Synthesis.

One of the most important ideas in Lundensian thought is the idea which Ljunggren, in connection with Luther's theology, calls "unity in contradiction."[90] That

---

[89] *Ibid.*, p. 61.
[90] Ljunggren, *Synd och skuld i Luthers teologi*, p. 174. Bring and Nygren object to this phrasing of the problem, claiming that the very idea of there being contradictions is due to the illicit introduction of theoretical considerations. When their attention was called to the matter, they admitted readily that Aulén's theory of a dynamic synthesis is equally outside the scope of the Christian revelation.

religious faith is a "dynamic synthesis"[91] is the deepest secret. Faith is the reconciliation of opposites through a state of religious tension. The undue stress on any aspect, or the rational following of its apparent implications, is the same as the exchange of the insight of faith for the darkness of reason. "The understanding of the necessity of this antinomy," writes Ljunggren, "is in the last analysis the only solution possible in this world."[92] "The characteristic distinctiveness of faith, from one point of view, is this permanent gliding between opposite poles which reciprocally condition each other."[93] This idea of revealed truth comprehended through religious tension, as through the dynamic balance of motifs, entails a most significant corollary: faith has its limits. The pursuit of individual motifs apart from the synthetic tension of faith leads to its destruction. Faith knows nothing outside the tension contained in the paradox of the Christ-deed. "Faith can bear to face unsolved problems. One thing, however, it cannot bear: the desire to know any other God than him whose heart it has seen in Christ."[94] Faith knows this to be a fact and willingly recognizes this to be its absolute limit. Faith cannot explain the problems of the world. The divine action is unknown by man. To try to know the ways of God with the world would be to listen to the voice of the tempter: *"eritis sicut deus."* "We cannot . . . . without becoming guilty of *crimen majestatis* try to defend the divine action before human reason or human standards of right. We can neither defend it nor understand it: we are not allowed to understand the world's process

[91] Aulén, *Den kristna gudsbilden*, p. 73.
[92] Ljunggren, *op. cit.*, p. 174.
[93] *Ibid.*, p. 165.
[94] Aulén, *op. cit.*, p. 197.

as God sees it. At every step we meet an impenetrable and mysterious dimness. To desire that this veil be lifted is to go beyond the limits set for the life of faith."[95] Christian faith is *keine Weltanschauung sondern eine Lebensanschauung*. Concrete illustrations may be helpful. Aulén affirms that both the final judgment, dualistically conceived, and *apokatastasis* fall outside the limits of faith, since the one limits the durability of God's love, while the other makes of it an external force. To explain the nature of Christ as to his birth in time or out of time, his sinlessness, the possibility of the Christ-deed, etc., is not the task of theology or within the competency of faith. Whatever is the incomprehensible in God's love, which is and will remain the great secret of existence, it defies all attempts at rational explanation. In another passage, the same author asserts with great vigor that historical-exegetical questions fall outside the limits of faith. Faith is the solution by dynamic synthesis, by opposites in balanced tension, by the trusting soul's assurance "in spite of it all." Whatever is abstracted from this state of tension, from this picture of God in the Christ-deed, is outside the limits of faith.

Without doing full justice, to be sure, but with as much empathy, correct proportion, and due emphasis as possible, we have presented the idea of God as pictured in Lundensian theology. The idea of man when seen religiously, that is, in relation with God, must next receive our attention, whereafter the religious relation of man, or man's fellowship with man when in relation with God, must form the concluding sections of this chapter. The idea of God, however, is far and away the most important in such a thoroughly theocentric ap-

[95] *Ibid.*, p. 229.

proach as the Lundensian. Without anticipating too much, it can almost be said that the system can be described as follows: God is the all-governing center who revealed himself in Christ and who continuously reveals himself dramatically against a background of evil, religiously comprehended as real. God is sovereign in all relations, however they may be interpreted, over cosmic evil, over man whether in wrath or in grace. But the sovereignty of God is the sovereignty of holy love giving itself victoriously. Whatever view faith must then receive of man, it accepts willingly, for God is the subject of faith which is the religious solution of problems through a state of tension inaccessible to rational understanding, a solution which knows its limits to be absolute except as enlarged through the divine persuasion. In the Lundensian relation of God to man, there is no self-pride, and from the conservative point of view no fallacious anthropology. Truly this theology is theocentric. God is first, last, and forever foremost.

II. The Idea of Man

The Lundensian view of man is a difficult topic on which to write, because most of the material is in the form of historical interpretation, no detailed exposition is available, and on many minor points there is considerable disagreement. The historical interpretation, however, is almost exclusively confined to the exposition of Luther, which, in Swedish theology, is the admitted means of expressing one's own views in the shelter of the great authority of the Church. Aulén's section on man in his systematic theology, moreover, must be the standard of interpretation, since this is a straightforward exposition of doctrine and contains its most important features. The minor points, again, must for reasons of space and general relevance be omitted from discussion. The interest of the exposition is in the general features of the Lundensian system, not in its minor divergences from the modern *Lutherforschung* or from the various shades of opinion in Sweden today. Bring's writings, by far the most extensive on this topic, are of extremely strategic importance because of his firm grasp on Lundensian fundamentals. Ljunggren's position in relation to Lundensian thought is highly disputed. He is claimed most vigorously as a supporter by the founders of the movement, and is found by Bring to agree in the fundamentals, yet is also considered by the latter to be insufficiently drastic in his separation of the aspects *coram deo* and *coram hominibus*. An objective observer finds, it seems, that the fundamentals of his thought are definitely Lundensian, but that Bring's observation is justified, namely that he is not drastic in his total elimination of all natural capacity in man, that he does tend to relate the Gospel to actual problems, even such as the genetic interpretation of sin, in accordance with the common understanding of Luther, and that his distinction between the aspects *coram deo-coram hominibus* is not cut with Lundensian sharpness. These differences, however, along with several others, are far too insufficient to preclude his inclusion within the Lundensian school of thought as a whole. Ljunggren without question represents the most vital, scholarly, and typical aspect of modern Swedish theology with reference to the doctrine of man. To do justice, therefore, to the Lundensian school of thought, to Ljunggren himself, and to divergent theological tendencies in Sweden, it may be said that he stands closer historically to Luther's actual statements than either the Lundensians with their intuitive interpretation of his deeper meanings, or the more liberal modernizers of Luther. All the Lundensian theologians, nevertheless, inclusive of Ljunggren, agree in seeing the problem from two points of view, *coram deo* and *coram hominibus*, absolutistically and empirically, and unanimously agree that the religious point of view is almost exclusively *coram deo*. This aspect, therefore, will be considered first. The second section will picture the Lundensian point of view *coram hominibus*. The third division will take up man's fellowship *coram deo* in its relation to man's fellowship *coram hominibus*, or the doctrines of the Church and the relation of Christianity to culture. In Lundensian theology the emphasis is overwhelmingly in the order of presentation.

A. Coram deo

1. The Nature of Man before God

Man may be viewed from two points of view: *coram deo* and *coram hominibus*. The theological point of view is absolutistic, devoid of any relative considerations. "*In loco iustificationis* there is room for only a totalitarian point of view: On the one side, nothing but man's sin and guilt, and on the other, nothing but God's grace."[96] With the same definiteness Aulén and Nygren both write: "Christian faith knows of no blurred intermingling of the divine and the human."[97] "The chasm between God and man is absolute."[98] Seen from this absolutistic point of view, *coram deo* man is *massa peccatis*. Like a symphonic theme constantly recurring until it

[96] Aulén, *Den allmänneliga kristna tron*, p. 319.
[97] *Ibid.*, p. 36.
[98] Nygren, *Den kristna kärlekstanken*, Vol. I., p. 167.

becomes the symbol of the symphony as a whole, is the Lundensian stress on man's total guilt before God. Man without the intervention of grace is totally worthless, unconditionally, spontaneously evil, completely egocentric, devoid of any worth or merit, attractiveness or potentiality. God is God and man is his religious contradiction. Idealism is the constant target of Lundensian attacks: idealism is the greatest enemy of Christianity; idealism is man's blasphemous assertion of containing something divine, of having a part in God by nature. Idealism is the sin of the ages. Over and over again runs the theme: *coram deo* man is worthless. Idealism is self-idolatry. What was the fault of Hellenism? Optimism about man. What was the fault of the Middle Ages? Optimism about man. What has caused the recent religious and even cultural crisis? Optimism about man. "*Factually* man is from his very beginning in the power of sin and belongs to the devil."[99] "Man is by nature . . . spontaneously evil. The evil will proceeds spontaneously from his inner self."[100] Man is *natura perversa*. "*Naturalia erga Deum plane corrupta.*"[101]

The fact is that man, religiously speaking, is totally sinful. Man, as seen through the eyes of faith, is sinful by nature, totally sinful, but not by nature in an abstracted sense. Nature as such is nothing but an empty form which, theologically speaking, i.e., as seen through faith, was created for God. Nature is no psychological entity apart from its content which is either God, contained in faith, or the objective powers of wrath. Man, outside of grace, is "bound by the objective powers of

[99] Ljunggren, *Synd och skuld i Luthers teologi*, p. 57.
[100] Bring, "Ordet, samvetet och den inre människan," p. 61.
[101] Ljunggren, *op. cit.*, p. 92.

The Relation of God to Man

wrath in existence."[102] "Man is sinner and nothing but sinner. . . . Man is either one thing or the other and in both cases unconditionally. Where wrath rules, it rules completely, and where grace governs, it governs without limit."[103] Or to turn to Bring, his concise, ever-returning thought is that the inner man or man's conscience is the man as a whole, all evil or all good. Concretely man is ruled like an animal by its rider.[104] In its natural condition the conscience is "altogether evil" and "directly wrong." "The conscience is governed altogether either by the Word or by the law."[105] But although conscience is occupied completely either by the Word or by the law, "this room is in itself nothing at all, no psychological entity apart from what it contains."[106] Conscience, or man's inner self, *coram deo,* is, consequently, according to Bring, an empty form, a passive mold, not a *conscientia* in the sense of a divine capacity, nor a synteresis in the sense of a divine part in man. To return once more to Ljunggren: man's "conscience is the subjective correlate to God's objective action. *Conscientia* and *imago Dei* are consequently synonyms. . . . All the perversion which rules human nature is reflected in conscience,"[107] making it totally unable to lead man to God. It is "an organ," a "passive medium," not a "created power within man."[108] Conscience is the whole of man from the eternal point of view, and is, as such, identical with *homo theologicus*. Ljunggren, in this instance not strictly Lundensian, acknowledges that according to

---

[102] *Ibid.,* pp. 208-209.
[103] *Ibid.,* p. 238.
[104] Cf. Bring, *op. cit.,* p. 46.
[105] *Ibid.,* p. 49.
[106] *Ibid.,* p. 51.
[107] Ljunggren, *op. cit.,* p. 113.
[108] Cf. *ibid.,* p. 113.

Luther there is somehow in man "a dim and shadowy picture of man's original fellowship with God,"[109] without which man could not be reached. The conscience itself cannot, to be sure, show the way, and is useless without the Word and the Spirit, but somehow it is needed, even though it contains nothing more than the faintest degree of discriminatory powers. Where Bring has at most stated that empirically there are degrees of faith, Ljunggren has, via Luther, made a least concession as to man's actual, temporally real part in the receptivity of faith. But even this is only in the most remote way to be thought of as a psychological endowment. As to Bring's position there is no question. His concise statement is unequivocal: "It is of course possible to speak of man from a psychological point of view, but in such connections it seems meaningless to speak of God."[110] All religious judgments as to man are the judgments of faith, and from the point of view of faith, in the strict Lundensian sense, it is entirely irrelevant to speak of any human categories. Faith as a human prestation would be a most insidious form of self-glorification and destroy the completeness of the theocentric orientation.[111] "Faith is God's acceptance of the sinner without any prestations on his part; faith is not a conditioning factor for God's grace."[112] Theologically considered, faith as man's means to salvation, however great a part in it God may play, "belongs under the concept of deeds."[113] To assume that faith, whether it is defined as *assensus* or *fiducia*, is in man or belongs to him, is, in any

[109] *Ibid.*, p. 114.
[110] Bring, *op. cit.*, p. 75.
[111] Cf. Bring, "Förhållandet mellan tro och gärningar inom Luthersk teologi," pp. 24-27.
[112] *Ibid.*, p. 25.
[113] Cf. *ibid.*, p. 33.

case, to psychologize the concept. Under such an assumption, man has faith as an organ or instrument of receptivity whereas faith is entirely a gift of God.[114] It is for this reason that the question of free will is entirely irrelevant to religion. *Coram deo* man is paradoxically both fully free and fully bound, but this has absolutely nothing to do with psychological or metaphysical categories. For faith the problem of freedom and determinism just does not exist. On this point it is well to let Bring himself speak: "Through faith man is fully determined by God. . . . As to whether man is a log or a stone, i.e., possesses freedom in relation to God, is entirely foreign to Luther's way of thinking. This way of putting the question involves the placing of a psychologically thought man against a metaphysically viewed God. . . . If it is said that faith implies a decision, this means only that man is compelled by God through faith. It is impossible to separate God's gripping and compelling man and his surrendering himself without landing in the metaphysical-psychological way of putting the question."[115] Most mistakes are made, according to this way of thinking, because theologians are unable to hold themselves to this *totus homo theologicus* which has nothing to do with the natural man's capacity, but only with his confrontation before God as a sinner totally and unexceptionally. It is of utmost importance to remember that total worthlessness is not a factual statement from a theoretical point of view but man's religious view of himself in the presence of God. Through faith man knows himself both to be fully unworthy and fully responsible before God.

[114] Cf. *ibid.*, p. 29.
[115] *Ibid.*, p. 239.

The reasons for man's sinfulness may be thought of in different ways. One thing is certain, the metaphysical view of sin as finiteness is definitely rejected. Sin is, as we shall see, perversion of will or unbelief. And this unbelief is total, this perversion is entire, due to the fact that all have failed to fulfil the law perfectly, and, absolutistically considered, the condemnation is complete. The question *coram deo* is not of degrees of punishment or reward, but of a fearful either-or. This sinfulness, moreover, is inherited, transpersonal, existent before man is born. No distinction is made between moral evil and sin; such a distinction is moralistic. All evil in man *coram deo* is sin. Inherited sin, as well as total depravity, is accepted. Sin is racially transmitted and man is congenitally devoid of all merit. Inherited sin is equal with the anti-religious bias of nature itself, not as an empty form, to be sure, but as concretely possessed by evil powers. "Sin, in this sense, is an *immensum et infinitum*, an *infinitum et aeternum*."[116] Nevertheless, Ljunggren also struggles hard to make sin personal by asserting that as soon as man functions, he is enmity against God by the very bent of his will. The real sin is inherited, the direction of man's will, but since man also expresses his will it becomes personal as well. In "work" sins, which are the symptoms of man's factual condition,[117] man expresses his personal will, i.e., as concretely possessed by evil. By logical priority, man is inevitably sinful before his first act, though the act cannot be separated from his sinfulness. "When man begins to act, when he is awakened to consciousness, he

[116] Ljunggren, *op. cit.*, p. 205.
[117] Cf. *ibid.*, p. 216.

is already caught in sin, he acts and thinks under the influence of a perverted relation to God."[118]

Sin is thus an inherited perversion of nature due to unbelief. Man is responsible, as Aulén says, not only for his own sins but for the connected totality. The voluntary acts, in a moral sense, are really a view *coram hominibus*. *Coram deo* man is totally guilty because of lack of faith. The lack of faith is the mystery of God, his election. Even if faith is in one sense man's receptivity, this, too, is God's work. "Moral idealism is the very incarnation, as an approach to religion, of man's rebellion against God."[119] If man could do anything, anything at all in himself, God's love would be motivated. This would mean the rending asunder of the whole Lundensian concept of God as unmotivated love. If we could do one thing, moreover, "God would be robbed of his absolute sovereignty over us. He would lose his 'liberty.' "[120]

Nor must it be thought for a moment that the Spencerian concept of will, i.e., that man always acts according to his inclinations but has nothing to do with their origin, that man, in other words, is by nature compelled to sin, mitigates the guilt in any way. Even though sin is inherited and transpersonal, universal and necessary, guilt is coextensive with sin. The whole theology of Luther, in the last analysis, is definitely asserted by Ljunggren to rest on the thesis that "inherited sin both is irresistible and burdens man with guilt. With the righteousness of this antinomy stands or falls Luther's distinctive theological conception."[121] This is also the

[118] *Ibid.*, p. 220.
[119] *Ibid.*, p. 94.
[120] *Ibid.*, p. 98.
[121] *Ibid.*, p. 367.

thesis of Ljunggren's entire book:[122] "Before God conscience affirms both the inevitability and the guilt of sin."[123] It is again to be noted that this is the feeling of faith, "the reason of religion," not the rationalism of the natural man. In some respects, Ljunggren seems theologically to go beyond the position taken by Aulén. This will become clearer when we deal with the problem of eschatology. On the point of sin and guilt, however, both heartily agree.

2. The Function of the Law

"Conscience is governed altogether by the Word or by the law."[124] Man's spirit, in the sense of the house of an objective power, whether fully good or fully evil, is in the case of the "old man," bound by the law. But the law has also a functional capacity *coram deo* to drive man to God. "The law makes demands on man as though he were an ethical-religious subject independent of God. Faith implies that God is subject of man; the subject of faith is exactly God. The law, therefore, by requiring that man be the subject of a morality of which God alone can be the subject, drives man to a religion that lies as far as possible from the implications of faith."[125] The law does not really indicate the good, for it demands good works, and good works are man's selfish way to God. Bring and Nygren both maintain at this point that in

---

[122] An Uppsala theologian related orally how Ljunggren was deeply grieved by the fact that Aulén's Olaus Petri lectures did not sufficiently emphasize the concept of man's inevitable guilt, but seemed to be more concerned with God's objective conquest of the cosmic evils by which he both reconciled the world to himself and was at the same time reconciled. In the third edition of his systematic theology, Aulén, however, has come exceedingly close to Ljunggren's view, and refers to it for further study on the subject.
[123] *Ibid.*, p. 376.
[124] Bring, "Ordet, samvetet och den inre människan," p. 49.
[125] *Ibid.*, p. 40.

one sense, of course, the law indicates the good but that the good is a matter never of the law but of faith's deeds through unconditioned love. The higher, therefore, the demands of the law, the more refined and inward man's efforts, the further man is from faith. "The conscience itself, being spoiled, leads in a diametrically opposite direction from the content demanded by faith."[126] A long note added by Bring can in this connection be summarized as follows: All attempts to fulfil the law are labored, not spontaneous, and labored righteousness is ever egocentric, and as such directly *contra fidem*.[127] There is, therefore, no inner man apart from God or the devil. The law requires of evil that it conform to the absolute good, i.e., be spontaneously good. This is obviously a contradiction by which the law shows man to be inescapably bound. In God alone is freedom. *Coram deo,* of course, there is no freedom for man except the freedom of God's compulsion. But this is man's intended freedom. The spontaneous freedom, therefore, which the Lundensians claim the law requires, reveals man totally lost, and becomes in this way a means to man's salvation. The law reveals man's hopelessness apart from God. In one of his most recent utterances on the question,[128] though still maintaining that the law as a way to salvation leads really farther away from God, Bring stresses proportionately much more than before that the Gospel and the law belong together, that the law is given by God, that the law drives man to God. The law is connected with faith in God's creation and signifies man's being bound to God from birth. Guilt becomes

---
[126] *Ibid.,* p. 48.
[127] Cf. *ibid.,* pp. 48-49, footnote.
[128] Bring, "Lag och evangelium."

personal because man does not follow this law which is "received into consciousness through the conscience."[129] Only insofar as man tries to reach God by means of the law, as a road to salvation, is the law evil. Although the old phrases recur, the tone is different in this article. In many respects, as will be seen, the sharp polemic attitude is beginning to soften, and even as Nygren, at least for a moment, could not conceive of *agape* without a structural background, so Bring in this article on "The Law and the Gospel" is finding both wider and firmer foundations for faith. The Lundensian theologians, it must always be kept in mind, maintain that all statements as to man's being driven by the law merely describe God's way of salvation, and thus reveal even more clearly that through the eyes of faith there is only one way between man and God, namely from God to man—that even man's activity in the process of salvation is, if seen religiously, God's ultimate activity of full and free salvation. *God* works in man, according to his wisdom, whether in wrath or in love. Through this assertion of faith, God's relation with evil becomes peculiarly pressing, for if one wonders how this statement is related to faith's vigorous avowal that God does not even allow evil, and that God's power and wisdom are unlimited, he begins to understand how the paradox of faith really reaches great degrees of tension. But faith is not an intellectual evasion, for it transcends and prospectively solves its problems through its hold on God through whose love, wisdom, and power all questions beyond the understanding of man will ultimately be solved.

We have thus seen that, in the eyes of faith, man is totally worthless, devoid of any good part, that man's

[129] *Ibid.*, p. 212.

nature is made for God, but that in itself nature is but an empty form to be filled by an objective content, that man is sold under evil, that sin is the perversion of will universally inherited, which, while logically prior to any sinful deed, is inseparable from the deeds themselves, that sin is, consequently, a total perversion of nature synonymous with total lack of faith, that guilt is as extensive as the rule of sin itself, and as such, though universal and inevitable, is, nevertheless, fully guilty, that the law as the expression of God's wrath, *opera aliena dei*, drives man to grace, and that the knowledge of the workings of God's wrath is a mystery not accessible to rational knowledge. It is now necessary to consider a little more closely the process of redemption as seen by faith, man's activity in it, and man's condition when in a state of grace. The only topic which then remains, *coram deo*, is eschatology.

3. The Religious View of the Atonement

The Atonement is the divine love-deed on the Cross. There God reconciled himself with the world by conquering the powers of evil. "The work of Christ completed on the Cross is seen by faith to be an act of God, an act of the divine love-will. This viewpoint has vital significance for Christian faith. As soon as it is no longer unconditionally central, as soon as it is broken by any thought with a different orientation, the basically Christian motif is dimmed, and the fact is clouded that the divine fellowship has its source exclusively in the divine will, and is entirely effected by this deed."[130] The redemptive drama is an objective historical reality in which God has atoned for sin fully and once for all. On

[130] Aulén, *op. cit.*, p. 253.

Calvary God reconciled himself with the world by conquering the real powers of cosmic evil. The Atonement is a cosmological-redemptive drama. But, on the other hand, God is himself reconciled, inasmuch as the powers of evil, even if not sin, are somehow thought of as expressing the divine will. Since "the hostile powers, or at least some of them, from a certain point of view, are thought of as serving the divine will and going its errands, the act of victory, the conquering of the Powers, is seen from this point of view, as God's being reconciled: he becomes reconciled by reconciling the world with himself."[131] "Even the devil can, in similar manner, be put in relation to the divine will."[132] "From this it seems quite obvious that the victory over the destructive powers contains a reconciliation as well. . . . Christ's victory through self-sacrifice is the means by which God reconciles the world with himself but by which he is also at the same time reconciled."[133]

If God was in Christ reconciling the world unto himself, *propter Christum* can be interpreted only as the spontaneous love of God which was revealed in Christ. The thought by its very nature and of necessity precludes the idea of atonement as man's offer to God. The offering motif in Christian thought signifies "that the offering deed performed in Christ by divine love has a reconciling meaning even for God himself."[134] Similarly, the punitive idea connected with the Atonement can mean only that "wrath is melted down and remelted into the divine love through love's carrying of wrath's

---

[131] Aulén, *Den kristna försoningstanken*, p. 11.
[132] Aulén, *Den allmänneliga kristna tron*, p. 258.
[133] *Ibid.*, p. 259.
[134] *Ibid.*, p. 263.

burden."[135] In relation to teachings of vicarious suffering, moreover, the thought is now that "the divine love has accomplished that which no human power could, and this, in man's place by means of the Christ-deed."[136]

It is of greatest importance to stress that the one theme sounded in connection with the Atonement is the idea that God has accomplished it, that no human achievement is possible; man, religiously speaking, is the passive recipient of God's grace; even man's activity is, in the eyes of faith, God's work; man is saved *sola gratia, sola fide*; even Christ in his union of natures did not suffer *qua homo* but *qua deo*. This is the ever-recurring theme in Aulén's Olaus Petri Lectures, where the classical thought of the Atonement is sketched in contrast to the Latin and the subjective. The classical alone has an uninterrupted way from God to man. In Anselmian theology, God, to be sure, takes the initiative, but Christ, in the last analysis, suffers *qua homo*. This at least ideally motivates God's love, demands that man in some way meet the demands of God's justice. The subjective theory is, of course, out of the question, as the blasphemy of idealistic self-glorification. Aulén's own thought is comprehensively stated in a summary of the view of Luther, who is claimed to have both revived and deepened the classical idea of the Atonement. And Luther's view, in the form of the organic unity of the modern *Lutherforschung*, is ever and always what a Swedish theologian called "the theological norm." "The entire structure of Luther's theology is such that the Latin theory of the Atonement simply *cannot* be contained within its frames. The background of the Latin theory of the Atonement

[135] *Ibid.*, p. 264.
[136] *Ibid.*, p. 265.

is the moralistic theory of penance—but to Luther this is an abomination. A leading motif in the Latin theory is the idea of an unbroken scheme of justice, the thought of justice as the principal expression for the relation between God and man. But Luther bursts through this very view of the relation of God to man by sharpening the demands: the law itself now becomes, from one point of view, a destructive power. The structure of the Scholastic theology is completely rational—Anselm's refrain is *'nihil rationabilius'*—but Luther's theology lacks entirely this aspect: of nothing is he more assured than that God's work in Christ, the Atonement, the forgiveness, the justification, carries the signature *contra rationem et legem*. The way of 'the law' and the way of 'reason,' according to Luther, belong inseparably together: they represent 'the natural man's way,' but God's way in Christ is totally different. When God's act in the Atonement, according to the Latin theory, is broken by the idea of what happens, so to speak, from below, this is in radical conflict with what to Luther is Alpha and Omega in the world of faith, i.e., that there is no other way to God than God's own way to man."[137] This idea is so central, so all-pervasive, so oft-repeated, that the Atonement can fairly be summarized as God's work in man. Whatever man may do psychologically, whatever way his will may be expressed when driven by the Word, in the last analysis, in the eyes of faith, everything is God's work. And *coram deo*, the question cannot even arise. "When he (Luther) denounces 'justification through the works of man,' he does not deny the engagement of the will of man. . . . The main thing is now that in the relationship of faith *all is stamped and*

---

[137] Aulén, *Den kristna försoningstanken*, pp. 204-205.

decided by the love of God. This relation to God is what it is through God's love which at the same time judges and saves. It is this power alone that overcomes and subdues[138] man, that places him in the communion of love and constrains him to go its errands."[139] "The forgiveness is not caused partly by man and partly by God —its 'possibility' and *reality* depend entirely on God's *agape*. But under such conditions there can be no rational explanation or motivation. Every such explanation should in reality destroy the very foundation on which the Christian faith in forgiveness rests. As to the 'possibility,' Christian faith can only say: 'with men this is impossible, but with God all things are possible' (Mt. 19:26). Forgiveness is totally an act of God, his gift. This does not mean, however, that in this relation with God there should be no human 'activity.' Christian faith speaks most unreservedly about man's seeking and receiving, about his turning and yielding himself, of his daring 'yes' to the divine love, etc. But this involves least of all that forgiveness should, to some extent, be a human achievement or have a human motivation. For, from the viewpoint of faith, this human activity is nothing but an aspect of the divine activity that works in man's world.... Salvation is, according to faith, altogether God's way to man."[140]

In no uncertain or wavering manner Aulén polemizes against the idea that God's forgiveness should not be fully free, should be motivated by human achievement or some supposed inner worth in man, no matter how these human prestations might be conceived. The idea that

---

[138] Aulén here uses "subdue" to render *betvinga*; this idea is especially prominent in the word.
[139] In *Revelation*, p. 303.
[140] Aulén, *Den allmänneliga kristna tron*, p. 332.

man's repentance should in any way condition the complete spontaneity of the redemptive love is a moralistic-ethical misinterpretation of the idea of atonement. Equally subjective, idealistic, and objectionable is the thought that man's love of God, man's answer to the loving call, should in any way justify God's free forgiveness of sin. God's forgiveness is yesterday, today, and forever his unconditional, unmotivated way to man, the great mystery of the divine drama which is inaccessible, completely inaccessible, to any and all rational comprehension. Forgiveness is a definitely "supra-ethical" act, "the innermost secret of religion."[141] Nygren, equally, finds in Luther this distinctly religious view: "To him God's forgiveness of sins and his creation of fellowship was so far from self-evident that he was rather forced to consider it a divine mystery which takes place 'contrary to all reason,' all morality, yes, even contrary to conscience itself."[142]

It is, surely, easy to understand from this that God's forgiveness, his prevenient and operative grace, is the only basis of the Christian life. Without God's election, his stooping to save that which by its very nature is eternally lost and incapable of effective initiative regarding its own salvation, man would forever remain in the miseries of his own selfishness, in his own self-centered attempts to fulfil the law, in his unenviable position under the doom of the Eternal. "The forgiveness of sin is the form for all fellowship with God."[143] "Fellowship with God is effected through God's forgiving act, and exists through faith."[144] This idea is well expressed by

[141] *Ibid.*, p. 223 ff.
[142] Nygren, *Filosofisk och kristen etik*, p. 281.
[143] *Ibid.*, p. 281.
[144] Aulén, *op. cit.*, p. 320.

Bring: "The thought of God as the subject of faith is a direct consequence of faith in God as the subject of the Atonement."[145] Faith seems to be thought of as the gift of God through the Redemption, the positive possession by God, the being filled or ruled by the divine *agape*. "Forgiveness is never without faith. . . . Faith has its foundation, its existence, its content through the divine act of the Redemption."[146]

The Lundensian theologians are most insistent that the fact that forgiveness is exclusively the work of God, the act of God's immeasurable grace, in no way reflects on God's unconditional opposition to all evil. The question as to why he does not freely forgive all is, unfortunately, not discussed. But in those whom divine love does forgive, forgiveness is no weak condoning of guilt, no soft overlooking of trespasses, but God's continuous opposition to sin in the very act of redemption. Forgiveness also, as we shall see presently, is not one decisive act, but a continuous process. This destroys all ideas of forgiveness as a preliminary step to fellowship with God. Redemption is no presupposition for faith. Atonement is not the negative preparation for fellowship, but the positive creation of harmonious togetherness. In truth, Nygren sums up this idea of forgiveness when he calls it a positive creation of divine fellowship in and through faith, on the basis of sin. Man's unworthiness, man's sin is ever his only quality before God. On this basis God's free, spontaneous, unmotivated *agape* creates a divine fellowship.

Before leaving this subject, it is illustratively helpful also to include Nygren's summary of the Atonement,

---

[145] Bring, "Ordet, samvetet och den inre människan," p. 53.
[146] Aulén, *Den allmänneliga kristna tron*, p. 323.

found at the end of *Försoningen* ("The Atonement"). It seems quite important to note that both Aulén and Nygren, especially the latter, are predominantly absorbed in the thought of God's free love, *sola gratia-sola fide*, and make mention of the worthlessness of man before God almost entirely from the viewpoint of what God's unmotivated love must presuppose in man.

"1. The meaning of religion is *fellowship with God*. For that reason, the Atonement is its most basic concern.

"2, 3. In relation to pre-Christian and non-Christian religions, which usually contain three stages: 1) gift offering; 2) the way of ethical prestation; 3) the way of humility, it can be said that the *Christian Redemption* signifies both their completion and their radical destruction.

"4. The common thought of redemption is *egocentric*; the Christian, *theocentric*. The classic expression of the latter is II Cor. 5:18 ff.: 'that God was in Christ, reconciling the world unto himself, not imputing their trespasses unto them.' God is subject in the act of redemption.

"5. Christian theologians have not always succeeded in following Paul. Usually they have remained satisfied with a *compromise between the ideas of egocentric and theocentric atonement*. The best example of this is '*Christus qua homo.*'

"6. Mankind has always dreamt of *a fellowship with God on the basis of holiness*. Christianity proclaims *a fellowship with God on the basis of sin*. This is the meaning of 1) Jesus' gospel: 'I have come not to call righteous, but sinners'; 2) Paul's doctrine of the Redemption: God redeems precisely sinners; 3) Luther's renewal of Christianity: '*simul iustus et peccator.*'

"7. *Redemption and God's agape* are fundamentally one and the same. From a Christian point of view, the outlook on redemption which does not rest exclusively on God's love has failed. *God's agape is the measure by which the Christianness of every theory of atonement can be tested.*

"8, 9. The testing of current theories of atonement by this measure reveals a general difficulty to reconcile the Atonement with God's love. *Either* the point of departure is God's love, and then *even the mention of atonement* appears superfluous (the parable of the Prodigal Son); *or* one starts from the Atonement, but then it can be reconciled with God's love only by placing alongside of it God's holiness. The Atonement is now thought of as *the synthesis between God's holiness and his love*, but not as a pure expression of God's love.

"10. For Christian redemption it is characteristic that *just God's love necessitates the Atonement*. Love is will to fellowship. Sin is, in the deepest nature, man's lack of will for fellowship with God. The Atonement means that the divine love accepts the burden that man's selfishness has caused, but refuses to carry.

"11. Christ's atonement, therefore, is literally a vicarious sacrifice, and a vicarious suffering. Here we meet the divine love as a 'lost love.' But only the love which so far sacrifices itself that it becomes a lost love, trampled by selfishness, is also *omnipotent* love. In that Christ's love on the Cross became a lost love, his Cross has become a *crux triumphans*."[147]

This sketch by Nygren of the Atonement is a complement to Aulén's approach to the problem. In both cases the stress is the same. God's love is the subject of

[147] Nygren, *op. cit.*, pp. 61-63.

the Atonement. There is but God's way to man. The Atonement is not rationally explainable, but the mystery of God's *agape*. The Atonement is God's free, spontaneous, unmotivated love creative of fellowship *sola gratia*. The Atonement is God's work in man, God's activity in man. Psychologically man may be thought of as a subject, because psychology cannot know God, but theologically God is the subject of forgiveness and faith.

Now if God is the subject of forgiveness as well as of faith, does not this imply that man becomes sinless, that man as the house of faith is completely possessed by God? Is not the relation *coram deo* absolutistic? From one point of view man is completely forgiven, but this forgiveness is also fellowship in spite of man's sin, and as such increases man's sense of guilt. The nearer man comes to God, the more he knows himself removed from God. This, of course, is not a logical conclusion, but the knowledge of faith. God's forgiveness is full, complete, yet paradoxically enough, just through it man knows himself simultaneously and continuously to be a sinner. God's forgiveness is not a sinless perfection, but a complete forgiveness and fellowship in spite of man's sin. Thus man is ever qualitatively different from God, ever needy of forgiveness, ever dependent on his mercy, but through faith, ever forgiven, ever free. Man is *simul iustus et peccator*. "Through the development of the thesis of this never ceasing dualism between righteousness and sin in the life of the believer, Luther drew the line between Catholicism and the Evangelical faith with such a sharpness that it can never be overcome."[148] This was a death-blow to all moralisms; this

[148] Ljunggren: *op. cit.*, p. 252.

was the complete destruction of the merit system. From moment to moment man depends on God's grace, is saved *sola gratia, sola fide*. And *sola fides* is ever and completely *sola gratia*. In a short space Ljunggren has defined *iustus et peccator* as used by the great authority of the church: "*Simul iustus et peccator* in relation to the situation of the believer does not refer, in the first place, to the mixture of good and evil by which the 'moral' man is characterized, but first of all to the *religious* dualism which is the source of the moral contradiction. That the believer is *iustus* means most of all his 'passive' state of being bound by the work and the souls' innermost '*Getragenwerden*' of which faith consists. In the same manner, that he is a sinner involves primarily the 'necessary' egocentricity connected with his temporal existence which makes him continually struggle against the word of God and against the realization of his becoming the eternal being which this intends him to be. As '*spiritus*', or as determined by God, the believer moves away from himself and from the judgment concerning his relation to God which founds itself on the reality discernible to *ratio* (*iustitia activa* or *sensitiva*); as *caro*, however, he is forever circling around his own self, his own deeds, his *experience* (*experientia*), his 'conscience' and his feelings. . . . In this dualism Luther is, in the last analysis, concerned with the struggle of two powers 'outside' man, that continually fight for his soul. The dualism involves that the law, hostile to the divine order, wants to crowd out the divine presence of the Gospel. When man is said to be at the same time spirit and flesh, this means that he is involved in a never ceasing struggle between God and his enemies. Man is righteous insofar as he depicts faith's self-originated movement towards God, flesh insofar as he tries to be reconciled to God by means of the law, either by spitefully depending on good deeds or through the excusing of evil."[149]

Closely related to the problem of *simul iustus et peccator*, and equally near to the next topic, the problem of eschatology, is the nature of faith as having and hoping. While Folke Holmström in *Det eskatologiska motivet i nutida teologi* goes to unusually comprehensive length to show that while in the first part of this century, especially in Germany, faith was considered a present possession, an extra-worldly realization; and while in the next period, on the other extreme, it was proclaimed an object for future realization, Lundensian theology has, nevertheless, always striven for a synthesis of the two. The content of faith is not only hoping, but having, and not only having, but hoping. Between the two there is always a tension beyond rational explanation. Since the promises of God are actually received through faith the possession is divinely present, but since the life of faith is ever a life under the conditions of sin, there can, on the other hand, never be any self-assurance on man's part. Faith exists only as a passive and continuous receiving. At the same time, faith is also a struggle against an opposition which is to be conquered, and, in this sense, faith is hope built on the promises of God. This completion is not only the fulfilling of the present good as owned in faith, but also the appearance of something entirely different. "The question is not only of the completion of that which now is, not only of the emancipation from all trammels connected with the present life of faith, but also in the

[149] *Ibid.*, pp. 270-271.

real meaning of the word, something 'wholly different.' This very doubleness of hope's perspectives, the tension between these two lines of thought, reveals in a most vital manner how the content of Christian faith appears as an incomprehensibility which lies outside man's capacity for comprehension."[150] Even as the relation of *simul iustus et peccator* was an *external* relation, i.e., a matter of being ruled by external powers and a continuous relation to both resulting from the fact that man is the scene of conflict between them, so the state of having and hoping is really, in the last analysis, not man's having but man's continuous receiving, man's eternal position *sola gratia*.

4. The New Interest in Eschatology

On the subject of eschatology Aulén has had his discussions on the topic in *Den kristna gudsbilden* and *Den allmänneliga kristna tron* complemented by an unusually comprehensive and extensive work, by a young protagonist of Lundensian theology, Folke Holmström: *Det eskatologiska motivet i nutida teologi*. In *Den kristna gudsbilden* Aulén dismisses the idea of eschatology as a theological topic as understood by a *loci*-theology. Eschatology does not deal with a certain temporal aspect of the Christian life, but characterizes theology as a whole. Eschatology is the tense background of every Christian pronouncement. There are two characteristics of modern eschatology: it is energetically cut from its Biblical forms only to receive, on the other side, "a more penetrating and ubiquitous appreciation of the significance of the eschatological motif *within* theology than ever before. . . . The eschatological motif cannot

---
[150] Aulén, *op. cit.*, p. 353.

be viewed solely as an appendix, as a complement to the rest of the Christian doctrines, but, from one point of view, it conditions the Christian faith as a whole. The Christian outlook as such, from one point of view, must be altogether eschatological."[151] Quoting Althaus at some length, Aulén agrees with him that eschatology is a tension between the world of fact and the world of value, between the axiological and the teleological aspects of life.[152] Apart from the moralistic implication in Althaus' view, he would also agree that eternity and time meet in the moral decision. With Aulén, time and eternity would meet in the spiritual gift which includes the state of both having and hoping. In this connection, he vigorously dismisses "the most extreme" position of the Barthians that *"das Christentum das nicht ganz und gar und restlos Eschatologie ist, hat mit Christus ganz und gar und restlos nichts zu tun."*[153] This, to him, is the very destruction of the reality of faith due to a false, metaphysically oriented outlook on time and eternity.

In *Den allmänneliga kristna tron*, Aulén also emphasizes that Christian eschatology has nothing to do with, or rather, is the very fortress against, all evolutionistic, idealistic optimism. The Kingdom of God comes not through any powers resident in the world, but only and surely through the will of God. The Kingdom has nothing to do with human progress, but is a gift of God outside the sphere of history. "To Christian faith the final rule of God—God's Kingdom—lies entirely out-

[151] Aulén, *Den kristna gudsbilden*, p. 371.
[152] While Aulén in this instance can possibly be interpreted as citing Althaus without direct approval of his position, it is important to note that Holmström wrote his entire work at the suggestion of Aulén for the sake of vindicating this double nature of Christian eschatology.
[153] Aulén, *op cit.*, p. 373.

side the sphere of history.... God's Kingdom has *nothing* to do with ideals of earthly happiness. From this point of view, the eschatological character of the Kingdom of God *can never* be sufficiently stressed."[154] But this does not mean that the Kingdom has nothing to do with this world. History is rather the field of battle where God wins his Kingdom. "To the Kingdom of God every generation is equally near—and equally far. The main thing in the relation of the Kingdom of God to history is this: the activity of the Kingdom of God."[155] Thus eschatology presents a solution, not rationally comprehensible, but a religious, i.e., a "dynamic," synthesis.

In his work on eschatology Holmström definitely sets out to elaborate the general sketch on modern eschatology given by Aulén in *Den kristna gudsbilden*. His theme is the idea that the one-sidedness of both the this-worldly theory of eschatology as represented by Ritschlian theology and by Bousset in the history of religions, and the extreme over-historicism as represented by Weiss and Schweitzer, were due to a false metaphysical antithesis, while in the last epoch, a synthesis is beginning to take place, not through philosophic speculation, but through religious insight, through a Biblical view which is beyond the problem of false abstractions. To prove his theme, Holmström advances an extensive and comprehensive discussion of the dominating points of view in the history of religions and theology in Germany and Sweden during the twentieth century and immediately before. The Biblical solution advanced is, in short, that eschatology is both deadly serious, presenting all-im-

---

[154] Aulén, *Den allmänneliga kristna tron*, p. 198.
[155] *Ibid.*, p. 199.

portant existential commitments, and also temporally real and decisively final. Eschatology is thus both individual and cosmological, and is, in both instances, the driving power and final sanction of religious decision. From this general thesis and in line with Lundensian methodology, he divides eschatology into four aspects, the first two of which deal with "faith theology," and the second two, with scientific theology. The four aspects are, respectively, eschatology as motivating power, as primary experiential content, as the general background of theology, and as a specially abstracted topic for study, yet withal possessive of a special sphere of intrinsic reality. The first of these is, naturally, the tremendous tension resulting from the seriousness of being the pivot between time and eternity, the scene of conflict between the everlasting "nay" and the everlasting "yea," the battlefield of God against the powers of darkness. Holmström often speaks of the spiritual decision even in terms of pietism rather than in those of Lundensian thought. Man can somehow accept or reject the divine call; man's choice is of utmost importance; upon it hangs his eternal welfare or doom. Yet, paradoxically, he also polemizes against man's efforts as conditioning his salvation *in toto* or *in parte*. Even Barth, for him, is too moralistic, since he stresses obedience, from one point of view, as a conditioning factor for salvation rather than God's mysterious election *sola gratia*.[156] Christian history is today the tremendous conflict between the geniuses of Luther and Kant, between religion and moralism. All prestations by man must be counted for naught. Those who cannot understand this paradox of God's election and the seriousness of man's choice

---

[156] Cf. Holmström, *Det eskatologiska motivet i nutida teologi*, p. 195.

are referred to the psychological history of Calvinism. Determination deepens the seriousness of life, not logically, but religiously. In this sense, religious eschatology is not a doctrine of the transcendent, but a transcendental doctrine; not a teaching of concrete events to happen, but a continually overhanging doom unless man is accepted in the period of God's grace. Eschatology in the first sense may be defined as man's consciousness, not of an eternal decision, but of a temporally limited decision for eternity.

The second aspect of eschatology relates itself to the primary content of faith, not as an intellectualistic synthesis between time and eternity, nor as the revelation of definite things to come, but as a religious understanding of eternity as divine and of time as human, and of the solution of the problem connected with them as a final victory of the divine. The end to come is definitely an end of time, a final decision made by God. Starting with time, man is ever its prisoner; starting with the over-historical, man's speculations become unhistorical. The content of eschatological faith is, therefore, this: decide now, or be forever condemned. The definite end of time as grace is set by God unknown to man; individually it may be at death—we know not—but one thing is certain: a definite, final, cosmic end is set. Individually and collectively, man will be definitely judged. The judgment seat of Christ is not forever; man's history is not his judgment; the end is final, unchangeable.[157]

[157] Cf. Hök, *Värdeetik, rättsetik, kristen kärleksetik,* p. 129 ff., wherein the author takes a definite position on the question: God's invitation has as its background doom, final, definite doom, after a limited period of grace which varies, not according to man's measure of sin, but according to the time of God's decision that this man's end has come.

The second two phases of eschatology are only the "scientific" rendering of the first two: the understanding scientifically, i.e., logically, of their content. Citations from Holmström himself may best give the author's thought: "The matter becomes even more complicated when through an expansion of the concept, eschatology comes to mean not only faith's tension between the future and the present, but also the abolition of the tension."[158] "Inasmuch as salvation through faith in Christ is even now revealed as eternally valid, yet at the same time ever partly concealed during the conflict of this age, eschatology can mean both complete abolition of this tension in the future, which is inseparable from all historical life, and also the present state of being existentially gripped by the assurance of salvation through tension-filled faith in the living God."[159] "Time becomes qualified as a history of revelation filled with the dramatic tension of decision and yet awaiting fulfillment. . . . At a definite limit unknowable to us, this interim truce is changed into eternity's fulfillment, when '*regnum gratiae*' becomes '*regnum gloriae*', when God's judgments stand eternally fixed as definite facts: 'eternal life' and 'eternal death'. For revealed faith, time is a historically given and a temporally limited invitation to the kingdom of grace. . . . The line between time and eternity is fixed by God, depending upon how long it pleases him to let the invitation of grace seek man in his wayward paths."[160] "If time is limited, eternity is not everlastingness—the thought would be an illegitimate passing over the border—but just a line that

---

[158] Holmström, *op. cit.*, p. 13.
[159] *Ibid.*, p. 14.
[160] *Ibid.*, p. 300.

marks the time that is ours from a conceived unlimited extension which is beyond our powers. . . . Eternal life is offered only during a temporally limited period of grace. When that is over, man's fate is eternally fixed."[161] "The main significance which, in our belief, eschatology has for theology, is the Gospel message concerning God's calling during a limited period of grace."[162]

With this viewpoint, Holmström naturally opposed Aulén's placing of the question beyond the limits of faith. In a footnote in his book he shows Aulén's wavering on the question: how, in the first two editions, 1923 and 1924, he accepts the annihilation of the wicked, but in the latest edition, on the contrary, he discovers annihilation to be nothing but the double result in disguise, and refuses to accept either a final doom or *apokatastasis*. Holmström, however, affirms that "the dualistic result is alone reconcilable with the existentially received faith which wants to keep its contact with the New Testament message."[163] Only such an eschatology can adequately correspond to the paradox of *iustificatio*: *"simul iustus et peccator."* "The consciousness of decision is reflected in the possibility of an eternal doom in hell; the consciousness of election, in the hope of an eternal happiness in heaven. This perspective of a double finality is the most consistent expression of the Biblical message of a sovereign God who deals with the sinner both in judgment and in grace."[164] With this point of view Ljunggren agrees without reservation: "Can faith in God as grace and *'eitel Liebe'* really be kept against the background of a double predestination? . . . Can

---
[161] *Ibid.*, pp. 300-301.
[162] *Ibid.*, p. 405.
[163] *Ibid.*, p. 309, footnote.
[164] *Ibid.*, p. 310.

this *ira severitatis* in any sense be thought of as an *ira clementiae*? Yes, Luther thinks so highly of faith that he believes it capable of passing even this hardest of tests. Reason, to be sure, fails. But, no matter. For this very fact proclaims the highest victory of the thought of election."[165] Faith sees in God's eternal punishment his eternal grace. "Just when man has been compelled to establish the *reality* of eternal condemnation, not only its *possibility*, does he stand before another and more powerful reality that convinces him that there is nothing in God's will which cannot unexceptionally be determined as love."[166] Here, then, is a difference of opinion in Swedish thought: Aulén, wavering from description of tradition to rational inference, refuses to accept the last depths of horror and perversion which have been attributed to God in the name of Christian faith.[167]

5. Immortality or Resurrection

In this connection, it seems best to take up the idea of eschatology disjunctively, from the point of view of individual destiny. The reason for this seeming discursion into the doctrine of immortality is the obvious fact that Lundensian theology has no such doctrine, on account of its doctrine of man, except as it forms part of eschatology. When Aulén treats immortality in connection with the church's prayer for the dead, he leaves the straight and narrow path insofar as he refers to the continuity of even human love, for this would, indeed, be a demonstrative parable against the use of which

[165] Ljunggren, *op. cit.*, pp. 471-472.
[166] *Ibid.*, p. 474.
[167] As will be seen in our discussion of eschatology from the point of view of the individual, Holmström himself, however, is less enthusiastic of late about the position taken by Ljunggren and Hök, leaning strongly toward the putting of the problem beyond the limits of faith.

Nygren so fervently inveighs, but, on the other hand, Aulén merely reveals once more his sensitiveness to the implications of *agape*. Immortality is also, and consistently, treated as that part of the doctrine of the Church which refers to the divine durability of its fellowship. First and foremost, however, immortality in Lundensian thought is eschatological, is definitely religious, founded not on the nature of the soul, nor on the nature of the universe, but on God's promises to be fulfilled in the last days. The soul is as mortal as the body. All attempts to base immortality, or to bolster it by means of spiritualistic or philosophic arguments are curtly dismissed. "Any connection between the living and the dead which is not determined by its relation to God lies entirely outside the sphere of faith."[168] Even the idea of immortality has the two usual eschatological poles: existentially, it means the assurance of the dependability of the divine promises of God; and, in its temporal relation, the idea of immortality means not only this qualitative aspect of faith, but a definite resurrection at the end of time. The problems which arise in this connection are not dealt with and evidently lie beyond the limits of faith. If man as the house for objective forces is destroyed, if man is mortal, body and soul, what is raised in the last day? Even if the recreated individual can be considered responsible for his guilt, even though it was inevitable to begin with, why should he be awakened to doom if God is *agape* and the realm of justice as such is abolished? The problem is not met in Lundensian thought, and perhaps should not be. For, after all, these are but rational speculations on the inscrutable ways and purposes of God. When Aulén,

[168] Aulén, *Den allmänneliga kristna tron*, p. 459.

nevertheless, breaks the descriptive methodology claimed for Lundensian theology, and maintains that souls may be saved after death,[169] a problem on which Holmström, as well, wavers, and this for the rational reason that otherwise the implications of divine love would be violated, i.e., human restrictions would be placed on God's free *agape*, one wonders just what is to be saved if there is no immortal part in man. Do men continue, though devoid of both body and soul, as qualifications of the cosmic powers, perhaps not even as empty houses, but as irreal identities in karmic unities? Was it for this very reason, or for the sake of the nature of *agape*, that Aulén in the first two editions of his systematic work on theology favored annihilation? When Ljunggren and Holmström stressed the necessity, not the possibility, of man's twofold destiny, their interest was Biblical. In his most recent article on eschatology, however, Holmström has caught up with Aulén in his worries about restricting the work of the Holy Spirit of God's love. The double outcome is, to be sure, most Biblical, least influenced by idealistic speculations; but can faith reconcile it with the picture it has received of God through the Christ-deed? Comparing his comprehensive book on the subject published in 1933, and his two articles in *Svensk teologisk kvartalskrift*, in 1934 and 1935 respectively, with his utterances in an article of 1936, "Eskatologiska slutperspektiv" ("Final perspectives of Eschatology"), a marked sensitiveness to the "weakness" of the dualistic outcome is evidenced, and dualism is seen to express "quite defectively" the idea that God's condemning zeal after all is in the service

[169] Cf. *ibid.*, p. 209.

of "the will of his holy love to create fellowship."[170] Aulén, having recognized that annihilation is but a form of the double outcome theory, which he cannot accept since it limits God's love, and being unable to accept the idea of *apokatastasis*, "for we must reckon with the possibility of an eternal hardening of the heart"[171] as well as with the possibility of salvation after death, finally dismisses the whole problem as beyond the limits of faith. And there we let it lie.

B. Coram hominibus

1. Religion and Ethics

The relation of God to man in the Lundensian system is incomplete without a consideration of its theological ethics. Much has been done in this field, but the most and best, by far, has been done by Nygren in his two books to which frequent reference has been made in the chapter on methodology. Aulén's small book, *Kristendomens etiska åskådning* ("The Ethical Outlook of Christianity"), has valuable corroborating material in relation to the Christian idea.

As an introduction to the longer and more detailed work of Nygren, Ljunggren's study of the relation of religion to ethics in Luther's theology will be helpful. From the point of view *coram deo* man is justified exclusively through faith.[172] "If faith as *faith* is already the highest 'morality', and not first through the deeds resulting from it, unbelief is in the same manner *eo ipso* the opposite of morality. . . . There is the most inti-

---

[170] Holmström, "Eskatologiska slutperspektiv," p. 123.
[171] Aulén, *op. cit.*, p. 208.
[172] Cf. Ljunggren, *op. cit.*, p. 179.

mate relation between religion and morality."[173] This justifying faith is not the deed itself, but an aspect of the deed making it acceptable to God. "Justifying faith is never an act alongside of other acts, but an aspect of every deed through which it becomes pleasing to God."[174] Faith inevitably involves ethical consequences. This must not be thought of, however, as though there were no ethical personality. "Personality as an ethical entity is necessary, and it is the product of the religious personality. But not *vice versa*, so that the ethical becomes the primary and crowds out the thought of the religious personality."[175] Yet even though the relation is so close, there are, nevertheless, two distinct aspects of personality, the religious and the ethical, and these must never be confused. "It has been noticed frequently how intimately entwined is the absolute religious point of view with the ethical and the relative. And yet this latter aspect is also strongly represented in Luther's theology. The totalitarian aspect does not exclude the idea of development and degrees either in lives of sin or of grace."[176] But "the ethical viewpoint must be kept apart and in its place."[177] "What we are before God must be separated from what we are before men."[178] "There must be no confusion between what belongs to *locus iustificationis* and what belongs to *locus perfectionis*."[179] The two are separate aspects. *Coram deo* man is justified as *spes*; *coram hominibus* man is ever *res*. But *spes* inevitably influences *res*. A quotation from Ljunggren

[173] *Ibid.*, p. 179.
[174] *Ibid.*, p. 215.
[175] *Ibid.*, p. 237.
[176] *Ibid.*, p. 238.
[177] *Ibid.*, p. 335.
[178] *Ibid.*, p. 340.
[179] *Ibid.*, p. 360.

will show how close the ideas of Luther as expressed by Ljunggren's and Nygren's more elaborate system are: "Faith *eo ipso* involves a change in the ethical content. Faith as such is *identical* with ethical goodness. . . . This does not mean an immediate change in the functions which constitute man's psycho-physical existence connected with his natural capacities of soul. The *renovatio* implicit in grace is, to Luther, not a magical intrusion in man's temporal conditions, but is located entirely on the personal plane.

"This conception of 'the person' as the real subject in justification does in no way imply a mechanical division between the two planes in man represented by *homo theologicus* and *homo politicus*. Luther here establishes the distinction according to which man finds himself in two basically different situations, as passive and receiving, or as active and doing. It is the same person, nevertheless, which is subject in both these positions. For this reason faith can never be without results in the more narrow sense of the ethical or active life. But the fruits of faith never appear except through the temporal laws under which man now lives. In this sphere the renewal can take place only gradually. Here there are no leaps in the development, but a closed continuity in orderly sequence."[180]

Bring brands this line of thought as moralistic. The reasons will appear when Nygren's system is given at some length. Any identification of faith and morality tends obviously to make faith appear to be at least an organ of receptivity in man. Faith in the Lundensian system, however, is never man's organ of reception, but totally a gift of God. When Ljunggren via Luther calls

[180] *Ibid.*, pp. 315-316.

faith an aspect of the deed which makes it pleasing or acceptable in God's sight, the *eros* motif from man to God is obvious. The relation between religion and ethics is neither sufficiently causal nor drastically clear-cut. Man is not merely a channel of God's *agape*, a means of transmission for God's grace, but somehow a distinct entity in himself. The notion of gradual development is naturally also inconsistent absolutistically with the notion of *simul iustus et peccator* in which man is at once totally sinful and totally forgiven. The general point of departure and approach in Ljunggren is, however, the same as in the Lundensian school, and his work was consequently hailed with delight by both Nygren and Aulén, but Bring is right that the Lundensian interpretation is more drastic on the one thesis: there is only one way from God to man, namely God's way to man. Consequently, all relativistic viewpoints are relegated to the aspect *coram hominibus*. Aulén, as usual, is quite consistent in his complete separation of the two aspects: "the one aspect deals with man *'in loco iustificationis'*; the other, *'in naturalibus.'* "[181] This differentiation between Ljunggren and the Lundensian school, however cursorily rendered, sets the problem which Nygren has labored diligently to solve.

In Nygren is found by far the most careful exposition of the relation between religion and ethics, between man's relation with God and that with his fellow-man. The best approach to his view seems to be in the order in which he himself gives it when discussing the Christian *ethos* in *Filosofisk och kristen etik*. Two points relevant to this topic were necessarily discussed in connection with methodology in order to present the credentials

[181] Aulén, *op. cit.*, p. 318.

of Christian ethics to be a legitimate content of the form found by philosophical ethics: the fact that Christian ethics is unreservedly dispositional and that it has a distinctiveness, a uniqueness all its own. With the former contention Aulén thoroughly agrees in his book on the subject: "There can be no question about it. *The Christian ethics is dispositional ethics.*"[182] With the same purpose, Hök has devoted most of his work to a refutation of all ethics of value or rights to show that Christian ethics is solely a matter of the heart's disposition. The distinctiveness of Christian ethics, again, is unnecessary to repeat, since the whole Lundensian system is built on the thought of the Christian *agape* as a gift from God completely unique and conclusively separate from all natural affections. As with Ljunggren and Bring, so also with the rest: God is the religious subject, and no matter who really is the ethical subject—and here, as we shall see, Nygren definitely endeavors to make room for man as subject—God's *agape* it is that characterizes man's ethically regenerate will.

It is necessary, however, to look more closely at the Christian disposition. "Can the Christian faith be shown to be so intrinsically related to the presupposed ethical disposition that the latter cannot exist if cut loose from the former?"[183] The question is answered systematically after two historical observations have been made in relation to Christ and Luther. Christian ethics is dispositional, and on that account uses the causal and not the teleological scheme. The relation is always: from the tree, the fruit; from the heart, the deed. In the second

---
[182] Aulén, *Kristendomens etiska åskådning*, p. 9.
[183] Nygren, *Filosofisk och kristen etik*, p. 218.

place, the specific ideal of Christian ethics is the disposition of Christian love. The two can be summarized in Luther's thought that a man must be blessed to do good, or also, that he must be loved in order truly to love. Nygren then turns to his systematic task to determine whether or not Christian faith is inseparably connected with an *ethos*, a disposition of which it is "the root and well." To do so he analyzes Christianity, endeavoring objectively to determine the specifically Christian. It is in this connection that the author analyzes Christianity under the aspect of the category of eternity.[184] With all religions it has four aspects: (1) the revelation of eternity; (2) the judgment of eternity; (3) the reconciliation of eternity; (4) the penetration of eternity. All these aspects are lighted by the Christ-deed. "The most compact definition of Christianity is this: *Christianity is the religion which finds all these aspects primarily realized in Jesus Christ.*"[185] In the first place, the nature of God's love is revealed through Christ. Secondly, the pure light of God's *agape* judges all inconsistent with it as sin. Thirdly, the Atonement is seen through and inseparably connected with the Person of Christ. Fourthly, God penetrates man with his *agape* as given in Christ, making a real fellowship possible and giving man a new center in which he is freed from his egocentricity and constrained by the love of Christ.[186]

It now remains to see whether the Christian ethics springs inevitably out of this systematic nature of Christianity, for only thus can the ethical ideal become legiti-

[184] Cf. *ibid.*, p. 238.
[185] *Ibid.*, p. 238.
[186] Cf. *ibid.*, pp. 238-239.

mately Christian. "But in spite of the fact that the nature of Christianity has been defined from a purely religious orientation, every aspect reveals that it has definite ethical consequences. Obviously, then, the question is of a truly religious *ethos* determined by the Christ-mediated revelation of eternity, judgment of eternity, reconciliation with eternity, and penetration by eternity. Thus our plan of exposition is also laid. It is our task to investigate every one of these aspects separately to ascertain its bearing on the Christian *ethos*."[187]

The first aspect of Christianity, the eternal revelation through Christ, involves an extended concept of fellowship within Christianity which results in important ethical consequences. This is naturally so, since the ethical category, Nygren likes to suggest, is fellowship. In any case, "wherever we talk of an ethical situation, the question is always one of fellowship (togetherness)."[188] Man is the subject of ethical relations in wider or smaller proportions according to the extensiveness of his relation with similar subjects. But the real question is as to the *how* of fellowship, as to the ethical idea. "The question is now how the experience of eternity through Christ affects and determines the ethical ideal, or, in other words, what character this ideal assumes under the influence of the Christian fellowship with God."[189] "While the non-religious ethics knows of only one fellowship, that of man with man, the Christian ethics knows it in two dimensions, the horizontal or human fellowship, and the vertical or divine fellowship."[190]

[187] *Ibid.*, p. 240.
[188] *Ibid.*, p. 241.
[189] *Ibid.*, p. 242.
[190] *Ibid.*, p. 243.

This new fellowship must inevitably affect man's ethical outlook. But all religions place man under the light of eternity, and to know fully the influence of Christianity on ethics, three manners of influence of the religious experience on the ethical experience must be distinguished. First, a comparison must be made between the religious and non-religious points of view in general in their relation to ethics; second, the influence of an ethical religion on ethics must be studied; and third, the special content of the Christian ethical ideal must be investigated. In the first instance, "the ideal is not affected as to its content, but receives religious sanction."[191] In non-ethical, primitive religions, the total life of the tribe depended on religious sanction. In the second instance, an ethical religion is bound to affect ethics and *vice versa*, since the fellowship both with God and with man is had by the same subjects. But this influence, Nygren asserts strongly, is never theoretical; man never has an influence from either side and then postulates a similar condition in another sphere, but man has experiences in both realms which experientially widen his fellowship. The two categories are distinct, autonomous, and are mistreated unless they are kept mutually independent. An experience of God is not immediately applied to man's ethical relations, but forces him ethically to weigh his fellowship with man. Similarly religion is never ethicized through human fellowship, for "religiously speaking, the concept of God is secondary; the experience of God, primary. Only if the experience of God is already ethical can, from a religious point of view, the concept of God have an

[191] *Ibid.*, p. 245.

ethical outlook."[192] The ethicizing of the concept of God must pass through a religious experience of God in order really to influence religion. In no uncertain words, Nygren then scorns the idea that the influence of ethics on religion is one-directional. The answer to the second phase, therefore, is that an ethical religion actually influences the ethical ideal: The widened religious experience opens a new vista that sees beyond the former ethical ideal. The third question concerns itself with the special influence of Christianity on its ethical ideal. He once again stresses the fact that the nature of Christian ethics is not the fellowship of might or of right, but of uncalculating love. Even though Christianity is once and for all theocentric, its ideal is not God's power, and it differs consequently from the fellowship based on rights or justice by *"the spontaneity of its love."* Christian love is no altruism, no sympathy, no enlightened generosity. "According to Christianity the 'motivated' love is human, the spontaneous and 'unmotivated', divine."[193] The influence of Christianity as an ethical religion on its ethical ideal can be thus summarized: The influence is an indirectly extended fellowship experientially effected through a concrete experience of God.

The second main division in Nygren's approach is the nature of ethics in relation to religion as the judgment of eternity, or as he entitles his division "The human fellowship *sub specie aeternitatis.*"[194] The problem in this connection is concretely defined: "to show that the ethical in Christianity is necessarily subsumed

[192] *Ibid.*, p. 247.
[193] *Ibid.*, p. 251.
[194] *Ibid.*, p. 252 ff.

under its religious aspect, or that its *ethos* is inevitably a religious ethics since the human fellowship can be viewed from the point of view of eternity."[195] The problem is then attacked by showing that the isolated I and the isolated moment are delivered from their predicaments when God and eternity respectively replace the confined natural units. When man is central, everything is calculated from his own point of view; when God's love is the center, man acts freely, spontaneously. From a Christian point of view that act or condition alone is good which has as its well and source the spontaneous Christian disposition of love.[196] "Only the causal relation can legitimatize an act."[197] Teleology is legitimate only secondarily as a furtherance or facilitation of the disposition of love. As always in Lundensian theology, all pragmatic and rational guidance of action is banned. Different actual actions are possible, but all are good if motivated by love.[198] That all Christian acts are the result of spontaneous, overflowing love, Nygren finds obvious, since man's acts of *agape* are exclusively the overflowing into the world of God's own love. "The Christian is placed between God and neighbor. Through faith he receives God's love, in love he passes it on to his neighbor. . . . The Christian love is altogether a work of God."[199] Taking over Luther's thought, Nygren writes further: "In relation to God and neighbor the Christian is to be compared to a pipe which, through faith, is turned upward, and through love, downward. All that a Christian has, he has received from God, from

[195] *Ibid.*, p. 253.
[196] *Ibid.*, p. 259.
[197] *Ibid.*, p. 260.
[198] Cf. *ibid.*, p. 265.
[199] Nygren, *Den kristna kärlekstanken*, Vol. II, p. 552.

the divine love; all that he has, he passes on through love to his neighbor. Of his own he has nothing to give. He is but the pipe, the canal, which conducts God's love."[200]

But if God is the subject of faith and love, has man a personality of his own, is he an independent ethical subject? If love is altogether God's work in man, does man as such love his neighbor? This problem in Lundensian theology finds many answers. Man's love is really spontaneous, says Nygren, since it is only "a reflex of God's love." The problem is after all psychological, affirm both Nygren and Bring, for religiously the problem does not occur. *Coram deo* there is no free personality; such a question is irrelevant. *Coram hominibus*, however, man may be said to have a free will. *Coram hominibus* man does not accept God's will blindly, but yields himself to it because he has experienced it as best. The accusation of ethical heteronomy is, therefore, based on a failure to distinguish two ways of looking at man. The Lundensian theologians naturally find it difficult to use the word "love" in relation to God, and consistently prefer the word "faith." The reason for this, says Nygren, is to keep the source of *agape* clear. After all, to be completely found by God in faith is the same as to love him with all one's heart. The main thing is this: if God is the source of love, if man's love is but the response to God's love, man is freed from all calculating motives. Even enemies may be loved without difficulty by this overflowing good will. But is man, the reader still asks, the ethical subject? Yes, comes the answer, for in God man is for the first time his true self, his whole self according to God's

[200] *Ibid.*, p. 553.

intentions. What Nygren at innermost wants to say, it seems, is that man is ethically a free subject who simply because of his religious experience autonomously does the good in his relation with his fellow-men. Such a phrasing of the thought is definitely in line with one of Bring's latest articles in which all natural good is on a different plane from the religious and good in itself unless it be used as a means of salvation.[201]

From this point of view Nygren emphasizes that communion with God is the indispensable prerequisite of Christian ethics. Fellowship with the eternal *agape* lets in a new light on man's entire situation. It is with this intention that Bring, as has already been noted above, similarly stresses that all good acts are good as such but absolutely evil when seen in the light of religion, i.e., as a means to salvation.[202] Before God, only the spontaneous acts prompted unconditionally by the very nature of the *agape* which he bestows are good, and these acts follow inevitably from man's communion with God just as the sun cannot help shining. Christianity, therefore, has a specific ethics resulting necessarily from its religious nature. "The spontaneous disposition of love is for Christianity the specific ethical ideal. The Christian disposition of love necessarily demands it, but, on the contrary, this ideal is demanded by no other outlook."[203] Equally definite is Nygren in *Agape and Eros*: "It follows that Christianity takes a unique place as a creative force in the history of human thought. It has revolutionized the treatment of the problems of religion and ethics; and in doing this it has

[201] Bring, "Några synpunkter på problemet om nåden och den fria viljan," in *Från skilda tider*.
[202] Cf. Bring, "Lag och evangelium," pp. 207 ff.
[203] Nygren, *Filosofisk och kristen etik*, p. 268.

treated them both together, not as two separate questions, but as one question. Christianity knows of no such thing as an un-ethical fellowship with God, or as non-religious ethics. Christian religion is ethical and Christian ethics are religious."[204]

We have now dealt with the first two points: religion as the revelation of eternity and religion as the judgment of eternity with respect to their effect on the ethical ideal of Christianity. The next two points—the reconciliation with eternity and the penetration by it—have to do with the realization of this ethical ideal. Inasmuch as the first of these has already been treated in our discussion of the Atonement, the main idea being, of course, that there is only one way between God and man, namely God's way to man as the subject of the Atonement, we can turn to the second part of the realization of the Christian ideal which deals specifically with ethics: "how can we go from this (communion with God) to the Christian fellowship of brotherly love?"[205]

This question is answered by the assertion that in the God-given faith man has a new center. "Whatever is not man's governing center is not his God."[206] "When man's egocentricity is destroyed through the religious experience, the foundation of all unethical conditions is also destroyed, and man receives through his fellowship with God a new foundation on which an ethical situation can and must develop. Negatively and positively fellowship with God destroys ethical improductivity."[207] This whole thought, of course, is that of the

[204] P. 31.
[205] Nygren, *Filosofisk och kristen etik*, p. 289.
[206] *Ibid.*, p. 289.
[207] *Ibid.*, p. 293.

Lundensian understanding of the relation between faith and love. Of both God is the subject. Through faith God's love overpowers man but flows through him into the world. Man is a channel, "a pipe," through which God's love reaches the sinful world. The subject of Christian love is not man but God, who uses the Christian as his tool or organ. It then follows, that "through the extended experience received through fellowship with God man's ideal, simply for ethical reasons, must, by necessity, become like unto it."[208]

From the previous discussion it is clear how suggestively the Lundensian theologians, as a rule, differentiate between the two aspects *coram deo* and *coram hominibus*. By considering all religious questions absolutistically and relegating all relativistic problems to the aspect *coram hominibus*, a unified religious system is possible. The one aspect from God to man provides a real structural strength. And this line of thought is practically always and uninterruptedly central. Another element of strength in the system is, unquestionably, its methodological isolation from philosophic and empirical problems insofar as these are secondarily, and not primarily, religious. In connection with the relation of Christianity and culture, we shall see anew how the empirical situation is concretely affected by the religious, according to the theological ethics sketched above; but first it seems best to deal with the Lundensian doctrine of the Church.

[208] *Ibid.*, p. 315.

C. The Church and Culture

1. The Church as the Continuity of the Christian Consciousness

With respect to the doctrine of the Church, Aulén's discussion of it in his systematic theology is undoubtedly the best. The center of Lundensian thought, here as always, is that all things Christian must be seen through the light of the absolute revelation in Christ. The problems of the Church, at least for theology as a descriptive science of Christian faith, are, therefore, not empirical but systematic.

The Church is not a human organization, not a human fellowship, not an entity of any kind alongside of God. The Church is, rather, an aspect of God's creative activity, and, it seems even more consistent to say, an aspect of his redemptive love creative of fellowship. The Church is the fellowship of those in whom God is the subject of faith and love. Perhaps here, again, the most objective method of depicting the view is to allow the author to speak for himself. "The Christian confession of one holy, catholic Church expresses something essential as to the manner in which the divine love realizes itself in the life of man, i.e., that in and through the Christian Church the divine fellowship which is of faith exists and is realized. To confess the Christian Church is to confess the God who creates fellowship. . . . In other words, to confess the Church is to confess God."[209] "In this spiritual fellowship God's Holy Spirit is the creative power . . . . and there is no question of comprehending the Spirit in the terms of Schleiermacher, as a sort of 'Gemeingeist'. This should mean that faith

[209] Aulén, *Den allmänneliga kristna tron*, p. 358.

were not a product of the Spirit, but of men."[210] "The Church is that fellowship in man's world which is created by divine love."[211] The Church is here plainly seen as conceived of according to the one-directional scheme: it is God's gift to man independent of man's endowment or effort; it is the descent of the Spirit into men binding them together through the new experience; it is God's fellowship with men conceived of collectively where men are *simul iusti et peccatores*; it is God's *regnum gratiae* among men; it is God's fellowship with men on the basis of sin, and yet on the basis of ever-new and complete forgiveness.

This view greatly simplifies and unifies the doctrine of the Church. The unity of the Church is attained: it is the unity of the Spirit. "It is a unity in and through the Christ-deed, through the Gospel as the organ of the Spirit."[212] The holiness of the Church is attained: it is the holiness of the Spirit. "The holiness of the Church means that it is not 'of this world'. . . . Its holiness guards against all tendencies to pull the Church down into this realm of human frailty."[213] The universality of the Church is attained: it is the universality of the Spirit. More open on the question of eschatology than some of the Lundensian theologians, and mindful of the fact that God according to the religious view is the subject both of faith and of love, Aulén writes: "The universality of the Church is an expression of the universal reach of the divine victory in Christ, for the universality of the Atonement, for the accessibility of

---

[210] *Ibid.*, p. 359.
[211] *Ibid.*, p. 360.
[212] *Ibid.*, p. 361.
[213] *Ibid.*, pp. 362-363.

redemption, for God's open and fatherly arms."[214] The Church is, therefore, prior, at least logically, to its members. It is not a relation among men except through or in God's *agape* creative of fellowship. The Church is not a human fellowship, not a spiritual kinship in the idolatrous terms of idealism or of mysticism. The Church is the indispensable prerequisite for God's grace to the individual. Outside the continuity of the Spirit revealing itself to the Church no individual is reached by God. In truth, and without institutional restrictions, Aulén can apply the famous saying by Cyprian: *extra ecclesiam nulla salus*. For the Church is the expanding continuity of the Christian consciousness of divine love without which no one can enter the Kingdom of God.

2. The Church and the Crises of Culture

Only one aspect of the relation of God to man in Lundensian theology remains to be considered: the relation of this spiritual entity, the Church, to secular culture. This is not, as yet, a burning question in Lundensian thought, except as it allows itself to become defensive with respect to its critics, who often accuse it of being hostile or negative to man's cultural tasks. The Church is admittedly not of this world and it cannot allow the directness and depth of its fellowship to become obstructed or to be made shallow by any primary concern with the relativities of human undertakings. In order ultimately to affect the world the more stirringly and healingly, the Christian fellowship needs to attain a new intensity and fundamental clarity. The chief mission of the Lundensian school of thought is, therefore, the purification of the distinctively Chris-

[214] *Ibid.*, p. 363.

tian, with the isolation, at least methodologically, of the truly religious from all false religiosities, with the reform of the world-transformed Church, with the effecting, in the words of Lindroth, of a "diastase," not a synthesis in theology.[215] Nygren has repeatedly stressed this task[216] as that of Swedish thought of today. One of Aulén's most recent books deals with "Christianity and the Crisis of Culture,"[217] and was specifically written to meet criticisms which had been directed at him on this point by a Stockholm journalist. The whole burden of the school with regard to theology and culture is *bene distinguere*.

When this has been said, however, the Lundensian school would greatly object both to the idea that it is a theology of world-renunciation, and to the idea that Christianity should not affect culture. It is a theology, it would claim, not of world-renunciation, but of world transcendence, and it affects deeply by its very nature the world around it. Aulén emphasizes that the isolation is chiefly methodological for the sake of allowing Christianity to work with the full strength of its genius. Nygren accentuates the fact that the isolation of the Church is more concerned with the destruction of an impeding religious synthesis than of a cultural synthesis. "There are two kinds of synthesis: one religious and one cultural. When there is only a question of a cultural synthesis, the danger to Christianity is less. Christianity can become connected with different kinds of cultures, provided that they are religiously indifferent, without necessarily being in danger of losing its unique-

---

[215] Cf. Lindroth, "Diastas och syntes i teologien," pp. 16 ff.
[216] Cf. especially *Den kristna kärlekstanken*, Vol. I., p. 191; Vol. II., Introduction and *Religiositet och kristendom*, passim.
[217] *Kristendomen och kulturkrisen*.

ness."[218] Both Lindroth and Nygren seem, however, to advocate, or hold to be necessary, almost a dialectical swing between synthesis and diastase. The present task imposed on the Christian theologians by the mysterious working of the Spirit in history is to free Christianity from entangling alliances. The task is reform. The religious alliances, *nomos* and *eros*, have already been considered. But culture, too, has its apparent friends to Christianity which seem to aid it, only finally to deceive it. The worst of these allies is idealism. The whole crisis of culture, according to Aulén, is the crisis of humanity, of a humanitarianism built up under the influence of idealism, on the false assumption of man's own strength. The reason for the crisis is that the Church became worldly and, losing its heavenly contact, and thereby its guiding light and motivating power, failed "to give life and power to human endeavor."[219] The Church alone, being not of this world, can provide the needed dynamic for social good, but only by remaining distinct, only by remaining not of this world. Similarly Nygren speaks of "a total change of face in the relation of religion and culture."[220] Not only has man begun to despair of the realizability of culture, but culture itself has begun, according to a new evaluation, to appear like a dubious entity. Religion, however, has ever been "the foremost factor in the criticism of culture."[221] Its eternal light has revealed the relativity of all human achievements, the evanescence of all things earthly. It has stood as a raging fire against all materialistic, eudaemonistic, or utilitarian ideals of human welfare.

[218] Nygren, *Den kristna kärlekstanken*, Vol. II, p. 16.
[219] Aulén, *op. cit.*, p. 37.
[220] Nygren, *Religiositet och kristendom*, p. 14.
[221] *Ibid.*, p. 15.

It has been an unshakable fortress against all rationalistic *"Kulturseligkeit."* And now it has arisen with spiritual power to prevent its own seduction by idealism into the relativities of the this-worldly realm. It will also continue to defend itself against all alliances with modern forces, whether religious or ethical, whether friendly to or critical of culture, against all forces which are based on un-Christian motifs, on man's strength or welfare, and not on God's unmotivated, groundless *agape*.[222] Bring, moreover, is quite consistent, from the Lundensian point of view, in his treatment of religion and culture. In his largest work on the subject, "The Relation of Faith and Deeds in Lutheran Theology,"[223] he consistently maintains that the religious and the civil spheres are distinct. *Iustitia actualis* deals with the whole man absolutistically in which sense man is totally *simul iustus et peccator*. *Iustitia civilis* deals with the relativities of human fellowship on the plane *coram hominibus*. The dualism of the two realms is not that of religion and morality as such, but that of the two understood as ways to salvation. Religiously speaking, *iustitia civilis* is always evil, always failing of God's demanded perfection both in motive and in content. The Lutheran system of thought has been accused of anti-moralism, of retarding social welfare because of the common but erroneous idea that morality must be teleologically motivated, whereas in the Lutheran system it is exclusively causally related to religion, out of which it flows with inevitable spontaneity. Nevertheless, when there is not a question of this religious reference, the Lutherans hold that the deeds may be called good in the sense of *iustitia*

---

[222] Cf. *ibid., passim*.
[223] "Förhållandet mellan tro och gärningar inom Luthersk teologi."

civilis, and as such they are, indeed, the necessary condition for human fellowship. From this relative point of view, the deeds are both necessary and good.[224] Here we may, indeed, speak of both *ratio* and *liberum arbitrium* but never *in iustitia actualis.* Religion, therefore, admits of the need for civil goodness, but declares it to be finally and inescapably under the judgment of the religious point of view. When it is obviously admitted, therefore, that man can do good *in naturalibus,* it always refers to *iustitia civilis.*[225] Similarly, in one of his most recent articles on the subject, Bring differentiates between the two spheres, the religious and the secular, identifying the former completely and unquestionably with the soteriological. Deeds are evil only insofar as man puts his trust in them and considers them his merits before God. Religiously man's powers for salvation are totally destroyed, but in the external, in the civil sphere, his capacity is, of course, not lost.[226] "If a man acts spontaneously, in unselfish mercy and helpfulness (cf. the parable of the Good Samaritan) this act is, without further consideration, *good,* and there is no need to ask for a psychological capacity for this, in terms of a psychologically conceived process of justification, or for a religious intention. . . ."[227] Bring goes on to claim that there is much good in common life seemingly unconnected with the religious life, but "wherever there is anything good, true, or honest, *it lies on the same plane* as the free deeds of faith. Thus the Gospel completes the law even in the case of the good that men do

---

[224] Cf. *ibid.,* p. 199.
[225] Bring, "Coram deo-coram hominibus," p. 175.
[226] Cf. Bring, "Lag och evangelium," p. 218.
[227] *Ibid.,* p. 218.

outside of religion."[228] We thus have good deeds performed outside of religion, "just good," and "on the same plane as the free deeds of faith," and evil restricted to deeds performed with a selfish intention. It is obvious that Bring is beginning to develop an aspect of theological thought where much is yet to be done. Religion and civil life must not be cut asunder lest culture become another religion. Bolshevism, Rosenberg's national religion, Friedrich Naumann's attempt to create a double standard of ethics—no, the tie between Christianity and culture must not be cut.[229] What, then, is the relation between the two, according to Bring? Man can do good outside of Christian faith, but only the *useful* or the *expedient*, never the truly good according to religion. There can never be a question of a principle eternally valid. The religiously good is that in which the eternal Goodness is always a member in man's fellowship. Cultures may come and go, but the foundations of the Church are eternal. Religion, nevertheless, affects culture by making man realistic. This is the bridge between the two points of view. Man in himself is selfish. The world's chief difficulty is selfishness. Religion lets God's *agape* remove all selfishness. Selfishness has veiled the light of the truly useful and expedient. When religion makes man become his real self, the veil is gone, and man through faith obtains both the will and the light to improve the social order. This is the practical Christian's position with respect to his social actions. This is the basis of adequate social ethics which requires both the will to see and the will to do. There is good in the world outside of religion, for religion is

[228] *Ibid.*, p. 219.
[229] Cf. *ibid.*, p. 221 ff.

solely a matter of fellowship with God. The Christian accepts this natural good as such, and as a free and wise man *coram hominibus* he performs his effective part *in loco civilis*. The main idea in Lundensian thought, in this respect, is, therefore, that the uniqueness of Christianity, God's *agape*, cannot help producing the fruits of the Spirit, and any alliances with forms of culture, however friendly or good in themselves, might cause the Church to lose its inherent strength as a factor in social improvement. It is only lately that thinkers like Aulén, Bring, and Nygren have begun to become concerned with this important question; and with their creative genius, and that of their younger disciples, it is to be hoped that more, much more, along this line of thought may be built upon their strong structure of religious interpretation.

CHAPTER IV

SUGGESTIONS TOWARD A PHILOSOPHIC CRITIQUE

As the descriptive part of our analysis has demonstrated, Lundensian thought aims at the invulnerability of theology, positively, by means of philosophic validation, negatively, by means of philosophic impotency. Positively it claims transcendental legitimation as a science from the fact that its object is derived from a form of experience a priori, universal and necessary, the prerequisite for experience as a whole. Negatively, Lundensian theology limits the sphere of philosophic efficacy to transcendental deduction and to the analysis of concepts. This reduction of the field of philosophy rests on the basic contention that inasmuch as value and knowledge are categorically distinct, no science can be normative. Knowledge deals with the form of fact; value is the experiential content of immediate commitment. Philosophy, theology, and ethics are all sciences. Philosophy deals with the totality of factual forms in their necessary interrelation. Theology and ethics as particular sciences deal logico-descriptively with their carefully delimited fields of fact; in the case of Christian theology and Christian ethics, with the organically distinct deposit of Christian faith.

The subject of this critique is accordingly fixed as the relation of philosophy to truth, of factual knowledge to value judgments, and of normative to descriptive thought. When a philosophic critique must be summarized into one lecture,[1] the nature of the study must necessarily be suggestively indicative rather than conclusively complete. For this reason, only the main features of the Lundensian system will be considered.

Lundensian theologians are no longer generally concerned with Nygren's Kantian foundation for his theological system, except possibly in its negative aspect. Critical philosophy is more a matter of proving rational theology impossible than of transcendentally deducing the category of religion. Lundensian theology, nevertheless, is built upon a Kantian foundation. If the younger Lundensians turn more and more away from transcendentalism to positivism, they gain in invulnerability at the expense of constructive adequacy. The skeptic is fortified behind the difficulties attending all constructive effort, but the theologian who builds on skepticism makes faith synonymous with indiscriminate credulity. Even though Nygren's transcendentalism offers points for valid criticism, his refusal to succumb to a supernaturalism which denies all relation between faith and constructive reason is wholly commendable. If positivism's contexts of meaning are substituted for Kantian transcendentalism, the very categorical foundation of Lundensian theology becomes reduced to a linguistic positivism where the content of faith has only a historic and psychological interest with no significant relevance for scholarly investigation apart from its possible practical usefulness. Nygren's Kantianism stands as a sturdy warning against this fate. Nor does it lack strong points. That different spheres of experience must have a rational normativeness in accordance with their distinctive

[1] Chapters IV and V were prepared as lectures on the Hyde Foundation at The Andover Newton Theological School.

genius, must have their own approach to truth, is a significant observation connected with Kant. Then also, Nygren's religious category on which the other validities are built bespeaks a basic unity in experience which Kant seems to have failed to depict even in his third Critique. Kant's practical postulates, moreover, cannot adequately achieve this unity. Perhaps it would be better philosophy to move from theoretical postulates to presupposed forms of knowledge rather than from practical postulates to contents of belief. Nygren's category of religion, moreover, the category of eternity, or of absolute validity above time and space, is a form both wide enough to include the greatest variety of historical difference and sufficiently relevant with its notion of permanence and change to embrace the deepest problems of religion. Many thinkers, moreover, would support him in making central to religion the problem of the permanent and the perishing. There is also virtue in Nygren's attempt to go beyond Kant's strict transcendentalism by his introduction of the transcendent, at least as far as forms of validity above space and time are concerned. These forms would insure as religious whatever content could legitimately be proved relevant; and since the deduction of the religious category started with definite, distinct religious experience, history must naturally contain a religious content as valid as experience itself. Christian faith could then be counted on to make a Christian choice and to witness for it with great confidence. To the author, this Kantian foundation for theology appears more attractive than any he has ever found.

It meets, however, with grave difficulties. The unity in experience does not necessarily presuppose a unity above time and space. The forms of consistency connected with the theoretical realm seem more certain and uniform than the unity of life itself. Even though consciousness is presupposed for the knowledge of these unities, consciousness itself flickers, and these unities remain standards of constancy. These unities, moreover, are both within experience and within time and space. We may have through experience knowledge of the absolute, but we have no absolute knowledge, not even of absolute forms. Kant's forms of consciousness in general can be no more absolute than experience in general, than that part of experience, at least, which is most permanently consistent. If experience is the field of knowledge, the criteria of knowledge must come out of experience and their validity cannot go beyond it. Only postulates or heuristic devices have any claim to partial knowledge, and then only when related to and made necessary by that experience. There is in Nygren's category of eternity an idealistic trend of thought which goes beyond Kant's critical limitation of reason; for even though Kant found principles of validity as forms of consciousness, universal and necessary, the presupposition for experience as a whole, he could not by his method find any forms of knowledge valid above time and space. It makes no difference that Nygren holds that no content of knowledge above time and space is possible; not even the forms of knowledge above space and time can legitimately be deduced according to the Kantian method. If, on the other hand, the category of eternity has to be inferred from the other fields of experience, it has no valid area of experience, *sui generis* and a priori, and cannot, therefore, in the very nature of the case have any distinct historical content. There is, in any case, an inconsistency between Nygren's deduction of the religious category from its distinctive self-witness on the one hand, and his attempt, on the other hand, to have the other realms of experience indicate the one ultimate category which is the religious. If experience itself, furthermore, is the starting point and the final criterion of philosophic truth, there can be no validity, even of forms, beyond experience. In this case Nygren seems guilty of reasoning in a circle. Recourse either to postulates from experience or to uncriticized faith alone remains as a way to the content of the realm of reality dealing with the ultimate beyond time and space. It is, indeed, difficult to build any theory of revelation on an empirical foundation except as extensions from it whether by rational inference or by faith's leap to the ideal. Nygren's attempt is, however, one of the most ingenious in the history of theological thought.

Absolute knowledge always stumbles on the fact that it must be received and interpreted by the relativity of experience. Experience contains certain forms such as those of logic or of mathematics which seem to be absolutely valid, but the greatest degree of validity that can be claimed even for these is that they are the most consistent forms observable in experience. Whitehead points out that there is not only a form of flux but also a flux of form, and Dewey with every right relates the laws of logic to their function and knowledge in experience. Nygren is thus, in one respect, too absolutistic in his approach; for not only can he not get to his knowledge of forms except through the previous knowledge of its content, but also neither can he obtain absolute content or absolute form within experience. The category of eternity as the category of religion, therefore, seems to be an unwarranted proposal. It will have to be supplanted by some less static and more empirically available concrete universal, such as, for instance, fellowship and the non-human factors which condition it.

Perhaps it is the feeling for this inadequacy in transcendentalism that is currently driving Lundensian theology to positivism. If theology claims for itself no more than the description and systematization of contexts of meaning obtainable from history, it appears to be entirely untouchable by criticism. Nor is this reduction of philosophic adequacy a reduction of faith, for that lies on a different plane beyond the power of reason to prove or disprove. Two things, at least, can be said of this position. Although it does recognize that faith must go beyond the reasoned factual content of knowledge, it also cuts religion loose from all rational moorings. In an age of change and confusion, the temptation to do so is strong, but so also is the need for reasoned criticism of the new whether for acceptance or rejection. Secondly, and of utmost importance, the claim that reason is utterly incompetent to form a world view or to criticize matter of ultimate reality is dangerously exaggerated. It must be granted, of course, that the categories which apply to our present experience may not hold beyond it; but if there is anything beyond it and if we know anything at all about it, the relation between the two realms must be at least appropriate. Revelation has no significance except as it has relevance to our empirical situation. However revelation thus gets into experience, if light from another realm does take the initiative in informing us of itself, still this revelation must be interpreted and understood in terms meaningful to human conditions. The claim is not, therefore, that reason can from itself and by itself go beyond experience, but that reason can interpret, compare, and evaluate, as well as describe whatever comes into experience in whatever way or from whatever source. This is a crucial question, the question with which the Lundensian philosophy of religion stands or falls; and we must, therefore, investigate, however briefly, the scope and function of reason in religion.

It seems a gratuitous assumption on the part of Lundensian thought that reason and faith deal with two entirely different spheres, operative on two totally distinct planes. The gulf between fact and value, between the actual and the ideal, is obviously an unmistakable part of experience; but to make it absolute is to fall prey to the fallacy of the unjustified extreme, the unwarranted abstraction, an inapplicable all-or-none theory. Values or ideals are known and desired only because they have been partially experienced in the world of fact. Whether or not values beyond those concretely experienced are objectively real in themselves or adjectivally, as modifying an Objective Reality, as far as experience is concerned, they are projections from it, the imaginative extension of our partly realized desires. Values appear only in an interest relation where there is both a subject and an object. Even though the nature of the object is, to be sure, a secondary consideration since the value judgment exists in any case, this fact should not lead us to think that value judgments are not connected with factual situations or rational criticism, for this isolated value judgment is artificially severed from its genetic continuity. With regard to experience, logical analysis apart from chronological understanding is disastrously inadequate. Value judgments as well as rational judgments originate in experience, and, indeed, not separately but conjunctively. In experience the two seem to be united. When the child experiences the outside world, this comes to it not merely as a set of ideas or as a set of values, but as ideas colored with values, or as values connected with and preserved by an association of ideas. Reason is practically never a detached describer of formal factuality, but is almost entirely a dynamic instrument of adjustment dependent upon a reservoir of previous reactions and reflections. Even if this view of reason be called sophistry by the Lundensian theologians, to consider reason apart from its dynamic activity in the service of life as a whole seems naive sophistication. A purposefully enforced methodological disinterestedness as in science or a spontaneously good deed seem only temporarily detached from the deeper sources of personal and social interest. Both reason and our sense of value are in the service of life, and both are organically complementary to each other; both are necessarily, functionally correlative aspects of growth.

This intrinsic, functional relation between fact and value, moreover, is not only individual but social in nature. Our knowledge of fact and value is, to be sure, individually assimilated and organized into a personal knowledge and a personal experience, but this knowledge is through and through and for by far the greatest part of it a racial heritage transmitted by direct communication and by powerful suggestion, and some even say by a racial collective unconscious through instinctual disposition and an inherited ideational background. Society is an ever-living organism, a stream of conscious and unconscious interactions, consisting of overlapping selves by means of which the experience of the race and its intellectual attainments are preserved. This stream is not only subjective but objective by means of inherited knowledge and attitudes compressed into languages, written records, and oral traditions. It would be preposterous to say that in this stream of experience value judgments have no relation to the rational interpretation of experience. Though value judgments differ, both superficially and radically, there is a considerable overlapping of positive interests which grow rather than diminish with the testing of experience and its fuller rational comprehension.

There is a problem connected with the relation of fact and value, however, that must be faced. Why is it that value judgments coming from fairly similar human experiences differ so widely? And why, futhermore, is the wisdom of the race and, for that matter, of the individual experiment so often flouted? Why does a Hindu prefer nirvana and a Christian, heaven? Why does an individual commit a crime or do a deed which his reason knows to be evil or unsatisfactory? The first of these questions can be partially answered by the pointing out that in general men prefer to live, not to die, to have good food, not bad, to receive social approval and friendship rather than disapproval and isolation, that is, that there are certain fields of generally common interest. Even if the Buddhist claims he prefers death, nevertheless, actually he clings to life, as most men cling to life. Then, too, nirvana or "the fourth state" is thought of as the self delivered from evil, suffering, and isolation. Nirvana seems also, according to recognized scholars in the field, to have a positive content. The Hindu thinks of the deepest existence as *saccidananda*: existence, plus intelligence, plus bliss; and his pantheism is, not to mention popular Buddhism and Hinduism with their ideas of gods and heavens, a losing of his isolated, suffering self, into the real, universal self. The idea underlying nirvana as well as heaven may be a deliverance from the evils of this world, from the *neti, neti,* or the not so, not so, of Buddhism, from the *maya,* or illusion, of Hinduism, from the sin and suffering of Christianity, into the fulfillment, freedom, and lasting reality of nirvana, *tat tvam asi,* or heaven. Perhaps all of them, deep down, mean the deliverance from the evil and the transient into the permanent and the good. The specific value judgments of people and societies in different religions must, therefore, be judged according to their specific situation, their historic background, and the inner intent of their judgment. It is surprising how interpreters stay on the surface without noticing the deeper general needs and problems which underlie the different religions. Fellowships of suffering like Buddhism will seek deliverance from it; fellowships of joy and creative power like Christianity will seek continuance and life more abundant. Similarly, the individual in acute distress may wish to die and take his life. His judgment is that his life is intolerable and that death is desirable, but this judgment is considerably conditioned by his circumstance, and the general judgment seems to be that life is worth living. The peculiarity of the judgment preferring death is due in great measure to peculiarity of psychological make-up and physical and social circumstance. Judgments must themselves be judged in the light of circumstance and inner intent rather than of specific content.

This brings up that great problem as to whether the most inclusive judgment is, therefore, the best or the truest. If value judgments, as Ralph Barton Perry contends, are characterized by preference, intensity, and inclusiveness, and the last of these is the only aspect which can be compared since the other two vary with every judge, then we seem to be left with inclusiveness as our only standard. This is obviously a fallacy of the descriptive approach to life. The Lundensians would say that no comparison is possible and we must therefore choose by faith what is best; others despair of reason as capable of establishing norms, and talk in terms of inclusiveness. Value in its relation to reason is, however, more than a counting of noses. Reason lives by the experience of the race as appropriated by the individual and the group. Its appropriation varies with its attainment, but its attainment is conditioned by its ideal. These ideals are found in history and in life. Reason has the power of comparing ideals and of choosing among them, and then of applying these ideals as abstracted from their peculiar setting and applying them to other concrete situations. This is the only wise method and the only true hope for a successful missionary enterprise. This problem, however, will be more thoroughly discussed in relation with the problem of the normative or the descriptive approach to theology.

That men do not act according to their best insight in no way disproves the actual relation between fact and value. It only proves that man must be considered dynamically in terms of a struggling self which is beset not only by ignorance, but by a deeper self that may cloud the biddings of reason or of an evil self that may go contrary to it. We did admit and stress the chasm that exists between fact and value, between the actual and the ideal; but it is no better to make this chasm absolute than to insist on the identity of knowledge and virtue. Both extremes are untrue to experience.

There are three aspects of this problem of positivism in its relation to religion and the religions which must be examined, even if only briefly and suggestively: the scope and function of knowledge, the actualization or the realization of religions, and the legitimacy of normativeness. As to the first, knowledge is most demonstrable and most objectively communicable at the extreme abstraction of either form or fact. Logic and mathematics are demonstrable rational consistencies upon which all the deductive processes in scientific thought as well as theory are built. With the greatest abstraction possible, deductive reasoning is at its maximum of validity. Similarly, an isolated fact controlled by scientific investigation and tested and demonstrated by several scholars is the abstraction of fact in connection with which induction has its greatest validity. All reasoning is a combination of inductive and deductive reasoning, a going from the particularity of fact to the inherited communicated generality of form, and by means of these forms to a greater knowledge of facts. This process is far too complicated for analysis in this connection, but it is sufficient to point out that validity in terms of objective demonstrability and of common communicability is in both cases at its maximum with the maximum of abstraction. As science develops its body of knowledge, its specific validity decreases while its general applicability to the actual world increases. From the point of view of life, adequacy must be obtained at the expense of validity. No one can live by the abstractions consistent with a high degree of validity, or demonstrable knowledge. The more interpretation moves from the two opposite extremes of fact or form into the midst of fullness of life, the more difficult interpretation becomes and the less validity it has, but the more it obtains applicability and adequacy. This process is obvious in the relation of the natural and the social sciences. In the field of religions it is even more so. The difficulty with this field, however, is that so often it moves away not only from validity or demonstrable knowledge, but also from applicability. Religious knowledge, if it is to be in the service of life, must be the daring interpretation of the fullness of experience with its ideals, with its hopes, as it ministers most fully to it. This means not that man is the center of religion, but that if faith is to make God central for religion, and if it is to have relevance for life, it must have such a view of God and of the ideal as is most consistent with an adequate and applicable belief in the light of the experience that we have. If revelation is held to be the divine initiative from without man's experience so that the best we have is considered not only a human achievement but a divine bestowal, then such revelation must be an ideal fulfillment of life, faith that can transform it and make it better, that can make it fuller and freer, or else revelation as the message of religion has no relevance for life and no claim to either applicability or adequacy.

One of the most challenging assertions of Lundensian thought is that there is no one true religion ascertainable by reason, no religion with a capital R, no *centrum* but only *centra* of religions, that religions are not actualized but realized in history. Once again we see an alliance of conservative theology with radical scholarship; for it is coming to be a commonplace assumption in certain circles that religion is merely an aspect of culture to be understood through and through in terms of its historical development and peculiar situation. Popularly this thought takes the form that each religion is best for the people who hold it, inasmuch as it represents their situation and corresponds to their needs. The missionary enterprise may be well-meaning, but it is in the last analysis a disruptive spiritual imperialism. Nygren is thus well fortified in his position that history produces religions with basically different motifs. Since the acceptance of these is a religious, not a theoretical judgment, no comparison of these intrinsically different religions is possible. All we can do is to preach faithfully the Gospel to which we have committed our lives. There are two especially strong points which favor this view of history: in the first place, real historical difference is both actual and desirable; in the second place, history loses its zest unless becoming is real, unless something really new takes place. As to the first point, the kind of monism which claims that history has already been realized in eternity, has perhaps been foreordained or foreseen by God, makes unreal and unessential historic difference. This view robs history of its challenge. History is more than a prelude to eternity. History is, at least, eternity revealed in the now. Even if the present is not conceded to be the focus of reality, it is, at least, the reference of all living meaningfulness. Historic difference seems to be of the essence of reality. Secondly, if history is eternally realized anywhere, the temporal struggle becomes the unnecessary drama of human imperfection and natural evil. It does us no good to solve the problem of evil by pushing it into an incomprehensible eternity. Somehow the new must be really new. Creativity must be a basic aspect of reality. There is nowhere static perfection. If God creates and redeems, God himself must be growing. He must be an expanding infinity. Growth seems to be in the nature of things; the ideal is not yet attained, and may be even eternally a flying goal. If real difference is contrary to monism, many would prefer pluralism religiously as well as culturally. If real potentiality is also contrary to monism, pluralism must be the choice of the vigorous and the brave. Only those who seek safety and dread adventure will prefer a universe where history is the unrolling of a ready-made film. We are not convinced, nevertheless, that the choice between actualization and realization is totally exclusive. If the understanding of the actualization of religion is that of one true pre-planned religion pushing back the historical religions until this one true religion becomes actualized in history, and if this religion be conceived of intellectually as a constantly fixed relationship outlined in detail, then we must reject actualization and with it also the ultimate unity of the universe. Actually, Nygren and his followers play in with radical tendencies which seem destructive of the meaning of Christianity. If, however, with actualization is meant not the unfolding, perhaps through identity of psychological endowment, of a static prearrangement, not the attainment of a particularized condition, but the existence behind all religions of a dynamic, eternal, creative Purpose which in joint creativity with his creative creatures seeks ever higher types of fellowship; then there can be a standard, a fellowship based on New Testament love as revealed in Christ and founded in the very heart of reality, in God himself, and yet at the same time be opportunity for all desirable and possible difference in the types of creative fellowship which are developed. The standard of Christianity is then not a formal belief in Christ, but the message about God and the ideal relationship which he is giving himself to achieve in history, first fully proclaimed and consciously embodied in the life of our Master. In this case, God does not know specifically what will happen, and if he did man's freedom would be unreal, but he is the Power, Wisdom, Righteousness, and Love which pushes history from behind toward this one true religion and pulls it from before by the ideals which are only partially disclosed to man. If this is so, difference is real and consonant with a high grade of fellowship, while potentiality is equally necessary; but this does not mean that there are no common standards or that there is no universally applicable Gospel of Jesus Christ. The Gospel is the glad news of freedom from the panic of fear because there is in the universe a Guiding Purpose who is also Redemptive Love, and who bids us create through love and hope, not through hate and despair, new heavens and a new earth, who created differences in color and of talent, and who offers to have them all used in his service and in the interest of good will among men. Thus, in the joint creativity of God and man the true religion is being both actualized and realized, for realization is but the historic side of that Purpose which works behind, through, and before history and man's opportunity to cooperate with it, whether for success or failure.

The last phase of the problem of knowledge that we must consider is the claim by Lundensian thought that no science is ever normative. With science is meant not the natural sciences, but knowledge as a whole which can be no more than descriptive, analytic, and systematic. Obviously, Lundensian thought is observing, in this case, a true aspect of knowledge. Reason itself does not initiate any standards, but these are extracted from experience for its effective guidance. These standards are thus produced by experience itself. Life precedes logic, but not entirely. The rules of life proceed from it, but not unbidden. Whatever rules are applicable and meaningful for life have first been taken from it, but not without the conscious effort of rational criticism. An illustration can be made of the relation of revelation to reasoned truth. No vital religion springs from a system of rational speculation. Every vital religion, on the contrary, springs out of concrete history. Every vital truth is thus far revealed. Man knows not entirely the ultimate source of his ideas and ideals, but they rise out of life, particularly out of its great personalities which reveal truth and value. Yet in this process reason plays its part. In the life of every revealer there are thought processes conditioned by the circumstances of his life. These processes are an indispensable part of the truth revealed to him. They condition his acts and his value judgments. Then again, those who observe his life apply a degree of rational judgment in the discernment of the superiority of his insights, his faith, and his way of life. Thirdly, religion may make out of his insights a system, which may, of course, both develop and distort them. In all these processes, there may, indeed, be little abstract, detached reasoning. The reasoning may, for the most part, be enveloped in strong emotions, which fact, however, speaks for the meaningfulness and relevance of the insights. Reason may also abstract these insights either in the case of the original seer or in the case of his followers and apply them to a realm beyond our experience. This feeling that the deepest truth is not discovered by us but disclosed to us, so that faith can make reason leap to an ultimate explanation of its source is what is meant by revelation and what makes of human thoughts and emotions a religious phenomenon. Even though it looks at the problem in a different way, this primacy of life over its description is a vital aspect of Lundensian thought. The real truth behind its contention is that the guiding truths, the revelations of history, must be rationally tested, but cannot be rationally produced.

In yet another aspect, Lundensian thought reflects the spirit of our times. The notion of oughtness, the idea of normativeness, is repulsive. In a confused world with passing and conflicting standards, religious rules and ethical laws seems out of the question. Surely, even if one has the right to demand that their adherents obey them, nevertheless, no one has the right to demand their universal acceptance, since no one can claim alone to possess final and ultimate truth. The works of Nygren in their acceptance of the complete rule of scientific method also reflect the modern mood. In circles of learning, the greatest virtue has been to be scientific. The tide, however, is fast turning. Science has proved itself unable to cope with the problems of the human spirit and of social evil. Almost everywhere outside the natural sciences, the question is now not whether the result is narrowly scientific, but whether it is socially adequate. Men are undoubtedly seeking and longing for the authority of normative rules.

The dismissal of normativeness, however, is unwarranted; for there are standards which are rational speculation based not on private prejudice but upon the carefully reasoned interpretation of experience. Our trouble is, obviously, that the method of physical sciences has been extended beyond the limits of its proper efficacy, has been unjustifiably and detrimentally extended to fields where it is neither relevant nor adequate. In the physical sciences, the method consists of the rigorous objective observation of uniformities, a method which is plainly entirely descriptive. The idea of oughtness is not required by a method which deals with no vexing problems of freedom. Functional regularity is the very presupposition of scientific method. If scientific formulas be merely statistical averages, they have at least enormous empirical applicability. In the meaningful sense of the word, therefore, scientific method is never normative. Normativeness becomes increasingly important, however, as freedom increases and exact knowledge recedes. These norms, moreover, are not arbitrary, but are extracted from experience. Thus in the realm of language, the norms are mostly descriptive, resulting from actual usage in the past. The norms of language are traditional, but they become normative in the sense that an ought becomes connected with their present use. Rules of grammar are what come from the past and for the sake of an orderly society are imposed on the present. As life changes, however, rules tend gradually to be modified by it. Grammar contains, nevertheless, a normativeness which is not arbitrary but based upon descriptive norms of experience which become the rules for further experience. Traditional norms thus become for growing generations pedagogical norms possessive of conventional, even if not compulsory, power. The same situation holds for medicine, which deals with the border-land between the regularity of nature and the freedom of the spirit. Medical rules are descriptive norms discovered in the past but applicable to the present. To be well, the individual ought to obey the rules which pertain to health. He ought to have sufficient rest, sufficient food and a well balanced diet; he ought not to expose himself to disease. There is no medical compulsion except in severe instances, apart from civic health regulations the significance of which may not be fully realized, but there is a powerful feeling of oughtness connected with these traditional norms which have become pedagogical. A realm closer to religion and ethics in certain respects is that of law. Laws change with new insights and changed conditions, but there is a "common law," a heritage of legal opinion, a collection of traditional norms, the abiding over long periods of time of constitutional or permanent rules, and in this case the traditional norms are not only conventional but compulsory. They ought to and must be obeyed. Few of us, too, are anarchists. We believe in laws. It is easy, of course, to say that only insofar as the grammarian, the medical man, or the legal expert studies the past is he a scientist; not when the grammarian teaches rules, not when the medical man prescribes preventions or remedies, not when the legal expert judges or legislates. The point is, however, that the two aspects cannot be artificially separated. Science and art are two aspects of every field of human endeavor. All effective judgments of what ought to be are dependent upon the descriptive norms which constitute the distilled wisdom of the race, and conversely no field of human endeavor can be justified unless it be more than a science. This does not mean that some investigators may not be exclusively concerned with one aspect, though more significant work is done if they are aware of both. It does mean, however, that there are normative aspects of educational endeavor which must not be minimized. Out of the best in the traditional norms are selected according to man's best discernment the ideal norms which are then gradually invested with the sense of oughtness. Thus consuetudinary norms become educational standards. Of the field of religion and of ethics the same is true. Its rules, as far as they are valid, are not arbitrarily produced from rational speculation apart from experiential content, but insofar as they are effective, applicable, and adequate, they are selected from the best ideas and ideals in man's experience of his superhuman and human environment. Even though the superhuman is essentially the field of religion, the human, that of ethics, the two organically condition each other. Ethics and religion are necessarily both descriptive sciences and practical arts. To reduce ethics to the history of morals and to claim that reason has no power to judge concerning it, is to fail to understand the ways of history. Religion, too, in spite of its large areas of disagreement, must patiently sift its material from imaginative myth, historical theologies, or rational philosophy, and find what in history pictures most truly and adequately the mysteries of experience. Every field of investigation shows disagreements, but every field has its function to fill and must go on with it, not in the spirit of resigned skepticism, but in the confidence of its importance in the service of life.

CHAPTER V

SOME PROBLEMS CONNECTED WITH CHRISTIANITY
AS *AGAPE*

There can be no question that Nygren's investigations into Christianity as *agape* constitute one of the most significant contributions to the history of theological thought. His works are winning immediate recognition among thorough and open-minded thinkers. It is most fortunate that the third part of his *Agape and Eros, the History of the Christian Idea of Love,* has now appeared in English; for in several ways this section is of basic importance to the rest of his investigations. Especially should his analysis of Augustine's treatment of love, a most careful, enlightening, and immensely stimulating study, be carefully considered by every one interested in the nature of Christianity. The writer's own feeling upon concluding the last volume of *Agape and Eros* was that he had read a work of such depth and filled with such significant insights as to be deserving of a place among the great books of theology. Several years of thinking through the problems contained in it have, on the whole, confirmed rather than weakened this opinion.

Of utmost theological importance is Nygren's analysis of motifs establishing *agape* as the distinctive and determinative element in Christianity. Contemporary thought is suffering from a fit of confusion. Having escaped from a narrow and unintelligent dogmatism where the uniqueness of Christianity was taken for granted as an essential aspect of God's only Revelation, Christian thinkers, in many circles, are now all too frequently ready to renounce as prejudice or lack of knowledge the Christian claim to have a distinctive message for the world. Those who still cling to the uniqueness of Christianity have usually either some vague notion of a supernatural variety expressed in a Christology where God revealed himself as God only once, in the Incarnation, or else some popular idea, seldom critically appraised, to the effect that Christianity is unique because it alone had a founder who fully lived and even died for his religion, that good will first became connected with religion through the life and teachings of Jesus, or that inwardness and spiritual freedom are the contributions exclusively of Christian faith. If only because of the general confusion and vagueness on this topic, the scholarly nature of Nygren's investigation has rendered us much service. His entire historical approach, which we cannot, of course, discuss in this connection, is more adequate as well as more challenging than any other with which the writer is acquainted. By it, in any case, he has opened up broad but rigorous avenues to historical investigation of religion which many a thoughtful scholar is likely to wish patiently to explore.

That *agape* is the determinative and distinctive motif of Christianity seems certain. This does not mean, of course, that it is either the most common idea in Christian doctrine or the most usual motive of Christian action. The investigation does not attempt to be descriptive in a sociological sense. Nygren is careful not to claim that *agape* is the characteristic element in Christianity from the point of view of either the number of believers in it or the quantity of historical doctrine. He himself claims only that it is the basic motif, in the light of which the distinctive genius of Christianity can best be understood. We have stressed, therefore, the notion of a determinative motif, since to some people the idea of distinctiveness would mean nothing more than that difference whereby Christianity can be set apart from all other religions. Nygren is very definite, however, that with "distinctive" is meant not only an additive notion, but also an essential idea without which Christian thought as a historic phenomenon cannot be adequately understood. In this assertion we can wholeheartedly acquiesce. Christianity cannot be completely comprehended except through its distinctive idea of love. There are many ideas which are called love. Christianity is more than a general theory of good will. It is a system of thought and a proposed way of life in which God's love is at the center, necessitating, according to its nature, a fellowship on the part of those who have received it. Reference to this freely given, uncalculating love meets us everywhere in the teachings of Jesus. To say this is not to assert that there are in the Gospels no ideas inadequate to *agape* or inconsistent with it, but it is confidently to affirm that the Christian idea of love is there as both the distinctive and the determinative idea. It seems obvious that we cannot understand the teachings of Jesus apart from such parables as the Prodigal Son, the Good Samaritan, the Laborers in the Vineyard, or apart from such injunctions as the love of enemies, or certainly not apart from a view of God as freely forgiving, as allowing his sun to shine on both the evil and the good. The entire Lundensian emphasis on the unity of the New Testament seen in the light of the Christian idea of love offers much to this old problem. Surely, the Christian idea of love is characteristic of both the Johannine and the Pauline writings, whatever be their points of irreconcilable disagreement. That the Christian idea of love is even developed and made more explicit both formally and practically in Paul and John, Nygren, himself, has pointed out. The writings of Paul and the Johannine literature go beyond this, moreover, for they also begin to interpret the life of Jesus, himself, in terms of the operation of the divine Love. The Christian Church has ever since continued this interpretation of Jesus as a part of the original Source of this *agape*. In so doing it has often, to be sure, become imaginative and even magical; but its fundamental insight has been unerring, namely that heavenly light came through a historic life, and that this life must itself somehow be connected with the Source of that Light. In any case, Christian thought as a whole and at its deepest cannot be satisfactorily understood, in spite of all directly contrary doctrines and practices, except in terms of *agape* as its explanatory motif. The essence of the Christian Revelation is that somehow there came into historical awareness in the person of Jesus an understanding of God and his relation with men which is unique in the history of the world. The basic idea contained in this understanding is that God is Love, willing to give himself for sinful men, to suffer with them, and to save them into a fellowship based not on man's merit, but on forgiving love. Be this idea accepted or rejected, the emphasis placed on it by the Lundensians as simply a historic truth is vitally needed.

Whether or not the notion of *agape* is to be found in any pre-Christian literature, or in any writings not directly dependent on Christian sources, is another question. The writer, in any case, is not aware of any non-

Christian literature where the full idea of God's *agape* appears. Stoicism's universal love of mankind is both too immanentistic and too pantheistic to be on the same personal level as Christian *agape*, while it is also far too much a matter of living according to reason and natural law to be totally uncalculating. Buddhism's use of "good will toward all the world," on the other hand, is too negative to be *agape*, the reference being not to active goodness freely giving itself, and solely concerned with the good of its object, but being, rather, the quiet cutting off of all enmity and evil desire for the sake of harmony and spiritual invulnerability. A much nearer idea is that implied by the supposed action of the Buddha when, upon his becoming enlightened, he denied himself the supreme privilege of entering into nirvana simply out of compassion for his fellow sufferers, that he might preach to them deliverance from evil, or better, perhaps, that he might teach those willing and able to understand the truth which alone can free them from their terrifying illusions. This idea did not, however, become the central principle of explanation in Buddhism, but remained an exceptional instance which really contradicted its inner spirit and meaning. The idea that reality at its very core is redemptive love, and that men to be saved must have this as the God-given source of their conduct, was definitely not a part of Oriental religions prior to their contact with Christian doctrines. The problem of the *bhakti* sects in Hinduism is too complicated to discuss in this short survey; but they are, in any case, post-Christian and may even be due to Christian influence. The full doctrine of Christian *agape* is, furthermore, and not to overstate the case, not the essential element in the *bhakti* approach. It is, far rather, a very emotional form of the *eros* motif.

The Chinese idea of *jen*, or mutual benevolence, seems to fall short of the Christian idea of love by its conception of mutuality. More important still, of course, is the fact that it is an ethical rule rather than a religious assertion as to ultimate reality. According to critical scholars and in the light of the total meaning of Taoism, in Lao-tse's famous sentence, "Recompense injury with *teh*," *teh* is not rightly translated by kindness; and Confucius' negative statement of the Golden Rule is hedged in by an express prohibition of meeting evil with kindness. Both Lao-tse's Taoism with its negative ontology and its passive ethics and Confucius' stress on the human source of morality preclude their meaningful comparison to the Christian idea of love. That the Old Testament has passages which approach the idea of *agape*, to be sure, Nygren freely admits. The great chapter in *Deutero-Isaiah* describing the Suffering Servant is, however, more of an explanation of what seemed unjust punishment and a propounding of the value of vicarious suffering than the full idea of God's indiscriminate love as the deepest interpretation of reality and as the highest rule for human conduct. Except for its particularity of reference, a certain passage in *Hosea* (11:9) comes close to the idea of *agape*: "I will not execute the fierceness of mine anger, I will not return to destroy Ephraim: for I am God, and not man." The correctness of the passage or the authorship makes no difference in this case, since it can surely be established that the verses are pre-Christian. Even if the idea of the great invitation in *Isaiah* 1:18 should originally have been negative rather than positive, this, too, is irrelevant inasmuch as this textual change also is without a doubt pre-Christian. The passage as it stands sounds very much like *agape*: "Though your sins be as

Some Problems Connected with Christianity as Agape

scarlet, they shall be as white as snow; though they be red like crimson, they shall be as wool." The fact that this version of it is very likely a sentimental misreading or change of the original and that it is found in a context where *agape* is entirely out of place, would make us very hesitant to count the passage as an indication of a full view of God, in his relation with men, and of men's ideal fellowship among each other. The psalmist's tender pronouncement, "like as a father pitieth his children" (*Psalm* 103:13) may, to be sure, in one breath stress the unworthiness of the object, but in the next, restrict the father's pity to those who fear him. According to recognized Jewish scholars, the Jewish apocryphal literature has statements about love, beyond that of love to God and neighbor, that approach the statements made by Jesus; but they seem not to treat love as the deepest reality in the universe and as the final standard of conduct. In Jewish apocryphal literature either the Law or Wisdom is the regulative norm as far as God's relation with the world is concerned. The Jewish pronouncement regarding love to God and to neighbor, although indicative of a strong stress on the idea of love, and although exceedingly prominent in pre-Christian Jewish thought, is, nevertheless, too much on the line from man to God and includes too much of the idea of calculation to be *agape*. Judaism has ethical precepts of going beyond the measure, of having a yielding, forgiving disposition, and this has some reflection in its view of God, but the writer has not found in Jewish literature the completely Christian idea of love. Indeed, although the writer does not claim expert knowledge of the history of religions, he has, at least, never come across in his readings in the field a complete statement of *agape* in any non-Christian literature. Plato's tender mention of God as the shepherd of mankind seems, like Stoicism's ideas of the World-Soul, to be nearly hid behind the stress on his reasonableness, and fails of that groundlessness characteristic of the Christian idea of love, of that unmotivated giving of itself solely because it is its nature to give. Outside Christianity, then, although there are certain ideas similar to that of the Christian idea of love, the resemblances are for the most part apparent rather than basic. We can say, therefore, with some confidence, that *agape* is not only the determinative but also the distinctive motif of the Christian religion. God's revelation in Christ must be understood in terms of the Christian idea of love as expressive of the deepest truth in the universe and as the highest ethical standard for mankind.

When all this has been said, however, there are a few fundamental problems connected with Nygren's definition of Christianity as *agape* that must claim our attention. If we grant that *agape* as the Christian idea of love is the basic motif of Christianity, we must be careful before accepting Nygren's full description of it. His central idea of it, for instance, is that it is exclusively God's way to man. It is, naturally, of utmost importance to understand that the religion of Jesus was centered in God: it was God, not man, who was to bring in the Kingdom; we should be perfect even as our Heavenly Father is perfect. This fact, however, should not blind us to the great part that humanism played in the thought and teachings of Jesus. Both in method and in substance of teaching, Jesus made much use of the natural and the human realms, arguing directly from them to God. On this point we need not be afraid of "the peril of modernizing Jesus." The point is too obvious even to need

Some Problems Connected with Christianity as Agape

demonstration. The power and relevance of Jesus' teachings are due primarily to the fact that he extracted the best in human relationships, applying this both to the supernatural realm and to the common ways of human life. The exceptional became the ultimately real and the rule for the commonplace. If even an earthly father can rise above the customary spirit and demands of the law and, by the power of his love, restore his erring son, how much more must God freely forgive those who seek him. If the shepherd for the sake of a lost sheep is willing to leave the ninety-and-nine, if he values the one sheep so highly, how much more joy will there be in heaven when a child of God's creation turns again home. If the master of a vineyard can take pity on those who have worked but an hour, how much more will God deal with those who serve him, not after their desert, but after his goodness. "If ye then, being evil, know how to give good gifts unto your children, how much more shall your Father which is in heaven. . . ." If even an earthly judge, for the sake of his own convenience, will give heed to the pleadings of an importunate widow, how much more will God, who is Love, be anxious to help those in distress who continue to seek his aid. The body of Jesus' teachings, moreover, seems shot through and through with worldly wisdom and practical advice. Those who wish to be saved must not be like the foolish virgins who did not plan ahead. Spontaneous goodness is not enough. Wisdom is also needed, even the wisdom of serpents. In spiritual warfare man ought to count the cost as much as the King who plans a campaign. There is even a question as to whether Jesus did not hold as the ultimate sanction of right action not the Sadduccees' right for its own sake, nor the Pharisees' right for the love of God, but the

Essenes' right for the sake of future reward in heaven. This point is at least debatable. Perhaps Jesus' double stress on inwardness and on future reward was the secret of his power with people who could not fully understand the depths of his instruction. Even the disciples seem to have been motivated by a desire for reward in the Kingdom, and to have been promised it as well. Then, too, Jesus undoubtedly did emphasize the value of the individual: Ye are of so much value that "even the very hairs of your head are all numbered"; "What shall a man give in exchange for his soul?" Jesus even spoke of being "rich toward God," of laying up "a treasure in the heavens that faileth not." There are instances in his teachings where even expediency on a very human plane plays a large role. To go into this problem, however, is unnecessary, for Nygren's attempt to interpret Jesus' teaching of *agape* as a totally unnatural, divine gift exclusively from God to man does not square easily with the New Testament. The philosophical and ethical objections to it which naturally arise are another question. In this instance, Nygren's reliance on a modern mood, not without Barthian coloring, which finds more response in the teachings of Paul than in those of Jesus, seems to have made less acceptable his doctrine of *agape*.

The notion that the Christian idea of love is entirely from God to man also makes for an artificial Christology which tends to remove Jesus from man. At the center of this dualism between God and man lies a substance philosophy where personality is not the ultimate of ontology. Gilson has pointed out what harm and confusion come from not making Being in personal terms ontologically ultimate. The full significance of this philosophical insight, however, is seldom applied to theology. We naturally agree that God's *agape* was revealed in Jesus because God took the initiative, because God entered actively into history; but we cannot separate Jesus from the solidarity of mankind. We cannot give him an artificial manhood. In a recent discussion, a Lundensian thinker, when pressed by the author, declared that Sabellianism was really no heresy; that the Trinity can be explained chronologically rather than analytically; that God the Father came down and became God the Son. Although this view of a younger disciple of the Lundensian school may not be representative of their view as a whole, nevertheless, it is indicative of a tendency wherein God's *agape* is somehow limited, in a special way quite beyond explanation, to the Incarnation. We can agree with Nygren that in the life and death of Jesus we see the majesty of God as the "sacrificial, self-giving majesty of love." We must, however, remain content with the historic doctrine that Jesus was both God and man, that God was in him, that the importance of Jesus is, first of all, that God was seen in him, but in a fully historic, human personality.

It is unfortunate, indeed, that the Lundensian view of philosophy precludes the rational evaluation of theological theory and the subsequent exclusion of whatever themes are inconsistent with its basic motif. Either its methodological limitation of theology to the description of the historical content of Christianity has made it necessary for Lundensian thought to include as Christian a great number of thoughts inadequate to or inconsistent with *agape*, or else the desire to keep intact traditional theology has helped not a little to fashion its theological method. Nygren, for instance, will maintain with great vigor that only that which can be explained in terms of the *agape* motif is Christian; but when confronted with notions such as eternal hell or other traditionalistic dogmas, totally at variance with the Christian idea of love, he will counter with the assertion that all we know about *agape* is to be found in the history of Christian thought. No rational criticism of such aspects of traditional theology which go contrary to the notion of *agape* is allowed, on the ground that *agape* is not a human love and cannot be understood in terms of human thought. In this way, to use a popular expression, Nygren manages to have his cake and eat it, too. He can be both a liberal stressing God's love as basic to Christianity, and, at the same time, he can, as far as he lets himself, be a theological reactionary, accepting those very ideas which, humanly speaking, go contrary to the Christian idea of love. Lundensianism thus contrives to make possible a powerful resurgence of traditional thought in the very day of its decay, protected, as it is, by its liberal front of the Christian idea of love. This alliance of the Christian idea of love with those ideas of traditional theology inconsistent with it seems like an impossible straddling of the fence, a dangerous and destructive halting on both sides. Philosophical and theological criticism cannot permanently be evaded merely by calling the content of faith alogical, paradoxical, or religion's own answer to its own questions. It is easy to see that the idea of *agape* and much in traditional theology clash with all violence. *Agape* as faith's final principle of explanation is an idea of ultimate hope and historic challenge; whereas traditional theology maintains a split universe, an unsolvable dualism, an eternal heaven and an eternal hell. The traditional view of God is also anything but that of God as *agape*; whatever love it has is tied up under doctrines and beliefs which smother it by their very contradictions of it. The resolute acceptance of the Christian idea of love and its application to all the spheres of theology would result in a liberal system of thought where everything is ultimately subject to God's love. It is strange, indeed, to magnify *agape* while scoffing at its most consistent advocate in the history of theology.

This inconsistency Lundensian thought maintains by confining itself to the nature of God and to his work as a Redeemer. It fails to connect God the Redeemer with God the Creator. Somehow, God, if he is all-good, all-powerful, and all-wise, is responsible for the world that he has made and for the children of his creation. It is easy, of course, to say that we must not measure God by the measure of man, but must he not be better, at least, than our best measure of him? Either man, history, and nature are not ultimately so evil as they are supposed to be, or else they are not made by an *Agape* that is all-powerful and all-wise. The doctrine of God cannot be isolated from that of the world. Lundensian thought has said little about the wisdom and the power of God. Although faith is supposed to hold that he is both all-wise and all-powerful, the point remains that either God is the Creator of this world, who knew what he was doing, and who will, in his own way, accomplish a completely good end, or else he is in some way limited. No matter what the nature of that limitation might be, if God is to be thought of as a sufficiently wise and powerful, completely good Will, the choice between a limited God and universal salvation stands. On this point every theologian must make up his mind. There has been too much equivocation on or outright evasion of this problem for Christian theology to be interpretatively adequate. Some day, the Lundensians must face the problem. To place it beyond the limits of faith is not satisfactory unless all ultimate questions are placed there, too. The proposition that God is perfect in every respect involves definite implications. God's ultimate victory, the identification of God the creator with God the Redeemer and with God the Conqueror of evil is, of course, a bold venture of faith. Surely it cannot be arrived at through a rational interpretation of actuality. Yet we dare to think that the need of Christian theology is to live not by despair, but by hope; not by fear, but by faith. Only when the Christian idea of love is applied not only to redemption, but to creation and eschatology as well, can Christian theology feed on the faith which is "the conviction of things not seen." It seems that the choice between such a baffling faith and a limited God offers the only alternatives for Christian theology.

In one place, Nygren points out that *agape* must exist in a constant tension with *nomos*. Undoubtedly, *agape* can never come into the fullness of its power as a principle of interpretation until it is organically related to both law and reason. *Nomos* involves those traditional norms which help to direct present experience. They are necessary aspects of historic development and personal growth. *Nomos* must ever be in the service of *agape*. Tension between the two, although likely, is, however, not necessary. Tension results only when means to life become its ends. This frequently happens in the case of moral and spiritual laws, wherein the keeping of laws itself becomes an objective. The reason for the law or the historic circumstances that brought it into being are not understood. Men begin to exist for the Sabbath when the Sabbath should exist for men. Religious practices or doctrines are maintained as sacred long after their function has passed, and even when they work hardship on the people they were designed to help. Personal relationships are hemmed in by man's own legal creations; the past suppresses and impedes abundance of life. In this case, *nomos* has become an end, and, being no longer in the service of *agape*, is evil. It is not this fact, however, that is considered by the Lundensians, but, rather, that the works of the law can become a way to God. Men may believe that by the keeping of the law they can earn their salvation. This is, of course, an altogether natural belief, since obedience and service are highly valued in family life and in social life as a whole. We hope, too, that right doing is acceptable service in the sight of the Lord. Antinomianism constitutes a real spiritual danger. If God seeks man's love, however, and desires him to love his neighbor, man can, naturally, not reach God simply by means of the works of the law. The father and the mother want more of their children than obedience and service; they want their love, their trust, and their fellowship. In the same way, the law cannot lead men to God, and fear of it often hides for them God's face. Or, on the other hand, if a person takes pride in the keeping of the law so that he is thereby hindered from knowing his own sins and failures and from knowing God more fully and serving him more humbly, then the keeping of the law can definitely separate man from God. Naturally, too, there is a tension between man's sense of independence, his wishing to earn his salvation, and the necessity of recognizing the primacy of God's grace and the reception of it with humble gratitude. When all this is said, however, the relation of *agape* and *nomos* brings up one of the basic inconsistencies in Nygren's thought: his insistence that God's fellowship with man is on the basis not of God's holiness, but of man's sinfulness. In Roman Catholic thought, it is held, the attempt is to lift men up to God to have fellowship with him upon the basis of his holiness, whereas in Protestant thought, especially that of Luther, the insistence is that man's fellowship with God is ever on the basis of man's sinfulness. The whole question, however, is falsely presented. Man's relationship with God is neither on the basis of holiness nor on the basis of sinfulness, since both are legal thoughts, but on the basis of God's love, the relation of a Father to his needy, misunderstanding, wayward children. The relation of parents with their children in an ideal family relationship is not primarily on the basis of good or evil, but on the basis of tender affection. The Prodigal Son came home and was received into the father's arms on the basis neither of sin nor of holiness, but simply on the basis of love and of sonship. The Lundensians, on the other hand, would keep the son a servant. Although the forgiveness would be complete, there would also be a constant cleft between him and his father. The legalism which offers a choice between sin and holiness as the basis of man's relationship with God is surely entirely inconsistent with the basicness of the Christian idea of love.

Naturally, the Christian idea of love must be related to the function of reason in religion. When asked why the Lundensian system seemingly had to give such an appearance of being a reactionary irrationalism, Nygren frankly replied that as yet time has not permitted him to work out the relation of love to reason. Bring's book on the question is, to be sure, a careful analysis of the different senses in which reason can be used, but is so negative as to fail fundamentally to deal with the deeper problems involved. Since the question is still open, our best procedure is to wait for a fuller and more final answer from the Lundensian thinkers. The insistence that it is not rational for a holy God to stoop to save sinners is, of course, ill-founded. If God is love, the most natural thing imaginable is that by his very nature he should desire to save the children of his creation. Since we have discussed this question in the previous chapter, it is enough to say in this connection that religion is not reasonable, if with a reasoned religion is meant the production of religious dogmas through rational speculation according to the inherent powers of the mind; for religion is through and through a matter of revelation, of faith's believing its ideals obtained from experience to be objectively real, beyond man's experience. If, on the other hand, with reasonableness is meant that religion is not revealed apart from the function of reason in its interpreting and testing of experience, then we hold religion to be without a question reasonable. The decision of faith or the moral decision may at the moment of choice lie deeper than immediate rational review, but it is ever and ever dependent upon the previous experience, at least in part rationally interpreted, of itself and of the whole race. Revealed religion can never be a direct contradiction of reasoned truth. Vital religion is, rather, the progressive synthesis of the ideal and the actual by both thought and deed.

This brings up our final problem. To be meaningful as the distinctive and determinative motif of Christianity, provided that faith holds Christianity to be universally adequate and applicable, *agape* must in some way be organically related to the whole of man, the whole of history, and the whole of nature. It would, however, be unfair to expect this of Nygren or the Lundensians, inasmuch as their chosen task is not synthesis but analysis. Nygren himself has stressed the fact that certain epochs of thought are synthetic in spirit, while others need the discipline of diastase. With widening horizons, Christian thought came close to being interpreted entirely in terms of Old Testament derivations, New Testament surroundings, and general cultural conditions through which it has passed, without any consciousness that it had a unique message, that as a religion it was decidedly distinctive. Then, too, not only was Christianity in danger of losing its identity because of a confused historical method, neither sufficiently critical nor rich in analytical insight, but also it was threatened by a vague rationalistic method, working from the generalities of experience without appreciation of the necessity of faith's choice among the historic traditions which through unusual personalities and historic communities have given certain answers to the problems of life reaching beyond any general theory that is dependent entirely on the rational description of actuality. In this way, revelation succumbed to reason, and theology became equated with the philosophy of religion. Reason can never by itself, however, working solely with average experience and without the compulsive power of faith, leap to the ideal which provides religion with social and personal adequacy. The ontological argument is primarily not rational but religious in nature. Every religion is conditioned by the will to believe, but the intent of this will is not, first of all, to obtain comforting or even helpful illusions in order that they might become effective reals, but, much rather, to discover an objective

Some Problems Connected with Christianity as Agape

truth that will sustain and make available the ideal which at times gleams like an unattainable star beyond the horizon of the actual. Religion in this sense is not man-made but God-made. Man can believe with religious power and devotion only as long as what he believes is more than his own creation. Religions are historic developments, not rational creations. Faith, to be adequate, must find its sum and substance in a historic religion.

Nygren has certainly performed an invaluable service by calling attention to the fact that the vague thinking of today, where religions are interpreted solely in terms of some general moral development, some common cultural conditions, or some broad, rational speculations, must give way to the critical analysis of a new day, where the distinctive point of view of each religion is recognized as faith's attempt to answer, not formal considerations, but the absolute questions of life. Nygren has not said that synthesis is wrong, but, rather, that it has its place. His point is, therefore, well taken that his task must first of all be a critical discovery of the basic motif of Christianity. This task represents a most important theological contribution. Careful analysis ought always to precede important synthesis. We must know what Christianity has to say about human motives before we can relate its demands to the whole man; what it has to say about the relationship of God and man before we can relate it to other religions; what it has to say about God's relation with the whole world before we can relate it to a rational interpretation of nature. We differ with Nygren, however, in our position that reason can compare motifs, and that it can relate these both to philosophic problems and to psychological data. If God has created us, the *eros* in our nature must somehow be related to the *agape* which should form the source of our conduct. In man himself, God's work as Creator and Redeemer must be reconciled. Hocking discusses the sublimation of instincts in the remaking of human nature, while A. A. Bowman takes issue with him in this respect, believing that a total transformation of man's distinctive drives is somehow necessary. The point is, however, that whether we have sublimation, transformation, or even destruction and substitution of natural drives, those drives have, in their way, fulfilled an important function in the development of God's creative plan. Only today's good can judge yesterday's evil; only tomorrow's better can judge today's good; only the ideal can judge the actual. Whether the actual serves as a way to the ideal, a necessary stage before it can come, or even as a contrast to it, the higher development, nevertheless, has no right to refuse to see its relation to it. Still, the ideal must inevitably, by its very nature, condemn the actual, for it seeks eternally its own concretion. If God is to be both Creator and Redeemer, and if man must be understood as capable of experiencing both *agape* and *eros*, some one must work out the relation between them. For this reason, we must think highly of Augustine's synthesis of *agape* and *eros* into *caritas*, for here *eros* is in the service of God's *agape*. *Eros* finds its fulfillment in incalculable love to God. We do not think that Augustine meant that love of God is consistent with man's highest selfishness, but, rather, that man's natural self-centered drive for satisfaction can find its release only in that love of God and neighbor for which it is meant. When man finds this love, he is delivered from his selfish drive for satisfaction by the finding of a satisfaction in God which so completely fulfils his inner cravings that his love of

Some Problems Connected with Christianity as Agape

God and men takes the place of his selfishness. The reconciliation of *amor Dei* and *amor sui* seems merely the restatement of Jesus' assertion that only by losing our lives can we find them. We believe that Augustine taught that by loving God man finds his highest happiness, but this kind of happiness is that fulfillment of man's self-concern which is also its destruction. We think that Augustine would say with Niebuhr that "self-love is never justified, but self-realization is allowed as the unintended but inevitable consequence of unselfish action."[1] In any case, when the analytical task of theology is done, the synthetical must begin, and *agape* and *eros* must again be synthesized into at least a genetic relationship. The author believes that a coordinate relationship also exists between the two motifs, and that this is the reason for man's being torn between the ideal and the actual, between selfish drives and the sincere desire to overcome them. In that case, *agape* would come not entirely as a sudden gift, nor as a total relationship, but would have its beginning and development in man's gradual growth under the constraint of God's Holy Spirit.

In the same way, Christianity as *agape* must be related to the other religions of history. If we take the fellowship through God's *agape* to be the highest form of fellowship, then Christianity surely has a distinct message to all other religions. Since this message declares a certain kind of fellowship, it must inevitably be proclaimed both in practice and in theory. It is for this reason that missions must be a matter both of evangelism and of service. Evangelism without service is the practical denial of the inner message of Christian theology. Christian theology without social service is the preaching of a form

[1] Reinhold Niebuhr, *An Interpretation of Christian Ethics*, p. 53.

lacking in meaningfulness apart from the practicing of its content. To this extent we agree with the Lundensians that religion is more than reasoned truth. If *agape* is true, moreover, the works of Christian love must inevitably overflow into the whole world, quite without regard to its acceptance or rejection. When this is said, however, it must also be emphasized that Christianity has an intellectual content of such a general nature that it can be universally applied. Then, too, important victories are first won in the ideal, which only gradually becomes embodied. Nor does Christianity as an ideal, any more than Christ, come to destroy, but to fulfill. The struggle between faiths, contrary to Nygren's assertion, is not entirely a struggle to death. Whatever in the different religions of the world is good, promotive of a higher form of fellowship, whatever ennobles and helps life, must be kept and used in the service of Christ. Christianity is, however, a Gospel with a definite message condemning whatever ignorance, thoughtlessness, or hardness of heart separates God and men, and men and men. Christianity must deny as wrong whatever springs from selfish motives, whatever results from fear, whatever oppresses man with ultimate despair. Sometimes doctrines must be challenged; sometimes practices must be condemned; in neither case, however, because they are not Christian in a sociological sense, but because they are destructive of the highest and best fellowship in the place where it is believed and practiced. The remarkable thing about the Christian idea of love is that it is wide enough to include all forms of fellowship, every kind of communal life. All forms of fellowship can be changed with *agape* as their source and standard. Christianity as the belief in the ultimate victory of a two-dimensional fellowship based on

Some Problems Connected with Christianity as Agape

agape must, therefore, be effectively related to every kind of fellowship this world has to offer.

A final estimate of Lundensian thought is difficult to give. There can be no question that it represents a theology of unusual depth, dealing vigorously with the central problems of the Christian faith. Its analysis of motifs with its emphasis on *agape* is by far its most important theological contribution. If the *agape* motif can be freed from its traditionalistic alloys and if the Lundensians will release it from an inadequate, anti-intellectualistic background and then apply it fearlessly to all the problems of Christian theology, the work of the Lundensian school may herald a new epoch in Christian thought. The emphasis on Christian love as explanatory of faith's deepest assertions and as the religiously sanctioned standard for ethics certainly needs to become central in Christian theology and sufficiently strong to determine every one of its doctrines. The constructive power and possibilities of Lundensian thought so far overbalance its deficiencies and limitations that whatever news will come in the future from this young movement in theology will surely be received with keen interest by every one deeply concerned with the meaning and truth of Christianity.

CHAPTER VI

DEVELOPMENTS IN SWEDISH THEOLOGY, 1939–1966
William A. Johnson

INTRODUCTION

A great deal has occurred theologically in Sweden since 1939, the date of the publication of Nels F. S. Ferré's epochal book, *Swedish Contributions to Modern Theology*.[1] The Church of Sweden endured World War II, and managed to survive the agonies and temptations of the period relatively unscathed. A land which has nurtured Ingmar Bergman and Pär Lagerkvist has demonstrated that it is capable of extraordinary cultural achievements as well as a persistent theological "wistfulness;" (to which *The Silence* and *Barabbas* might bear witness).[2] Theologians still become bishops of the Church; and bishops still become ecumenical leaders.

[1] There are two general surveys of Swedish theological thought in English: Gustaf Wingren, "Swedish Theology Since 1900," *Scottish Journal of Theology*, Vol. 9, No. 2, June, 1956, pp. 113–134 (reprinted in Swedish, "Svensk teologi efter 1900," *Andra Tider-Samma Tro* 20, 1958 (Stockholm, Sveriges Kristliga Studentrörelsens Bokförlag); and Gustaf Wingren, "The Main Lines of Development in Systematic Theology and Biblical Interpretation in Scandinavia," published by the Library, Union Theological Seminary in Virginia, Richmond, Virginia, 1964. *Cf.* Edgar Carlson, *Reinterpretation of Luther* (Philadelphia, Westminster Press, 1948) which deals with the Luther renaissance in Sweden; also Leiv Aalen, "Principal Systematic Problems of Present Day Scandinavian Theology," *Lutheran World*, Vol. III (1956), pp. 44–49; J. W. Heikkihen, "The Basic Principles of Anders Nygren's Theological Thought," *The Lutheran Quarterly*, Vol. I (1949), pp. 123–134.

[2] This theological "wistfulness" of which I speak may be seen best in two books by a priest of the Church of Sweden, Olov Hartman, who is also director of the Sigtuna Foundation (an institute of the Church of Sweden which endeavors to initiate conversations between the world of modern culture, psychology, sociology, politics, economics and the Church). His books are *Holy Masquerade* (*Helig maskerad*) (Grand Rapids, Wm. B. Eerdmans Publishing Co., 1963) and *The Sudden Sun* (*Innanför*) (Philadelphia, The Fortress Press, 1964). Hartman himself describes the purpose of this latter work: "I wrote *The Sudden Sun* because voices of doubt and agony, voices which I know from my own thoughts and from people I meet in daily life, began to speak from within. In the novel these voices are answered by someone who takes them more earnestly than we do ourselves in our bitter protest against life."

Sweden's most distinguished theologian, Anders Nygren, left his professor's chair in Lund to become Bishop of Lund. He has subsequently retired and is now actively engaged in reworking his philosophy of religion. Gustaf Aulén too has retired from his bishopric in Strängnäs, and has become Sweden's theological elder statesman. Einar Billing, Tor Andrae, Torsten Bohlin, Nathan Söderblom and Yngve Brilioth have all died. Ragnar Bring (the third member of the Lundensian triumvirate) divides his retirement between Lund and the United States. Other theologians who figure prominently in Ferré's portrayal of the Swedish scene have faded away, others never developed their inherent potential, and still others were denied professorial chairs, because of the unique arrangement in Sweden which allows for few men to become professors. (Of the four universities maintained by the Swedish state—Lund, Uppsala, Stockholm and Gothenburg—only Lund and Uppsala are represented by theological faculties, and at Lund there is only one professor in each of the disciplines of Church History, New Testament Exegesis, Old Testament Exegesis, Practical Theology, Philosophy of Religion, and Comparative Religion, and two in Systematic Theology [divided into Dogmatics and Christian Ethics].) Other theologians became bishops without first having had the opportunity to serve as professors at Lund or Uppsala.

For more than four hundred years the Church of northern Europe has been distinctly Reformation Lutheran. As a result, the Scandinavian countries constitute the most purely Lutheran concentration of nations in the world today. The Reformation came to Sweden through the work of Olavus and Laurentius Petri, as they labored over the translation of Luther's and Melanchthon's writings. Olavus Petri is recognized as the "Swedish Reformer." He was a student in Wittenberg during the stirring years of 1516–1518,[3] and was in direct contact with Luther there. The Swedish Church acknowledges

[3] There are two books in English which describe this period: Conrad Bergendoff, *Olavus Petri and the Ecclesiastical Transformation in Sweden* (New York, Macmillan, 1928); John Wordsworth, *The National Church of Sweden:* The Hale Lectures (London, Mowbray, 1911). Still the classic work of this period in Swedish is Hjalmar Holmquist, *Svenska kyrkans historia*, Vol. III, *Reformationstidevarvet* 1521–1611 (Stockholm, Svenska kyrkans diakonistyrelses bokförlag, 1933).

a continuity with the medieval Church, so that there was at no time an awareness of a new Church initiated at the Reformation. It was the application of the truths of the Gospel (as redefined by Luther) to the life and teachings of the Church which gave Sweden its Reformation.

The Church of Sweden can readily point to the continuity of an apostolic bishopric. This fact has often led to friendly overtures by the Church of England; however, the Church of Sweden, with notable "high church" exceptions, has placed no particular significance upon this succession.

By 1523, Sweden had gained political independence from Denmark, and successfully completed the religious separation from Rome. This parallel break, national and ecclesiastical, has been important to the genesis of the "national Church" or "folk Church" concept, without, however, ever subordinating the Church to a lower position than the state. 1531 marks the date of the first Lutheran liturgy and in it, the term "Mass" was retained—a term which is still employed today. This date also marked the period when the leaders of the Swedish Church pledged themselves to "the Evangelical Faith, with the Scriptures as the norm for Christian teaching." It was not until 1571 that a *Church Order* directing Church polity and the liturgy was drawn up. The Archbishop of Uppsala, Laurentius Petri, was the guiding spirit behind this document. Not until 1593 did the Church adopt the Augsburg Confession as its creedal standard.

The characteristic emphases of the modern Church of Sweden grow directly from this historical background. The high church movement in Sweden is still flourishing, even if its influence is localized and its converts come mainly from the younger clergy. The high church movement is conservative in a traditional sense; that is, it attempts to reintroduce the "Catholic" element into the life of the Swedish Church and does so by emphasizing the theological and ecclesiastical continuity between the Church of Sweden and the "Holy Catholic Church." Representatives of this movement emphasize apostolic succession, the liturgical renaissance (which Gunnar Rosendal and others really anticipated), and the theological necessity for creedal and dogmatic affirmations. It is sacramental in a special sense (for the Church of Sweden has fostered a happy union of preaching and the celebration of the Eucharist in its corporate worship). It insists that the Church can be reformed only when all liberal and popular phases have passed, and the Church returns to its *unique* witness, that of the centrality of the Holy Sacrament.[4] The high church movement has its counterpart in other countries, of course. Its interest however, outside of Sweden, is in the Early Church (and patristic studies), and it endeavors to encourage the contemporary Church to emulate its apostolic origins. But within Sweden the high church movement is characterized by an enthusiasm for the medieval tradition, and is highly suspicious of any positive direction toward the Early Church. Within Sweden too, the high church movement consciously disassociates itself from the academic study of theology, which has usually concentrated heavily on historical studies of the Early Church and the Lutheran Reformation. The Early Church and the Reformation are considered by Lutheran scholars (especially Nygren, Aulén, Bring and Wingren)[5] to be "true and normative" interpretations of Biblical Christianity.

The Church of Sweden continues vigorous theological conversations with the Church of England, and retains its privilege of intercommunion with that body. It was Yngve Brilioth, who rose before his death to the exalted position of Archbishop of the Church of Sweden, who contributed the most to the Church of England–Church of Sweden dialogue. He was trained as a Church historian, was a professor in Lund during the years 1928–37, and wrote primarily in the area of practical theology (*Predikans historia* 1945: *The History of Preaching*). He visited England as a young student and his friendship with the Church of England grew from that time and never subsided. His most important work, which reflected both

---

[4] Ferré's observations (p. 23) are still relevant.
[5] Gustaf Aulén in *Reformation och katolicitet* (Stockholm, Diakonistyrelses Bokfölag, 1959), published in English as *Reformation and Catholicity* by Oliver & Boyd, Edinburgh, and Fortress Press, Philadelphia, 1961, discusses the Roman Catholic contribution to the ecumenical movement, and reflects a significant development in the process of *aggiornamento* on the part of Lutheran theologians!

his interest in Anglicanism and his blossoming ecumenical spirit, is his study of the Holy Communion, *Eucharistic Faith and Practice*.[6] Brilioth is a much more important figure in the development of the modern Swedish Church and the ecumenical movement than most realize. While he was Archbishop many considered him Uppsala's most important theologian. Wingren provides an interpretation of Brilioth's contributions to the Church:

> Brilioth sees the existing denominations which are to be found all over the world as having their origin in certain periods of Church history, their principal features having been. moulded at one particular period. As an Archbishop Brilioth also thinks in terms of Church history, which means that he thinks ecumenically. He sees the different denominations throughout the world as individualities, about which little can be done. Brilioth has little inclination for dogmatic thinking, and he often emphasizes with a light touch of self-depreciation that he does not understand Systematic Theology—but his self-depreciation is always tinged with a slightly ironical reference to the systematic theologians! In a way Brilioth has also contributed to the peculiar "historising" of Swedish theology. But Brilioth sees hardly any single period in the past as being *right* in contrast to any other period. *All* of them, he holds, have their contribution to make to the church life of the present day. This attitude of Brilioth's towards the past in itself implies a great readiness to understand the individual characteristics of the present-day denominations. Brilioth naturally takes a leading place as well in the present Faith and Order movement.[7]

Recently, women have been ordained to the priesthood of the Swedish Church, not without great conflict and difficulty, and, of course, much to the chagrin of the leaders of the high church movement.[8]

Roman Catholicism is developing in number in Sweden, not indigenously, but as a result of the migration of peoples from central and eastern Europe. "Lutheran" Sweden accepts them readily and the process of acculturation and assimilation appears to take place quickly.

[6] (London, S.P.C.K., 1953)
[7] Wingren, "Swedish Theology Since 1900," p. 127.
[8] *Cf.* Tord Simonson, *Kyrkomötet argumenterar* (Lund, Gleerup, 1963), which is a "critical analysis of the types of arguments used in the Church Assemblies of 1957 and 1958 in the debate on the competence of women to be ordained to the priesthood of the Swedish Church."

The Free Church movement appears to have passed its zenith, and most of the churches which belong to this characterization—the Covenant Church (Missionförbundet), the Methodists, and the Baptists—are greatly reduced in number and influence. The Pentecostals remain strong, probably stronger than ever before, as Sweden, too, nurtures its own sectarian movement.

Luther is still studied eagerly by every postulant for the priesthood of the Church of Sweden. A never ending series of studies of Luther has appeared in Sweden since the first expression of *Lutherforschung*.

One hears of attempts made by the Social Democratic majority in the Swedish parliament to disestablish the State Church, but to this point little has been done to place the historic Lutheran Church in less than its favored position in relation to the state. The instruction of religion is still required in all of the schools. The Swedish clergy is now revising the religion curriculum, recognizing that in Sweden too the Christian faith must live within a secular environment.[9] Significant Roman Catholic conversations have been initiated, albeit they are still for the most part academic. But they do contribute creatively to continental developments in this area of the work of the contemporary Church.[10]

Finally, a number of Swedish theologians, including Per Erik Persson and Gustaf Wingren, professors of theology at Lund, participate in the Faith and Order Movement of the World Council of Churches.

I. CONSTRUCTIVE DEVELOPMENTS IN
CONTEMPORARY SWEDISH THEOLOGY

Nygren, Aulén and Bring continue their creative theological work within the traditional Lundensian framework. But it is clear that their corporate influence has been superseded in Sweden by the

---

[9] A standard textbook for religion in the schools is Gösta Lindeskog, *Handbok i Bibelkunskap* (Stockholm, Natur och Kultur, 1959)

[10] Per Erik Persson, *Sacra Doctrina* (Lund, Gleerup, 1957), which is a criticism of St. Thomas according to Lutheran categories; cf. also Persson's *Romerskt och evangeliskt* (Lund, Gleerup, 1959) and Hampus Lyttkens, *The Analogy Between God and the World* (Uppsala, Almqvist & Wiksells Boktryckeri AB, 1952) and *Nythomismen: en religiös filosofi* (Stockholm, Diakonistyrelsen, 1962), a serious attempt to look at St. Thomas in the light of contemporary philosophical concerns.

figure of Gustaf Wingren. His is the name most to be reckoned with in Swedish theology today. He is a bold and brash young theologian, who appears as the new light on an already glittering Swedish fare. Although his tenure as professor of theology at Lund has been of short duration, he has already turned the main stream of Swedish theological thought away from the orthodox Lundensians. And it is to Wingren that we must turn for an appreciation of the substantial contributions which come from contemporary Swedish theology:

A. *Luther Studies (and Motif Research)*

Wingren's first book reflects his training in the richness of the traditional Lundensian program, and was one of a long list of Luther studies which had emerged from the University of Lund. It was entitled *Luther on Vocation* (Philadelphia, Muhlenberg Press, 1957) (Swedish title: *Luthers lära om kallelsen,* 1948).

As we have discovered, systematic theology in Sweden at that time had been given an historical emphasis. Because of basic methodological commitments, Swedish theologians devoted themselves to an investigation of the history of Christian thought, especially the period of the Lutheran Reformation. This period has now been researched with a great deal of energy, and results have been penetrating and exciting.[11] But though this research has contributed a richness of Luther studies to the theological community, it has neglected many of the pertinent problems of contemporary theological thought; in addition, there is some tendency to divorce historical research from specific theological (dogmatic) concerns. The emphasis on Luther research too has permitted a definite parochialism as Swedish scholars investigate their own (Lutheran) ecclesiastical origins.

In Swedish Luther–research a direct line can be drawn from the Bible to Luther. Luther is affirmed as the restorer of original Christianity, the restorer of the primitive Church in the midst of a

[11] A survey, in English, of the interpretive studies of Luther by Swedish theologians, is given in Edgar M. Carlson, *The Reinterpretation of Luther* (Philadelphia, Muhlenberg Press, 1948). Carlson (p. 28) says that "the history of theology in Sweden is a history of Luther research." The development of an individual and distinctive theology in Sweden may clearly be correlated with the advent of the interpretive studies of Luther.

corrupt and deviationist medieval Church. It was Luther, the Swedish scholars believe, who reintroduced the Bible within the context of a Church imprisoned by Aristotelian categories, and it is for this reason that Luther can be considered "the theologian for the whole of Christendom, a restorer of what is truly catholic." [12] Luther is isolated from the other Protestant Reformers and is considered to be the Biblical theologian par excellence. It is for this reason, too, that the Luther-research theologians are opposed to the medieval scholastic Church, the period of Lutheran orthodoxy, Lutheran pietisms of every sort, and also to much of present-day denominational Lutheranism.

But Luther can also serve the Church in an ecumenical way. He becomes the theologian for a "true and authentic Christendom." Liberal theology, especially as represented in Germany at the turn of the century by the Ritschlian school, is pointed to as failing to define a normative Christianity. The Early Church and the Lutheran Reformation are seen to be essentially one in theological import. Both are regarded as *true* (and normative) interpretations of Biblical Christianity.[13]

Swedish Luther-research has concentrated on a number of theological problems: the relationship of law and Gospel, the concept of revelation, the nature of the Church, the doctrine of the Atonement, and the concept of the "calling" (*vocatio*). The Swedish theologians have lucidly demonstrated the method of "motif research" in their analyses of Luther. The method must be *resolutely historical:* it must seek to understand Luther and his concepts in the historical setting in which they properly belong. It must also be systematic, but in a special sense. All of Luther's concepts relate back to his central affirmation, that of God's forgiveness expressed to the sinner through the death of Christ. Luther's historical significance does not lie in the particular ideas he expressed; rather it lies in the fact that his theology points to the *essence* of the Gospel—God's *agape* expressed in Christ, the justification and forgiveness of sins.

Gustaf Wingren's study of Luther is concerned with a central

---

[12] Wingren, "Swedish Theology Since 1900," *op. cit.,* p. 116.
[13] *Ibid.,* p. 117.

theological idea, that of *calling* or vocation. Wingren intends to investigate Luther's doctrine of vocation in an historical way. He writes:

> The task to which we address ourselves in this investigation of Luther's doctrine of vocation is purely historical in that its only aim is understanding Martin Luther's thought on one special point. . . . Our aim is [rather] to integrate Luther's statements about vocation with his basic theology, that is, to present expressions concerning *Beruf* in the context of his fundamental concepts—law and gospel, the work of Christ, freedom, sin, etc. The correctness of an interpretation of Luther's doctrine of vocation cán be shown only by its clarity and congruity with his *total outlook*. Our main purpose therefore makes our treatment of the material *systematic* in that our quest is the total view of a definite historical person, Luther.[14]

In this way, Wingren places himself consciously within the Lundensian school and the theological task of motif research. (But he does so without acknowledging the philosophical presuppositions that determine the task of theology to be that of searching for motifs.) The doctrine of the "calling," or vocation (the Swedish word is *kallelsen;* German, *beruf;* Latin, *vocatio*), is of crucial importance to Luther's theology, as well as to the subsequent development of Lutheran theology. For Luther, the doctrine of vocation constitutes the point at which the Church enters into the social order. The Christian life is to be a life which expresses itself in the acceptance of the responsibilities which one's vocation demands.[15] When the Christian fulfills the tasks to which he has been assigned, he is serving God.

Combined with the idea of the "folk Church"—that is, of a Church which expresses in its institutional structures the activity of a gracious God—the doctrine of vocation provides one of the most characteristic features of both Swedish cultural and religious life.[16]

---

[14] Wingren, *Luther on Vocation, op. cit.,* pp. vii–viii (italics added).
[15] Carlson, *op. cit.,* p. 35 ff.
[16] Carlson characterizes the "folk Church" and its impact upon Swedish cultural life in the following way: "The Church type that seems to the Swedish theologians to give the most adequate expression to the universality of grace is the folk Church. The institutional type and the association type attempt to draw boundaries where none can be drawn. The folk Church assumes that the activity of God is as inclusive as the total community. The visible Churches, through the Word and the sacraments, bear

Wingren interprets Luther on vocation in relationship to Luther's social ethical theory. Constitutive for Luther's social ethics is his conception of the two kingdoms: "the realm of the law over the body on earth and the realm of the gospel over the conscience in heaven," the one temporal, the other eternal. The two kingdoms, the earthly and the spiritual, however, are not hostile to one another for both are in God's hands.

But Luther introduces another tension within the conception of the two kingdoms, that of the kingdom of Christ and the kingdom of the Devil. Christ and the Devil are mutually antagonistic and their powers affect the two kingdoms. Man, in the context of the struggle between Christ and the Devil, is the individual who, in his vocation in the earthly kingdom, anticipates the heavenly kingdom. The heavenly kingdom is introduced to him by means of the Gospel, but it will not be fully revealed to him until after death. Thus man is located between heaven and earth, subject to the power of God as well as the Devil: "His vocation is one of the situations in which he chooses sides in the combat between God and Satan." [17]

Wingren discovers that Luther presents his doctrine of vocation in a dualistic way, that is, there is a constant relationship (and tension) between stability and mobility, freedom and constraint. Life in vocation, for Luther, is at times subjugation to a fixed reality; at other times it means freedom in the response of faith to God's grace. "The duality of stability and mobility gives its peculiar color to Luther's view of creation." Wingren does not attempt to remove or resolve the dualism in Luther's thought, but insists rather that this

---

witness to the total group and offer God's forgiving grace to all men. The holiness of the Church does not consist in the holiness of its members, but in the message that is proclaimed through the means of grace." *Ibid.*, pp. 33-34. Gustaf Wingren in *Creation and Law* (Edinburgh, Oliver and Boyd, 1961), p. 147, believes that as the present split between the Church and the State widens, and as the Church tends to isolate itself from the world more, the concept of a "folk Church" may again become relevant. *Cf.* also Gustaf Wingren, *Kyrkans Ämbete* (Lund, Gleerup, 1958) and *Svenska Kyrkans Ekumeniska Ansvar* (Lund, Gleerup, 1959). The theologian Einar Billing appears to be the guiding spirit behind contemporary affirmations of this kind of Church. Perhaps it is for this reason that Gustaf Wingren promises in the immediate future a volume on Billing's thought.

[17] Wingren, *Luther on Vocation, op. cit.* p. xi.

duality lies at the *center* of his theology. God and the Devil are always present to man: "The devil uses a static *vocation* for his purpose, and God replies with free new creation. The devil uses man's freedom to promote anarchy, and God replies by setting compelling barriers against freedom." [18]

The term *vocation,* as used by Luther, means "outer status or occupation," that is, one's earthly work, one's "station" (*Stand*) and office. Luther distinguishes between the *sinful* orders (the orders of popes, bishops, priests and monks, as well as the sinful activities of robbery, usury and prostitution) and the *just* orders, which are *ordained* by God and whose existence is not contrary to God's will (exemplified by husbands and wives, sons and daughters, lords and ladies, governors, regents, judges, officeholders, farmers, citizens, etc.). The order of soldier is also included: "because it is from God that a soldier receives his fitness to do battle, he may serve therewith, serving with his skill and craft whoever desires his services; and he may accept wages for his labor. For his too is a vocation which issues from the law of love." [19]

But the term vocation is also used by Luther in a variety of contexts. Sometimes the term describes a particular position one may occupy in life—a judge, a son, or a servant girl; or the term may be used to make a distinction between the ruler and his subject (Luther insisted that there was an inherent recognition of the fact that when two people meet, one is superior, and that this inequality is divinely ordained in order to bind one to another in the bonds of obligation); or the term may be used to describe the major associations or groupings of which man finds himself a part: marriage and the family, the political and economic societies, and the Church. However Luther uses the term, vocation represents a part of the created order. One serves God when he fulfills the responsibilities which his vocation thrusts upon him. One's place in a "station" (that is, one's vocation) is determined by God. The station is so created that it enables the Christian to serve the well-being of another.

[18] *Ibid.,* p. xii.
[19] Weimar edition of Luther's works, WA19, 659. Cited in Wingren, *ibid.,* p. 4.

"All stations are intended to serve others." Luther can then remind the Christian that he stands always *in relatione*, that he is always bound in creation to another. It is clear that every Christian occupies a number of offices simultaneously; he may be father to his children, husband to his wife, master to his servants, as well as a legislator within the government.

The station itself is the ethical agent. By means of it God is active through the earthly law. Wingren interprets Luther on this point:

> Here we come across what for Luther is the decisive contrast between God's self-giving love and man's egocentricity. The human being is self-willed, desiring that whatever happens shall be to his own advantage. When husband and wife, in marriage, serve one another and their children, this is not due to the heart's spontaneous and undisturbed expression of love, every day and hour. Rather, in marriage, as an institution something compels the husband's selfish desires to yield and likewise inhibits the egocentricity of the wife's heart. At work in marriage is a power which compels self-giving to spouse and children. So it is the "station" itself which is the ethical agent, for it is God who is active through the law on earth.
>
> What is effected through these orders of society is not due to an inner transformation of the human heart. The corruption of the heart is amended in heaven, through the gospel of Christ. There the human being is a "single person" and there inquiry is made into his inner wickedness, even if on earth it has been ceaselessly repressed and hindered from outer expression. On earth and in relation to his neighbor he fills an "office"; there the main point is that creation is sustained, e.g., that children receive food, clothing and care. This work of love God effects on earth through the "orders"—the order of marriage, of teacher and pupils, of government, etc. Even persons who have not taken the gospel to their hearts serve God's mission, though they be unaware thereof, by the very fact that they perform the outer functions of their respective stations.[20]

Wingren's second major work is a study of the second century theologian, Irenaeus.[21] Again, Wingren works within the framework of the traditional motif research program of the Lundensians. He discovers that the *central* theological problem for Irenaeus is that of

---

[20] Wingren, *Luther on Vocation, op. cit.,* pp. 6–7; *cf.* p. 10, "So vocation belongs to this world, not to heaven; it is directed toward one's neighbor, not toward God. . . . When one does that, God's creative work is carried on."

[21] Gustaf Wingren, *Man and Incarnation: A Study in the Biblical Theology of Irenaeus* (Philadelphia, Fortress Press, 1959) (which is the English translation of *Människan och inkarnationen enlight Irenaeus* [Lund, Gleerup, 1947]).

the relationship of man and the Incarnation. Wingren believes that an analysis of these motifs in Irenaeus' thought will provide important material for the contemporary theologian, who must develop an anthropology which is adequate to the modern world, but which also must be faithful to the witness of the Bible, the Early Church and the Reformation. Wingren recognizes, of course, that a study of the relationship of man and the Incarnation is *not* a popular nor a modern theological problem. But just because it is not a contemporary problem Wingren proposes to deal with it. He believes that the Early Church opens up to us a world of thought largely untouched by our modern theological controversies. The juxtaposition of the theological doctrines of man and the Incarnation permits us to understand Irenaeus and his age in terms of the uniqueness of that period, rather than in terms of the way these doctrines are discussed in the modern period.

Irenaeus lived wholly within the period of the Gnostic attack upon the Church. He responded to this heresy by providing the Church with an anthropology based on Scripture. For this reason Wingren believes that Irenaeus is instructive to the modern theologian in terms of anthropology. He can become the modern theologian's guide as an *authentic* interpreter of Biblical theology. Wingren argues that Irenaeus, unlike the modern theologian who sets God and man in opposition to one another (so that the omnipotence of God becomes a limitation to man's freedom and man's freedom becomes a limitation to the sovereignty of God), deals with *man* only in terms of the Gnostic's false idolization of man. God and man can never be conceived of as in opposition to one another. When they are, some men are thought to be *pneumatic* and others *sarkic,* the former capable of salvation, the latter incapable.

According to Irenaeus, man in this life is in bondage to sin. However, because man was made in the image of God, man's temporal destiny is to become like Christ, who is the image of God. Man possesses this destiny within himself: it is the image of God within him. When he becomes like Christ he becomes *completely man.* But it is only within the Church (the Body of Christ) that this transformation into the likeness of Christ is realized. The transformation is complete only in the Resurrection from the dead in the Kingdom of the Son when God becomes all in all. Wingren explains:

> Thus, in the Church the original Creation breaks through afresh and extends towards the resurrection, when the Devil and death will be destroyed and annihilated. Not until the Consummation will Creation be fully realized, for not until then will God's primal decision concerning man, *Let us make man in our own image* (Gen. 1:26), be accomplished, and this fulfillment of God's purpose is wholly dependent on the fact of Christ's becoming man, His conflict, and His victory.[22]

Recapitulation is a central concept in Irenaeus' thought. Recapitulation occurs through Christ, but it is also achieved by man: "It is the plane of Creation breaking through in the Incarnation and in the victory over evil through the temptations and Passion of Jesus by which our captivity is destroyed and a way opened from death."[23] Within the Church, and in the Resurrection, man is included in the recapitulation so that he realizes the original purpose of his creation:

> Recapitulation (ἀναχεφαλαίωσις) means the accomplishment of God's plan of salvation, and this accomplishment is within history, in a time sequence, and is not an episode at one particular point of time. It is a continuous process in which the οἰκονομία, *dispositio,* of God is manifested by degrees. First, and most important of all—and the basis of our whole salvation—is the event of the birth of Jesus when the Son of God became an actual man. . . . If we keep to the metaphor of conflict which we employed earlier, we might put it this way, that after a power stronger than the occupying power has invaded the enemy-occupied territory, the sequel of this primary event, i.e., the defeat of the enemy, is often a *fait accompli,* but it is a sequel which is accomplished in conflict—victory ensues in a series of events, and not timelessly as a logical consequence of the fact that the invading power is stronger than the power of the enemy.

It is the Incarnate One, the One who has been made flesh, who recapitulates. All that Christ does from His birth at Bethlehem until the judgment of the world He does as the One who was incarnate. His humanity, His flesh, is part not only of His passion and death, but also of His Resurrection and dominion over the world—He never gives up the humanity which he

[22] *Ibid.,* pp. xiii–xiv.
[23] *Ibid.,* pp. xiv, xv.

bore during the days of His earthly life. . . . While Christ is active, recapitulation continues "till he has put all the enemies under his feet" (I Cor. 15:25) and "himself be subjected to him" that God may be "all in all." (I Cor. 15:28) [24]

Recapitulation means more, however: it is a purificatory movement pointing backward to the first Creation; Jesus' struggle against the Devil in a conflict which repeats the history of Adam, but with the opposite outcome; man's restoration, perfection or consummation (man's growth is resumed and renewed); the assembling of men under Christ as Head, the resumption of the contact with the source of life and the renewal of life in men's public and private lives; the final consummation when Christ will become king in visible form.[25]

Irenaeus affirms that God alone saves through Christ, that salvation is offered to all, and that all men are equal before God. The Incarnation is the locus of God's entrance into the world of men, which means finally that man is actually sought by God.

Wingren is faithful in his analysis of Irenaeus to the juxtaposition of man and the Incarnation. Man is created by God "in the Son" to become the image of God. The Son of God is with God from eternity. But man stands in the middle of a conflict between God and the Devil. It is the Devil who once fell and caused man to fall. Man is drawn into association with the Devil and thus is made captive to evil. The mastery of sin means bondage, an unnatural occupation; all of life falls under the power of the oppressor. Man's bondage to the Devil disrupted his appointed end, to become the image of God.

Only the Son of God, who existed before man, and in whom man was created, can rescue man from bondage. For this reason, Christ becomes man Himself. The Incarnation means that both God and man are involved in the struggle against evil. In Christ, man meets man as he was ordained to become in creation. But this man must endure the same struggle against evil as every man. The

[24] *Ibid.*, pp. 81–82, 82–83; *cf.* also p. 79 ff.; 122 ff.; 170 f.; 192 f.
[25] *Cf. ibid.*, pp. 173–174.

culmination of the struggle is victory over death. Incarnation leads directly to the Resurrection. And thus recapitulation is accomplished.

Wingren's next book, *The Living Word*,[26] marks the beginning of his departure from the characteristic Lundensian motif research. This work also marks the beginning of his constructive systematic thought.

He indicates what is to be his task in *The Living Word:* "We are, accordingly, setting out to analyze preaching, the *kerygma,* the Christian message, in order to discover its essential nature. Ours is not a historical task, in the sense that we are trying to provide a picture of the Early Church proclamation, or of the preaching of the Reformation," [27] (which, of course, would have been a classical Lundensian endeavor). Wingren's purpose is much more practical: it is to attempt to answer the questions "What does it *mean* to preach? What is the *content* of preaching?" To answer these questions, Wingren must turn to the primary sources, first and foremost the Bible, but also "to those who laid bare for their contemporaries the Word of the Bible and especially to those who did that in the classic ages of the Church's history, for example in the first Christian centuries and in the age of the Reformation." [28]

It is clear, therefore, that Wingren is not prepared to leave his Lundensian background behind altogether. The periods which have most to teach us, he says, are those in which the Biblical message had to contend with teachings inimical to the Christian faith. Therefore, the Biblical period, the period of the Early Church (which was anti-Gnostic) and the Reformation stand out as "the most instructive ages of Church history."

The nature of preaching must be considered in itself. It is not necessary for this purpose, Wingren insists, to discuss theories of the philosophy of religion or to attempt to establish the scientific nature

---

[26] Gustaf Wingren, *The Living Word (in the Preaching and Mission of the Church)* (Philadelphia, Muhlenberg Press, 1960) (English translation of *Predikan,* Lund, Gleerup, 1949).
[27] *Ibid.,* p. 20.
[28] *Ibid.,* p. 21.

of theology (which had been Nygren's contribution). "No one has insisted on such a setting for preaching; compared with theology, preaching is a relatively independent entity, which can be made the subject of a systematic theological analysis." [29]

Wingren asserts that it is the "primacy of the Word" which is most characteristic of Protestant preaching. It was, of course, the Reformation which asserted the authority of the Word as over against the authority of an ecclesiastical hierarchy. Wingren assigns this place to the Word:

> The Word cannot be reckoned under any other category, whether under the teaching ministry of the Church or as a common conception of life, without thereby losing the standing that it has in Luther. If the right interpretation of the Word is that which is given by the Church then the primacy belongs to the Church and not to the Word. But the Word is first since Christ is first; so that the incarnate Word may sound forth he sends out his apostles—that is the correct order. There it is the Word which directs, the Word which fashions. Otherwise it becomes itself subject to direction and being fashioned. Similarly the Word is deprived of its position when theology begins with a clearly defined view of life involving certain fundamental questions to which the Bible and other Christian documents have got to give an answer. In this case the fundamental questions are provided without reference to the Word. The claim that the Word makes, however, implies that it has the right to formulate these questions itself. The Word loses part of its content when it is made to reply to questions other than those that spring from the Word itself. Since, then, the Word must be the starting point and the centre, there is much which indicates that, in determining the task of theology, we must, more consciously than heretofore, collect the threads about the concept of the Word, so that we may then look at other entities *from that viewpoint*. It is in this way that we should approach not only the Reformation but also the Early Church and, above all, the bible.[30]

Once Wingren has this basic affirmation before the reader, he can then discuss the situation in which the sermon is preached and the dilemma which the preacher faces as he attempts to preach the Word of God. One of the "false dilemmas" which the preacher faces, Wingren says, is that of the antithesis between objective and

[29] *Ibid.*, p. 23.
[30] *Ibid.*, p. 22.

subjective preaching. The antithesis is usually put this way: *either* preaching is concerned with the Word, the *objective* element, *or* it is concerned with men, the *subjective* element. Wingren finds that such an antithesis is foreign to the witness of the Bible and, furthermore, provides the preacher with an impossible task. Wingren explains:

"Subjective" preaching sets out to serve the cause of the cultivation of the mind and the building up of character, that is, it tries to develop religious personalities. "Objective" preaching, on the contrary, is unique in trying to bring to the world of men something that that world lacks, something that cannot be developed or produced from what is human. Consequently the "objective" type tends to establish its own Christian and ecclesiastical style of life, to generate out of the given revelation something specifically Christian for the shaping of life. Here again, to all appearance, the two types are antagonistic, but as usual, they really have a common root. For both of them it is more or less foreign to think of ordinary loyalty at work, the service of others, as that for which man needs to be set free.[31]

But that is not how Luther looked at the matter: "He deduces no ethic out of Christian doctrine, but plunges right into human life as it is and finds that all evil in the world comes from our own sin, from our slavery. We have no need of being fashioned into something or other; we only need to be set free, and then to take the place that is ours in our usual calling." [32]

The "slavery" that the New Testament speaks of simply means that *we cannot be men*. But when man is freed from the clutches of the Evil One he can be man again—he is redeemed. This conception of the restoration of one's humanity will become important for Wingren's later constructive theological thought. Wingren too is dependent upon Irenaeus' interpretation of recapitulation on this point. And Wingren argues that the Reformation shares with the Early Church the view of the goal of redemption as "the restored life of man."

If we think of the *kerygma* against its background of man's slavery under the Devil this way of looking at things becomes natural: the message of Christ's cross and resurrection restores the enslaved, that is, it gives man his natural

[31] *Ibid.*, p. 30.
[32] *Ibid.*, p. 30.

life and thus redeems him. Subjective and objective preaching are alike in this that they have got to make something out of man's life, either a "personality" or a "churchman"—to be just a man seems too tame. A characteristic action of Jesus as a healer, to which the Gospels bear witness, is his sending of those whom he had healed back home again to their everyday life. Christ looses the bonds of the prisoners and bids them return to that place in the life of the community to which they belong.[33]

Preaching is therefore the addressing of the Word to the congregation. The preached Word is both Gospel and Law. Both must "strike home" so that the death and Resurrection of Christ (which is the core of the *kerygma*) can take place in the listener. "To the history of redemption belongs the preaching of the Bible's message," Wingren asserts. The Bible itself preaches. The preacher who preaches from the Bible reproduces its content—and that content is the message of victory and the promise of the coming kingdom. "Preaching binds together what God did in the past and what is yet to be." Preaching holds together the acts of God in the form of a message, a promise and a summons—and it is just this which makes up the unity of the Bible.

B. *Methodological Questions*

Wingren is critical of what he calls the "anti-liberal" theologians, especially Karl Barth, who, he believes, sets God and man in opposition to one another to such a disproportionate degree that preaching is forced to retain an antithesis between subject and object. Liberal theology placed man in the center of the universe. Barth reacted against this starting point for theology, emphasized God's significance, and placed Him in the center. As a result the "speculative antithesis" between God and man remains unaltered. The Word must be Absolute in a world of relativities, for it possesses a transcendent element which can never be imprisoned in the historically given Scriptures. For Barth, the Incarnation must operate in the same way as the Biblical witness: it must point away from itself to the divine. The human in Christ reflects the divine, but the incarnate Redeemer never bridges the gap between God and man.[34]

[33] *Ibid.*, pp. 30–31.
[34] *Ibid.*, p. 31.

Wingren believes that Barth's rejection of Luther's doctrine of the unity of the human and the divine in Christ, the doctrine of *communicatio idiomatum,* is the cause of his difficulty. God and man do not stand opposed to one another as two incompatible forms of being; rather God and the Devil stand opposed to one another. They are the enemies. "Man is God's creation who has been brought into captivity to the enemy of God. Christ's task is to enter human life, destroy Satanic might and free man." It is the task of preaching to enter the fray against the powers of the Devil. The Devil trembles with fear when the Gospel of the forgiveness of sins is preached. The forgiveness of sins means that man is snatched from the Devil's grasp.

In *Theology in Conflict* Wingren criticizes Barth for not fully grasping the sense of the "active power" of sin. Wingren argues that Barth's theology is characterized by the total *absence* of a tyrannical, demonic power that subjects man to slavery, which God destroys finally in the work of redemption. Barth lacks the demonic in his theology because there was no conception of evil power in the liberal theology against which he continually reacted. Wingren indicts Barth for being imprisoned within "liberal" categories— which Wingren says he has simply turned upside down, replacing man with God. "It is clear," Wingren argues, "that Barth remains within the framework of Schleiermacher's theology, but rearranges freely within this frame so that God's freedom and superiority become clearly expressed." [35]

Wingren also objects to Barth's frame of reference, which he believes forces Barth into a nineteenth century theological mold and thereby destroys the possibility of a Biblically oriented theological system. Wingren interprets Barth's system in the following way: God and man have natures which are ontologically *dissimilar.* God is transcendent to man. God is superior, man inferior. Man has no knowledge of God until God decides to reveal himself. The revelation occurs in the person of Jesus Christ: "The Word became flesh." The Incarnation, thereby, becomes the center of Barth's theological system and, properly understood, is the revelation of God to man.

[35] Wingren, *Theology in Conflict,* (Philadelphia, Muhlenberg Press, 1958) pp. 25-26.

All of these elements—God, man and revelation—appear to be Scriptural. But are they? Wingren believes not. For one thing, *revelation* stands in the place where *justification* or *the forgiveness of sins* ought to stand. The essence of the Gospel, Wingren insists, is the forgiveness of sins. If revelation replaces it, then the meaning of the Gospel is other than what Paul meant it to be (cf. Romans 3:21 ff.: "But now the righteousness of God has been manifested apart from law, although the law and the prophets bear witness to it, the righteousness of God through faith in Jesus Christ for all who believe. For there is no distinction; since all have sinned and fall short of the glory of God . . ."). When *justification* stands in the center of a theological system, it is assumed that man *already* is in possession of something, that is, that God has already revealed himself through his work in creation (cf. Romans 1:20). But God has not disclosed his plan of salvation in his creation. Man is therefore driven to pursue righteousness—but he does *not* attain it. "He stands there, not without knowledge but 'without excuse,' consequently with guilt, just because already as man he has had to deal with God and therefore knows how he ought to live. The uniqueness of the Gospel, therefore, is that it reveals a new righteousness, apart from the law, a righteousness from God through faith in Jesus Christ." [36]

It is this emphasis upon God's revelation in creation which will appear later in Wingren's mature theological system. But it is clear that his criticism of Barth is based upon an interpretation of the Gospel (in a Pauline-Lutheran framework), which asserts that in Christ a righteousness by grace is revealed which is not based on the works which man is able to do. In Wingren's terms, Barth's frame of reference, including the three elements, the being of God, the being of man, and revelation, cannot deal adequately with the essential meaning of the Gospel. The Incarnation (the Word of God assumed in the humanity of Jesus Christ) is significant because it is God (a being of whom man has no knowledge) who reveals himself to man (so that man receives knowledge of God from Christ).

[36] *Ibid.*, p. 29.

Wingren also indicts Barth for not speaking of God ruling the world through his law.

> When the idea of revelation becomes the governing point of view, man's realization of the revelation becomes in fact the dominant point of view. But if God's activity is permitted to occupy the center, there is every reason to speak of God's work in creation even before the gospel. God's activity in the salvation of humanity comprises a long series of acts which God has done, does, and will do. We can start at any one point and proceed backward and forward.[37]

Wingren endeavors to place "God's activity" in the center of his theological structure, so that he can speak of God's activity in creation even before the revelation of Christ in the Gospel. Such a conviction leads Wingren to his two-volume work in systematic theology, *Creation and Law* and *Gospel and Church*.[38]

Wingren is also critical of Bultmann (in *Theology in Conflict*) for his uncritical appropriation of the philosophy of existentialism, particularly as it has been articulated by Martin Heidegger:

> Bultmann asks first whether "the Christian understanding of being" is the same as "man's natural understanding of his being." This would mean that the New Testament has discovered an insight which in principle is available to all men. Now, when philosophy (and especially Heidegger's philosophy) has disclosed the real quality of human existence, nothing more need be expected from the New Testament. Philosophy has replaced theology. We now know that man is not "tangible" like things; that he does not have qualities, but rather "possibilities," which means that he lives in "the decision." He can lose himself and remain imprisoned in the past; or, he can open himself to the future by throwing away all security and thereby attain to his "authentic nature." This is what existentialism maintains, and this is, as far as Bultmann is concerned, scientific truth. This is identical with what the New Testament suggests by "faith." [39]

Wingren believes that existential philosophy *controls* Bultmann's interpretation of the Christian faith. "Existentialism seems to be an abbreviated Christian view," Wingren writes, "a dogmatics without

---
[37] *Ibid.*, p. 35.
[38] Gustaf Wingren, *Creation and Law* (Edinburgh, Oliver and Boyd, 1961) (English translation of *Skapelsen och lagen,* Lund, Gleerup, 1958) and *Gospel and Church* (Edinburgh, Oliver and Boyd, 1964) (English translation of *Evangeliet och kyrkan,* Lund, Gleerup, 1960).
[39] Wingren, *Theology in Conflict, op. cit.,* p. 49.

God and without eternity." [40] The existential emphases upon man's life as concentrated between birth and death, and the decision man must make for his "authentic being," Wingren believes, make it impossible to have anything more than an "abbreviated and compressed content of the New Testament."

Bultmann defines guilt as the lack of self-realization, while salvation *is* self-realization. Wingren believes that it is important to place these two theological concepts in perspective in terms of the New Testament. He insists that there is a clear order of events in the New Testament: the death of Christ, the Resurrection, and the preaching about that death and Resurrection. When Bultmann deals with these events, he does so in the context of what he calls "concrete events" (*Weltfaktum*). A "concrete event" is an event that is perceptible to everyone and can be understood under the categories of cause and effect. The "content" of the *kerygma* is the death and Resurrection of Christ. The death of Jesus is a "concrete event," perceptible to everyone. But the Resurrection of Christ is a "concrete event" *only* in the preaching of the Apostles. This means, says Wingren, that the series of these three events in the New Testament is reduced to two: the death of Christ and the preaching of the Apostles. "The resurrection lies hidden in preaching. Preaching is the only form in which the resurrection of Christ is present and reaches the hearer." Wingren interprets Bultmann's understanding of the Easter faith as faith in the Word of preaching. But this must mean that if we remove preaching, the death of Jesus would simply be the tragic end of a noble life.[41]

Bultmann is ultimately rejected because Wingren believes that his existential interpretation of the New Testament is too restrictive and cannot deal adequately with the great New Testament themes. The forgiveness of sins is dealt with as *Tat Gottes,* but, Wingren insists, the Resurrection from the dead must also be considered as *Tat Gottes.* Bultmann's understanding of sin is comparable to Heidegger's *Verlorenheit;* righteousness is comparable to true exist-

[40] *Ibid.,* p. 54.
[41] *Ibid.,* p. 63.

ence. The New Testament affirmation of the deliverance from death as an act of God can never be reconciled with Heidegger's *Sein zum Tode*—so Wingren argues.

Wingren is also critical in *Theology in Conflict* of his predecessor in the Chair of Systematic Theology at Lund, Anders Nygren. In fact, it was Wingren's book which resuscitated interest in Nygren's earliest philosophical writings, *Religiost a priori*, *Dogmatikens vetenskapliga grundläggning*, and *Filosofisk och kristen etik*. Wingren intended in *Theology in Conflict* to criticize Nygren's methodological presuppositions.

A spirited debate between Bishop Nygren and Professor Wingren took place at the University of Lund in February, 1956. The debate was sponsored by the Theological Society of Lund, and a large segment of the university community attended.[42]

It was clear that this debate signaled a radical revision of the traditional Lundensian theological categories. At issue was the heart of the Lundensian program: the question of the function of the discipline of the Philosophy of Religion, its relation to theological methodology, and the task of the discipline of Systematic or Dogmatic Theology. Ferré has shown us that, for Nygren, the Philosophy of Religion functions in such a way as to ask categorical questions ("a presuppositional analysis in a given area of experience"); the Philosophy of Religion is a method of critical analysis, it is "an application of the *universal* science which philosophy represents in the area of theology." The Philosophy of Religion, for Wingren, is not that at all, but is rather a *special* science, comparable to the Psychology of Religion—which views religion from a perspective *different* from that of Theology—and is, finally, a discipline *alien* to Theology. For this reason, Wingren insists that the Philosophy of Religion may contribute nothing to the development of a theological methodology.

[42] A report of the debate has been given in an American theological journal by an American theologian who was there; cf. Bernard Erling, "Swedish Theology from Nygren to Wingren," *Religion in Life*, Vol. XXX, Spring 1961, pp. 196–208; especcially pp. 204–205.
The Swedish theological journal, *Svensk Teologisk Kvartalskrift* included the position papers of Nygren and Wingren; XXIII (1956), pp. 20–41, 122–160, 284–322.

But let us examine a little more closely the criticism of Nygren's philosophical presuppositions for theological methodology. In 1921 Nygren published an article, "The Fundamental Problem in the Philosophy of Religion," and his doctoral dissertation, *Religious A Priori*.[43] In these two works he sought to define the task of a "critical Philosophy of Religion." The task of the Philosophy of Religion, he said, was to determine whether religion was an a priori experience. The concept of religion as "a fundamental value" (an a priori categorical experience) which enabled religion to be incorporated into "a system of universally valid values" highlighted Nygren's methodological concerns in these early works.

"Theoretical knowledge represents one fundamental value, the ethical experience a second, and the aesthetic experience a third." The good, for example (the ethical category), is unique, an experience *sui generis,* which cannot be derived from the true (the category of knowledge) or the beautiful (the aesthetic category). Employing such an analysis, Nygren attempts to discover whether religion has an independent value similar to these other recognized fundamental (categorical) values. He finds that religion is *different* from the aesthetic experience, from theoretical knowledge, and from the ethical experience; that is, it possesses a unique and independent *value*. But he also finds that religion possesses *validity,* that is, as he says, it is "a necessary and indispensable human experience." Nygren employs what he calls the "transcendental method,"[44] or the "transcendental deduction of the category of religion" in his analysis of experience. However, religion is also "the presupposition upon which all of culture rests."[45] Religion becomes, therefore, the ground upon which a system of culture is

---

[43] Anders Nygren, "Det religionsfilosofiska grundproblemet," *Bibelforskaren,* XXXVI (1919), pp. 290–313, and XXXVIII (1921), pp. 11–39, 88–103; *Religiost a priori* (Lund, Gleerup, 1921).

[44] "That which must be valid in order that experience as a whole shall be possible is necessarily and universally valid and is therefore a priori. This is the transcendental method described in its briefest form. In order to show that a certain knowledge is a priori it must be proved that without the presupposition of its validity no experience is possible." *Religiost a priori,* my translation, p. 110, *cf.* also Wingren, *Theology in Conflict,* pp. 4, 5.

[45] *Religiost a priori,* p. 237.

built, which embodies the true, the good and the beautiful (the theoretical, ethical and aesthetic categories).

The transcendental deduction of religion yields *eternity* as its primary category ("the fundamental category of religion"). Eternity is presupposed in the total system of culture. Nygren goes on to assert that eternity is only "assumed" in the forms of culture, and in the theoretical, ethical and aesthetic experiences. Religion, however, "presupposes" eternity, which assures religion a primary place in the cultural life of man.

Nygren's employment of the Philosophy of Religion has established therefore that it is a meaningful and legitimate philosophical task to ask about the category of eternity. However, the *content* of religion has not yet been given. All that has been established to this point is that religion is a *form* of human experience (an a priori categorical form of experience). But it is a form which is empty of content. The content of religion lies in the theological answers which are given to the question of eternity by the concrete, historical religions of mankind.

The task of theology follows upon the establishment of the "objective reality" of the historical religions. Theology, Nygren says, "deals with the question of the objective reality of a given religion such as Christianity, or it deals with the validity of its claim to transcendence." Theology *describes* Christianity, and nothing more. It attempts solely to present the historically given religion in a descriptive way. It is then possible for Nygren to search for the fundamental motifs of the historical religion known as Christianity. Nygren writes:

The question is philosophically formulated, the answer must be found in the given historical reality. . . . What the fundamental motif is in any particular outlook can be determined only by immediate observation of its appearance in history, and this process involves the same conditions as are found in any other historical investigation.[46]

The task given to Dogmatic Theology has been defined by the Philosophy of Religion. The Philosophy of Religion *establishes* the

[46] Nygren, *Filosofi och motivforskning* (Stockholm, 1940), p. 44 (my translation).

categorical and fundamental questions for the phenomenon of religion. But these questions are empty and formal. The answers are found in history where the different existing religions struggle against one another. Dogmatic theology presents *one* answer, that of the Christian faith. But it is an analysis free from any kind of valuation.[47]

Nygren goes on to designate the task of Philosophical Ethics as defining the area of competence for Theological Ethics. Philosophical Ethics establishes the categorical and fundamental questions for all ethics. These questions are also empty and formal. The answers are given in history where existing types of *ethos* struggle with others. Theological Ethics provides one answer, that of the Christian faith. But again, it does so in an analysis which is free from every kind of valuation.

Both of these Christian answers may be summarized by the term *agape*. The fundamental motif for Dogmatics, as well as that for Theological Ethics, is *agape*. It is *agape* that brings man into relationship with God. It is *agape* that is constitutive for man's relations to his fellowman, and defines the specific Christian *ethos*. But it is God's *agape* to man that determines, and is the source of, man's *agape* for his fellowman. Dogmatics and Ethics are thereby intimately related. The Christian Ethic is derived from Christian Theology. That union between Ethics and Theology has been made possible by the categorical and fundamental questions which have been asked of historical material by the discipline of the Philosophy of Religion. Nygren makes it quite clear what he is attempting to do when he defines *motif research:*

Motif research operates on the boundary between philosophy and history. It contains both a philosophical and an historical problem. In regard to its starting point it belongs with the presuppositional, philosophical analysis and the principle of categories there developed. It is in the confrontation of these categories, established by the presuppositional, philosophical analysis, with the concrete historical material that it becomes necessary to inquire about

---

[47] It is for this reason that the History of Dogma (with Theological Ethics) belongs to the department of Systematics in a Swedish school of theology; on the Continent, of course, the History of Dogma belongs traditionally to the department of Church History.

fundamental motifs. Motif research does not approach the historical material with indifferent kinds of questions, and consequently not everything or anything can be seized upon and regarded as a fundamental motif. It seeks answers to very definite questions; viz., the fundamental questions of categorical nature. Consequently only that which is appropriate as an answer to such a categorical question can be regarded as a fundamental motif.[48]

But if Nygren asserts that the historical material gives an oblique answer to the philosophically defined question, then he is really saying that the question was not completely formal. A formal question is one which is without content. The question is not supposed to clash with anything in the concrete material. Historical material flows into the form, provided that form is empty. The task of critical philosophy is to clarify fundamental questions until they become completely formal. But motif research is dependent upon various conceptions, and attitudes of life, which give a *content* to the questions; the pure formal nature of the question is thus illusory.

Wingren comes to the heart of the criticism of Nygren's methodology in the following quotation:

The Christian message of God as forgiving Agape is, according to Nygren, an answer to a question posed by philosophy, a formal question devoid of content. *"The question is philosophically posed, the answer must be derived from the given historical reality."* Against this proposition we can on good historical grounds advance the following thesis: the Christian message of God as forgiving Agape is in reality an answer to a pregnant question, viz., the question of guilt. This message is meaningless unless the man who hears it is standing under the claim of God even before he hears the gospel. There is a continual danger that in Nygren's theology the center of the Christian faith, the gospel, becomes erroneously interpreted, since the gospel is divorced from the question of guilt and tied to a formal, philosophical question.[49]

Wingren insists that Nygren *cannot* interpret the New Testament gospel correctly. His approach to the historical material makes this impossible. *Agape* is a fundamental motif which answers a formal

---

[48] *Filosofi och motivforskning* (my translation), *op. cit.,* p. 44 ff.
[49] *Theology in Conflict, op. cit.,* pp. 16–17. Another cogent and comprehensive criticism of Nygren's methodology is found in Hjalmar Lindroth's lengthy article *"Anders Nygren und der Kritizismus," Studia Theologica* (Vol. X, fasc. II, 1957), pp. 89–188.

question when it is asked from both the contexts of religious faith and ethics. But the *content* of the question which the message of God's *agape* answers, that is, *the question of guilt,* cannot be found within either of Nygren's contexts. Nygren's error, according to Wingren, is that the purely formal character of the question directed to the New Testament *prevents* a correct interpretation of the New Testament:

> The formality, i.e., the lack of all content, ought to make the question really open so that the material would completely determine the answer. Instead we find that this formality disturbs the comprehension of the material. This must mean that the formalism itself, the critical approach, the striving after a formal, critical philosophy of this kind contains in reality a concrete, pregnant conception of life which clashes with the concrete, pregnant faith which is found in the New Testament. What is said in the New Testament is based on the presupposition that God has done a great deal in reference to mankind *before* he sent Jesus Christ into the world. It is impossible to come to this historical material with a question that is not determined by the biblical faith, and then select from this material only this one part, the New Testament, in order to force an answer from these sources to a categorical and fundamental question which is unrelated to those sources.[50]

C. *Gustaf Wingren's Systematic Theology*

The groundwork has been laid and all is now prepared for Wingren's positive theological statement. *Creation and Law* was written as a natural consequence of Wingren's concern for preaching and theological method. But *Creation and Law* cannot be considered without viewing it in relation to *Gospel and Church:* "one cannot discuss Gospel and Church *in vacuo* without affecting the proper interpretation of Creation and Law." Wingren contends, too, that he is concerned with the content and not the method of theology.[51]

---

[50] Wingren, *op. cit.,* p. 19.

[51] Wingren's *Theology in Conflict* dealt with methodological questions but only in a negative way, illustrating that Nygren, Barth and Bultmann's description of the content of Scripture was *dependent on the method* each used. The chief intention of *Theology in Conflict* was therefore that of asking basic questions about theological *method* without at the same time resolving those questions. The response to *Theology in Conflict* was twofold: there was a call for Wingren to deal with his own understanding of theological method (this was H. Richard Niebuhr's point in his American review of *Theology in Conflict*), as well as with his own explanation of the content of Scripture. Wingren insists that these two volumes deal with the *content* of Scripture. *Cf. Creation and Law,* pp. 192–193.

The Apostles' Creed and the Nicene Creed are Trinitarian in form, Wingren asserts. Faith in God the Creator, in Jesus Christ crucified and risen, and in the Spirit and its edifying work in the Church, was a *regulative* principle in the theological affirmations of the Early Church, which has been articulated in these two creedal formulae. But it was the affirmation of God's Creation which was first in the Trinitarian Creed, and part of a confessional act which was not articulated with full force until the time of the Gnostic heresies. Belief in God's creation was *not* a point at which the Christian Church became forced into creedal difficulties with their Jewish brethren. God, as the Lord of all creation, to whom "every knee shall bow, every tongue shall swear" (Isaiah 45:23) is prefigured in the similar statement about Jesus in Philippians 11:10. The New Testament, however, does not fail to give full value to the affirmation that God has created the world. This dogma emerged as soon as the Church encountered the Gentile world. Creation stands first in the Trinitarian Creed, because it is first in the Holy Scriptures—that is, in the Holy Scriptures which the Early Church used.[52] The primary works of God, which are spoken of in the confessions of faith of the Church, are recited in the order in which God has performed them (and continues to perform them)—Creation, the Incarnation, the Death and Resurrection of Christ, the outpouring of the Spirit and the Last Judgment. The congregation which assembles for an act of Baptism or the Eucharist and confesses the Trinitarian Creed, is also confessing that they are God's creations and possessions and that the account of the fall in the Bible describes their own condition. They are confessing that Christ is their Lord, and that his power is still contending with evil, and that the Spirit is gathering them to form the Church, in which community they await the coming Judgment and Resurrection.[53]

Wingren is critical of any attempt to put the doctrine of Creation in a secondary place in relation to the revelation of God in Christ. This attempt is misguided, he says, in that it assumes that we men

---

[52] Wingren, *Creation and Law, op. cit.*, p. 8.
[53] *Ibid.*, p. 10.

may acquire certainty about the work of God in Creation *only* by hearing and receiving the Gospel of his activity in the Incarnation. But that assumption, he asserts, is one which places man and the knowledge of God (or the lack of it, without revelation) in the center of theology, rather than God and his works. Revelation is necessary to understand Creation; without it, there is *no* natural knowledge of God. Such a conception of revelation, however, does not comprehend Creation as "the continuing work of God, which is independent of the Gospel." Wingren wants to reintroduce the notion of God and his Creation into the central place in theology, which coincides with the first article of the Creed. By so doing, he rejects all "liberal" attempts (including the "anti-liberal" Barth) which makes man and his knowledge (man's progress from the lack of knowledge to the attainment of knowledge) the essence of the idea of theological creativity.[54]

Wingren rejects a theological framework in which the sequence of God's events is disrupted at a particular point, even if that point is the revelation of God in Christ. Wingren notes that in the theology influenced by Barth, the relation between present time and the eschatological future is not characterized by the note of expectation that God will continue to act in the future. The Nicene and Apostles' Creeds enumerate the events which have taken place, but when they pass from the present (God's work is Christ's rule at the right hand of the Father), the verbs become future: "He shall return," "He shall judge," "of His kingdom there shall be no end." The belief in the work that God has already done points directly to what He still shall do. The theology which begins with the

[54] Wingren's criticism of Barth on this point is crucial: "From the theological aspect, the critical point in these writings of Barth is the role which *knowledge* plays with regard to the order of precedence in the doctrines with which he is dealing. Since the Law is revealed and its meaning fully perceived only when the Gospel is revealed, Gospel has priority over Law. Since social righteousness is comprehended within justification, justification has priority over justice. And since only the Church is aware of the basis on which the State rests, the Church has priority over the State. This theological approach makes human knowledge and insight the organizing principle for the sequence of the acts of God within the confession of faith. In so doing, however, it displaces the order of God's acts, and in fact it is the sequence in which we acquire knowledge of God which comes to determine the order of the confession." *Ibid.,* p. 13.

second article of the Creed (that is, the revelation of God in Christ) assumes that the meaning of God's work in Creation is gained only through the Incarnation. "It therefore clearly tends to let the relationship of the aeschatological consummation to the present time be conditioned by the fact that the future—which, according to the New Testament, will bring perfect vision, sight face to face—will bestow still greater certainty than faith in Christ at present possesses." [55]

What Wingren is anxious to reintroduce into modern theology is Luther's use of "personal pronouns," the *pro mei, pro nobis,* to describe to whom God's work is directed. The mighty acts of God are intended for man, man in Creation, man who receives his life from God, and man who is sought and redeemed in these acts by God who is *both* Creator and Redeemer. Much of modern theology, Wingren insists, is built upon an already existing philosophical anthropology (as in Bultmann), with the result that theology is based not upon the whole Bible, but upon the New Testament alone. The Bible, however, Wingren reminds his readers, is the Word which God speaks to man concerning Creation, the same man who later defies God. To begin with Creation and man in Creation is to begin at the point from which the mighty acts of God develop which point these acts "recapitulate." [56] Wingren's original thesis may be summarized as follows:

The main point which I shall make is that it is only on the basis of the Old and New Testaments together, and by commencing with the work of Creation, i.e. the order which the trinitarian Creed represents, that it is possible to escape the false alternative of an early Christian faith expressed in a purely theoretical form, or an anthropology derived from philosophy. The Old Testament describes a humanity which has been created by God and has turned from God, and which, represented by the peculiar people who had been chosen for the salvation of the whole of the human race, could do no more than await the outpouring of the Spirit. This humanity which awaits the Spirit, created by God, and subject to the discipline of the Law, is the same humanity into which the Spirit comes in the present time through the Gospel and the Church. The Old Testament fulfills the legitimate theological need of

---

[55] *Ibid.,* p. 14; cf. *Die kirchliche Dogmatik,* Vol. III, pt. III.
[56] *Ibid.,* p. 16; cf. pp. 18 ff. for discussion of Irenaeus' relation to the Old Testament doctrine of Creation.

an anthropology, and deals with men on as high a level as the New Testament. All that the New Testament bestows and promises—the forgiveness of sins, the resurrection of the dead, and life eternal, which in part is already a present experience, and in part is still a future hope—all these blessings are not given in a vacuum, but are always given to *man,* whose creation and defeat are described in Genesis. In the "new covenant" the works of God right up to the Last Judgment are always works of restoration and recapitulation.[57]

Wingren's anthropology, then, is one which is derived from the conception of man in the Genesis account of Creation. Man is born, and lives, yet never ceases to be *created* from beginning to end. The relationship of God to man is given in and with life itself. This relationship may assume the characteristic of wrath and judgment, or of forgiveness and mercy. Whatever form it takes, it begins by being the relationship between God, the creator, and man, a *living creature.* Wingren makes it clear too that the relationship is not dependent upon any intellectual assent to the existence of God. Man may question God's existence and doubt his presence in the world. But the relationship between God and man is given with life itself, and even after man ceases to use the term God or believe in him, he is related to him.

The doctrine of Creation forces us to speak of God in an anthropomorphic way:

As soon as we begin with the work of Creation as the first of God's works, it follows clearly that we must adhere to a simple anthropomorphic account of the subsequent works of God, to which both the Bible and the Creed testify. In the extension of the act of Creation there lies the life of a man (Jesus Christ), whose circumstances form the substance of the Gospel (the second article), and the Church, the very gathering of which initiates the events of the last period (the third article).[58]

Such a conviction, however, has important methodological implications for Wingren. The most adequate starting point for methodology, Wingren writes, is "that which proceeds on the one side from a given empirical fact, e.g., the fact that certain scriptures have

[57] *Ibid.,* p. 16.
[58] *Ibid.,* pp. 23-24.

been and are being expounded to men." On the other side it makes few assumptions concerning the significance of this fact. Wingren calls this interpretation of Scripture the phenomenological starting point for the relatively exact historical discipline of theology; at the same time, there is room, he believes, for systematic judgments regarding those facts: "The actual demands under which man lives are reinterpreted by the proclamation which is directed to him, and which extends to a belief in Creation from which these demands take their meaning." [59]

Wingren believes that he has rid himself of extraneous philosophical presuppositions for his theological methodology. He argues that philosophy seduces man into affirming and believing a total world view, an outlook which philosophy is incapable of supporting. A world view (and an attitude toward life) is possible only in religion. The Christian faith provides a world view *precisely* because the Christian faith is concerned with a belief in Creation and all that follows from that affirmation. When belief in the Creation is lost, the theologian must then attempt to find a world view elsewhere, and it is just at this point that he is tempted by alien philosophical systems. To begin with the second article of the Creed is to be seduced into accepting a philosophical framework which intrudes into a Biblical interpretation of the *kerygma.*

Wingren stresses his conviction that the Christian faith is primarily faith in Creation. If Creation is denied, many of the essential doctrines of the Christian faith are irreparably altered. The doctrine of Creation must be the starting point for Christian theology. Only then does Christian theology deal with God as he is related to human life in all of its ramifications. Wingren's point of departure is, therefore, the fact of Creation itself, i.e., the fact that man lives, and that he has been given life.[60]

Wingren believes that his interpretation of man and Creation avoids many of the difficulties of natural theology. By asserting belief in Creation one does not mean primarily that the world has been

[59] *Ibid.*
[60] *Ibid.*, pp. 27, 29, 31.

created, but rather that "God has created me and all creatures." Man's relation to the Creator is given through *life* itself. With this affirmation as the starting point, Wingren believes he can avoid many of the perplexing problems in theology, especially those which are centered about the doctrine of the *imago Dei:*

> To say that man, as a creature who has been born on earth, is created in Christ, is to use a term which is quite unmythological. It means simply that what man is offered in the incarnate Son is "life." The Creator who lets man live and who thereby creates him, creates him in His image (Gen. 1:25f.), and this image in which every man has been created is Jesus Christ, who is "the image of the invisible God, the first-born of all Creation" (Col. 1:15). The "new man" whom the believer in Christ "puts on" (Rom. 13:14; Gal. 3:27) is Christ Himself. This is what God the Creator intended man to be in Creation. To become like Christ, therefore, is also to conform to God's will in Creation and to receive "life" (cf. Col. 3:10; Eph. 4:24).[61]

The first article of the Creed testifies to the life which man possesses, which he will continue to possess as long as God bestows life upon him. Man can be regarded in a correct relationship to God, as the one who receives his life from the Creator. The central significance of the second article of the Creed is not the attainment of *knowledge,* but rather the fact of Incarnation. When Creation is permitted to describe man's relationship to God—in God man lives, moves and has his being, that is, man receives life from God *unceasingly*—then the Incarnation can serve to mean the work of salvation that restores man. Wingren quotes Hebrews 2:14 "Since therefore the children share in flesh and blood, He himself likewise partook of the same nature, that through death He might destroy him who has the power of death, the devil." The work of salvation, which restores man, takes place on the basis of Creation. "The article of the Creed which refers to Creation must precede the second article which deals with redemption, even when the Creation referred to is Creation in Christ." The order of these two does *not* represent the sequence in the acquisition of knowledge of God, but always the sequence of God's dealings with us.

[61] *Ibid.,* p. 35.

Wingren introduces the doctrine of the Law within the context of the doctrine of Creation. When the Gospel is preached, that is, the proclamation of Christ's birth, life, death and Resurrection, it is preached to men who have the events of Genesis 1 and 2 in their own history. Creation is repeated in every birth, the Fall in man's egocentric attempt to guarantee his own freedom. The condemnation of the law is experienced by every man in the midst of his bondage and constraint. But when the Gospel is preached, it permits man to interpret his life in the light of the faith-declaration: "I am God's lost Creation: I believe—help Thou mine unbelief!" It is left to man to make this interpretation; he may acknowledge, or refuse to admit, that life has been given but has been wasted.

The demands of the law, Wingren believes, bind man inextricably to the Creator. The content of the law is marked by its ability to act as a continuing rein on evil. This positive conception of the law is necessary for Wingren, in order for him to affirm the unity of the Bible, that is, that it is the same God who is at work from the beginning to the end of creation. The *pedagogical* function of the law and the *regenerating* work of the Gospel both aim at the realization of God's decree for Creation, *making man into the image of God*, that is, *making him like Christ, who is the "image of God."*

The law is *regulative* in human life, that is, it functions in such a way as to legislate regarding right behavior in society, and to protect and preserve life. But the law has another function; it "puts to death":

God's will to chastise, but also to give life and to sustain, which according to Gen. 3 and 9 was the consequence of human sin, and issued in the covenant after the flood, is so deeply implanted in all human life and so fundamental, that all life is lived only under this divine decree. Daily toil, the punishment of the murderer, and conception and birth are all part of it. Death too is part of it. God uses death in His government of the world (Gen. 9:5f.) in order to protect life, and preserve it by means of death. [62]

But the quality of mercy is also present in the law. The law is the "hardened" will of God, but it is the same divine will which God

[62] *Ibid.*, p. 133.

revealed in his gift of life to man in Creation. But now his will is opposed by all of that which must die—sin, the devil and the "old man." When the Sermon on the Mount forbids man to resist evil with force, it is in a real sense commanding him to love his neighbor. Wingren explains this apparent contradiction:

To employ force for its own sake is to set oneself over the wicked neighbour, even though he is guilty. But it is characteristic of civil office or "government" that it never considers its own ends. When a judge punishes harshly, it is not he himself who has been wronged, and if it is, he has no right to judge his own case. The judge is not representing his own personal reaction to the offense, but the reaction which God wills to be produced by any violation of His commandments. The judge is merely the instrument of God in effecting His will. God then uses human hands and voices in order to check the course of evil, just as He uses the judge or soldier to protect and benefit even the judge's or the soldier's own fellow beings. It is this same power, love of one's neighbour, which in my case compels me to abandon all use of force, but for my neighbour's sake compels me to take up arms to defend and "serve" him.[63]

Wingren recognizes that the powers of an earthly government can also be abused. But God can use for good what man misuses for evil.

Wingren ascribes two uses to the law. (In this it is clear he is adopting Luther's conception of the law.) The first use of the law is its *civil* use, that is, the law as it is operative in the external world. The second use of the law is its *spiritual* use, the revelation of God to man's conscience (the judging and guilt-revealing function of the Law). However, it is in Creation that both uses of the law are discovered. God's demand that men should continue to "have dominion" over Creation is part of his continuing Creation of the world. But his wrath and judgment are also evident in Creation, even when man is evil, disobedient and hostile.

The first use of the law is summarized by Paul in the single commandment "You shall love your neighbor as yourself" (Rom.

---

[63] *Ibid.*, p. 137. This argument is crucial for Wingren's social ethic. He asserts that we often display greater kindness toward our neighbor and interest in his well-being in the use of force than in our refusal to take up arms for his protection. The mercy of earthly government is God's own mercy!

13:9; Gal. 5:14). For Paul the love of one's neighbor is the same as the love of God, which means the same as man's free dominion over the things of Creation. Man's act of sin in the Fall disrupts all of these relationships. The sinner who separates himself from God also separates himself from the neighbor. Sin, therefore, has broad ramifications—it disturbs one's relationship to God, his neighbor and the world. The sinner, who separates himself from God (in isolation from him), also separates himself from his neighbor (in isolation from him). "Fear of 'losing one's life' is a part of unbelief (in relation to God) and suppresses any willingness I may have to give of myself (to my neighbor), and forces me to bow down and cleave to some part of God's good creation (in idolatry)." [64] When the Bible sums up all of the demands of the law in love for one's neighbor, it is stating the fact that the law has the power to compel all men to act on behalf of their neighbor.

The second use of the law is its "essential" use. The law, employed in this way, burdens man's conscience with guilt, sets him as guilty before God, and designates him as a captive and a sinner. Guilt *coram Deo* cannot be separated from the guilt one feels in regard to one's fellow man. The guilt which man experiences is occasioned by a concrete experience of guilt (in man's refusal to trust in God and love his neighbor). There is therefore a relationship between the first and second uses of the law in regard to guilt. When guilt is defined in terms of the first use of the law, it is the force which compels men to act for the advantage of others. But it also speaks of man who *does* the law: the first work of the law, that of compulsion, passes to the second work of the law, that of accusation.

The second use of the law, seen again in terms of the phenomenon of guilt, may be considered as an indicator of *health,* that is, health in the form of revealing to me what I ought to be. It bears in itself the image in which I have been created. Even as it accuses, it points to the original condition of Creation, and recommends me to him who alone can make me human again (Col. 1:15; Gen. 1:26).

[64] *Ibid.,* pp. 150–151.

The volume *Gospel and Church* completes Wingren's systematic theological statement. Wingren begins by asserting that preaching and the sacraments are events through which Christ encounters man in the present. When preaching, baptism and the Eucharist are received by man as gifts from God, then the Church comes into being. Those who are in the Church are the recipients of these gifts. The Church becomes, therefore, the "gathering together of those whose lives have been restored, redeemed, and delivered under their Lord in whom all things have been created from the beginning." [65] Their lives have been created by God, but they remain fallen creatures. When Christ comes to them in grace, he gives them back the lives they have lost. The salvation which Christ offers to man is the restoration of his corrupt humanity.

The Gospel must, of necessity, precede the Church. The Gospel gave birth to the Church, and governs the ongoing life of the Church. The Church is "the first fruits of a restored humanity," which means that it possesses already in essence, albeit in anticipation, the fulfillment of God's promises to man in Creation. The man in the Church is, therefore, man in the created world, man who has been freed to use God's creation in a proper way.

The Sacraments celebrated by the Church enable man to be included within Christ's continuing work of the restoration of humanity. The Sacraments of Baptism and the Eucharist have no meaning in the present apart from man's participation in them. Man who participates in the Sacraments has been made in the image of God, but is far from realizing that image. Man's real life consists in what he tastes and experiences, and not in what he is in himself.[66]

---

[65] Wingren, *Gospel and Church, op. cit.*, p. 5.
[66] *Creation and Law, op. cit.*, p. 196. "For them [men in the Church] the Sacraments are the means of participating in Christ. The work of Christ is the opposite of the work of Adam, and the course of events described in the Gospel is the opposite of that described in man's prehistory. The new Creation has already begun, and therefore the Church is filled with the song of praise. Since the work of Christ in His ministry on earth reverses Adam's fall, it has the effect of restoring and recapitulating human life. The centre of this saving work is His death and resurrection, and we are ingrafted into Christ in His death and resurrection through Baptism. The Adam who is snatched from the dominion of darkness and given in Baptism the life for which he was created is no more a creature of the past than Christ is, but is man, this man who is being

The original purpose of man is fulfilled within the Church. To be incorporated into the Church is to become truly man and be released from a life which is less than human to a life in which humanity is complete. Baptism makes a man truly human, and not simply a member of a particular church. The Eucharist enables man to die and rise again here and now "on the level of daily life."

Christ's death and Resurrection can become objects of hope for man, but also for all of humanity. We can never become truly human, Wingren says, unless we participate in Christ's death and Resurrection. Participation may occur within the Church, within a congregation of men and women who have experienced God's activity in the world, and who have the same humanity as everyone else, the same sorrow, sin, temptation, joy, etc.

The Eucharist is the celebration within the Church of God's presence in Christ within the Christian community. In the Eucharist, God gives himself to man, and acts on man's behalf; he comes in Christ and gives salvation to those who await him. "The Gospel is at work in the Eucharist, and in it Christ is continually giving Himself anew to His gathered people." The Eucharist must also be understood in terms of its social relevancy, in terms of the Christian's service to his neighbor. Christ's real presence in the Eucharist highlights the work that Christ is doing right here in the world.

Baptism brings man into the events of the death and Resurrection of Christ, the same Christ who comes to us in the Eucharist, who brings us there face to face with the events of our death and Resurrection. The communicant who participates in the Eucharist reaches out in faith to "that which is to come" (the eschatological motif) *just* as he leaves the table to become involved in the world and the affairs of men.

It is the Word which comes to man in the Sacraments and in preaching. It is not primarily a written Word but a spoken Word.

---

baptised. Recapitulation takes place in the Church, and is still going on. The epic and narrative aspect of the Sacraments and the Gospel is essentially the same as the epic character of man's prehistory and the narrative of Adam and his descendants. But the Gospel is the account of abundant life, while man's prehistory was the account of the onset of death." *Ibid.*, p. 196. *Cf.* also *Gospel and Church*, p. 9.

It is first the Word of the Creator through which all things have come into being. The Word became flesh in Jesus Christ, who lives and creates again in every Word he speaks to man. By the Word the Church comes into being and is built up. The Word underlies the Sacraments. The Sacraments derive their validity from the Word of God which was spoken by Jesus Christ. Preaching may be conceived of in the same way. The Word of God addresses man in the congregation. The Word commands and also gives, gives of itself. Christ is present, Christ who gives himself to man in the Church.[67]

The Gospel, which the apostles were commissioned to preach to all the nations, must be considered in relation to the Sacraments. The Gospel is first of all a message about something that has happened which is of great importance to those who hear it. This is the "Gospel" in the New Testament. The term Gospels may also refer to the documents which are kerygmatic in character, which proclaim the death and Resurrection of Christ. But as soon as the Gospels tell the story of the last events in Christ's life, the Resurrection and the ascension, they come to an abrupt conclusion.[68]

The Gospel is also the Word which, when preached in the world, is received in a variety of ways—it is a judgment, it effects a crisis in man's life, it points to the end of time, the final judgment, the final separation and fulfillment of man's hopes and fears.

The Gospel is ultimately related to Creation, and in this sense we see its recapitulatory action. "The Gospel is brought to all nations —all those nations of whom the prehistory in Genesis speaks, all of them created, fallen, and disobedient. Every human being on earth is 'in Adam.' But now men are born anew and find their true life in the Gospel which is the creative word and able to bring a 'new creation' into being." [69]

The relation of the Gospel to Wingren's conception of the new Creation is very clear in the following quotation:

[67] *Ibid.*, pp. 18, 19.
[68] *Ibid.*, p. 20. Wingren is dependent in this discussion upon C. H. Dodd's *Apostolic Preaching*, and acknowledges this dependence.
[69] *Ibid.*, p. 21, cf. also, p. 25.

Thus the last times have already begun. Christ has already passed through death and the resurrection and now declares the Gospel from the right hand of the Father. Those who hear Him have not reached their goal but are on the way and death is still ahead of them. But when they hear the Gospel with its word about the Son of man they come to see themselves as they really are and even now have come to their appointed end before the time. Now—in the word of the Gospel—is their judgment and now the offer of life is being made.[70]

In *Gospel and Church* Wingren also employs the concept of recapitulation to delineate the work of the Church. The narratives of prehistory in Genesis deal with other nations beside Israel. But from the call of Abraham onward, the other nations disappear into the background. The New Testament conception of "world mission" brings these other nations back into the picture. God's dealing with Israel has now come to its fulfillment in his dealing with men in Jesus Christ. The situation of the beginning times repeats itself. But the movement is not now from creation to death, but the reverse —from sin and death to life. And it is just for this reason that the Church "stands open on one side to welcome fallen mankind, while on the other side it looks out to the resurrection of the dead." The appeal for conversion on the part of the Church comes to man who is "in Adam." The history of Adam is every man's history. But the Church proclaims that Christ's death and resurrection are events which are opposite to the events of Adam's life. "Baptism brings the individual personally into this experience in which what happened to Adam is reversed and brings him through death to the resurrection." In this way, Wingren attempts to unite the eschatological and recapitulatory elements of the Church with Christology. The Word which goes forth in preaching is an event of the last days, but also the event of the restoration of Creation. But the Word can never be separate from the cross and Resurrection.[71] What occurs in the life of the Church is simply the continuation of what hap-

---

[70] *Ibid.*, p. 22.
[71] In this context, it is evident that Wingren (like Luther) is reluctant to make a sharp distinction between *kerygma* and *didache* in the New Testament.

pened when Christ became man. He became man to restore what God had originally created, that is, life for the "new man."

D. *Biblical Studies*

Uppsala University has traditionally been the scene of the most creative Biblical exegetical work done in Sweden. Biblical studies there were encouraged primarily by the important work of Anton Fridrichsen, who was professor of New Testament Exegesis from 1928–1953. He founded the Uppsala Society of Exegesis and was responsible for the annual *Svensk exegetisk årsbok*. Cosmopolitan by nature, he enhanced his reputation by his unique ability to gather doctoral candidates about him. *En bok om kyrkan* (A Book on the Church) (1942) and *En bok om bibeln* (A Book on the Bible) (1947) both contain important contributions from his pen. *The Root of the Vine* introduced Fridrichsen and other Uppsala Biblical scholars to a larger English-speaking audience, and also revealed the controversial nature of his work.[72] Those scholars influenced by Fridrichsen include Gösta Lindeskog, G. A. Danell, Krister Stendahl (now Frothingham professor of New Testament Theology at Harvard), Harald Sahlin, Harald Riesenfeld, and Bo Reicke (who is at present Professor of New Testament in Basel). *The Root of the Vine* is an important book for an appreciation of what has been called the "Uppsala New Testament School." For Fridrichsen and his followers, the New Testament is a homogeneous book, and the apparently diverging parts are seen to have essentially the same fundamental view of God and his work in Christ.

The idea of the Church (and the early Christian conception of the Church) became central for New Testament exegetical studies at Uppsala. Practically, this meant a close association between the academic community (at least on the part of the New Testament scholars) and the everyday life of the Church.

The dominant figure today in New Testament exegesis at Uppsala (and perhaps in all of Sweden) is Harald Riesenfeld. His interests

[72] Anton Fridrichsen, *The Root of the Vine* (London, Dacre Press, 1953).

are broad and include Biblical and Systematic Theology. He, too, has had a profound influence upon the high church movement in Sweden. His doctorate was entitled *Jesus Transfiguré* (1947). A recent work, *The Gospel Tradition and its Beginnings* [73] criticizes Bultmann's *Formgeschichte*. He argues that Jesus taught the apostles to memorize his words and to communicate them to the newly converted Christians.

Another contemporary New Testament scholar at Uppsala, Birger Gerhardson, in *Memory and Manuscript* (which has as its subtitle "Oral Tradition and Written Transmission in Rabbinic Judaism and Early Christianity"), examines the New Testament in relation to two "traditionalist" groups of materials, those of Rabbinic Judaism and the post-apostolic Church.[74]

Also at Uppsala, the young Biblical scholar Bertil Gärtner has contributed works of importance. *The Theology of the Gospel according to Thomas* and *The Areopagus Speech and Natural Revelation* are important theological studies and have made him known to a wider academic audience than often is the case for a Swedish Biblical exegete.[75]

Hugo Odeberg, professor of New Testament Exegesis at Lund (appointed in 1933, and recently retired), an authority on the Aramaic language of Jesus, has long insisted that New Testament scholars take seriously the Hebrew Scriptures as a background for an understanding of the New Testament. He wrote an important book in 1929 on the Gospel of John entitled simply, *The Fourth Gospel*. More recently he has contributed a *Commentary on Paul's Epistle to the Corinthians* in the Swedish series "Interpretation of the New Testament." Ragnar Bring's *Commentary on Galatians* appeared in the same series, and was published in English in 1962. Anders

---

[73] Harald Riesenfeld, *The Gospel Tradition and Its Beginnings* (London, Mowbray, 1957).

[74] Birger Gerhardson, *Memory and Manuscript* (Uppsala, Almqvist & Wiksell, 1961).

[75] Bertil Gärtner, *The Theology of the Gospel according to Thomas* (New York, Harper, 1961) and *The Areopagus Speech and Natural Revelation* (Acta semin. neotest, upsal., Vol. XXI, Uppsala, 1955).

Nygren's important *Commentary on Romans*, written in 1944, appeared in English translation in 1949.[76]

Henrik Ljungman, a young student of Odeberg's recently published a monograph in English which analyzes the Pauline conception of faith. This work is entitled *Pistis; a Study of its Presuppositions and its Meaning in Pauline Use*. Evald Lövestam, also at Lund, has published (in English) two works of significance: *Son and Savior; A Study of Acts 13:32–37*, and *Spiritual Wakefulness in the New Testament*.[77]

Old Testament exegesis at Uppsala has occasioned controversy over the past half century. The "Uppsala School" of Old Testament studies is a designation used to describe a group of scholars in whose work there is a common emphasis and a common type of solution. Great emphasis is laid on the importance and reliability of oral tradition. The scholars active in this field are for the most part anti-evolutionary in their interpretation of the development of religion, and seek to affirm the continuing positive influence of the cult, and the importance of the role of both king and prophet in the development of the cult. Two aspects of the contributions of the "Uppsala School" to Old Testament research deserve mention here:

1. Biblical Criticism

Ivan Engnell, who was Professor of Old Testament Exegesis at Uppsala before his recent death, asserted that a large part of documentary analysis, indeed of literary criticism in general, must be reworked, because it has performed its function without an adequate appreciation of a reliable oral tradition in the formation of the literature of the Old Testament. The Old Testament developed, he said, not in the "scissors and paste" way advocated by the

---

[76] Hugo Odeberg, *Korintierbreven* (Stockholm, Svenska Kyrkans Diakonistyrelses Bokförlag, 1944) Vol. VII, *Tolkning av nya Testamentet;* Ragnar Bring, *Commentary on Galatians* (Philadelphia, Fortress Press, 1962); Anders Nygren, *Commentary on Romans* (Philadelphia, Muhlenberg Press, 1949).

[77] Henrik Ljungman, *op. cit.*, Lund, Gleerup, 1964. Evald Lövestam, *Son and Savior; A Study of Acts 13:32–37*, (Lund, Gleerup, 1961), and *Spiritual Wakefulness in the New Testament* (Lund, Gleerup, 1963).

literary critics, but rather by the process of oral transmission within circles or schools of tradition: wisdom literature handed down by the scribes and the wise, Psalms by priests and the Temple singers, laws by other priestly groups, the prophetic teaching by communities of disciples, and so on. The material was fixed because it was written down. The process of oral transmission preserved, arranged and expanded material into collections of a specific form.[78]

Professor Geo Widengren, Professor of Comparative Religion at Uppsala since 1940, asserts on the other hand that oral transmission is far less important in the literature of the Middle East than the Old Testament scholars assert. He finds parallels between the literature of Islam and pre-Islamic Arabia and affirms that the mode of transmission depended largely on the general state of scribal culture of the period.[79] Engnell rejects Widengren's approach with its analogies to other oriental literatures, and asserts that the Old Testament literature is *sui generis*.

2. The Theory of Divine Kingship

Engnell, in his doctoral dissertation, *Studies in Divine Kingship in the Ancient Near East* (1943), uses a broad history of religions approach to assert that there was a common king ideology in the Ancient Near East with an accompanying cult pattern of worship among the kings. In the Old Testament, Engnell asserted, the king was regarded as the son of the deity, and at the same time, embodied in himself the entire community. He played a central role in the cult and especially in the New Year and enthronement festivals. The king was responsible for the victory, success and prosperity of the people, and fulfilled his role at the great dramatic cultic festivals in which he literally played the role of the god. At the annual festival the god's epiphany was portrayed, along with his marriage to the

---

[78] Engnell's work is dependent upon the research of others: H. S. Nyberg, *Studien zum Hoseabuche* (Uppsala, 1935), H. Birkeland, *Zum hebräischen Traditionswesen* (Oslo, 1938), and A. Bentzen, *Introduction to the Old Testament I* (Copenhagen, 1948).

[79] G. Widengren, *Literary and Psychological Aspects of the Hebrew Prophets* (Uppsala and Leipzig, 1948).

fertility goddess, his battle with the enemies chaos and death, and his death and resurrection. On the one hand, he was the suffering servant of Jahweh, atoning for the sins of his people; on the other, he was the victorious king who overthrew all alien powers.

Engnell discovers parallel sacral kingships in Egyptian, Mesopotamian, Hittite and West Semitic materials. And although he speaks of a complete fusion of the Canaanite and the desert traditions, he does leave room for a Jahwistic reaction. The prophets who demanded exclusive loyalty to the God of the desert, he asserts, inherited more from Canaan than they had realized. Their idea of God was syncretistic, a combination of Jahweh, El, and Baal; the tension was between contrasting conceptions of the *one deity,* one element of which represented history, the other nature. The prophets were not openly hostile to the cult as is commonly believed, nor was there a complete absence of hope in their message.

The "Uppsala School" of Old Testament Studies has prompted scholars everywhere to revise and rework their interpretations of traditional Biblical material. Although the kingship theory of Engnell and others has stimulated Old Testament scholarship, one would anticipate that it will modify profoundly, rather than replace, the great enduring prophetic interpretation of the Old Testament.

The Professor of Old Testament Exegesis in Lund, Gillis Gerleman, has devoted himself to an examination of the Syriac and Greek translations of the Old Testament. He also contributed the volume on Ruth to the *Biblischer Kommentar, Altes Testament.*[80] Gerleman is also editor (with Lindeskog and H. S. Nyberg) of the *Annual of the Swedish Theological Institute* (ASTI).

II. ADDITIONAL DEVELOPMENTS IN SWEDISH THEOLOGY

It is quite clear that Gustaf Wingren is the leading figure on the theological scene in Sweden today. He has attracted an international audience by his writings, by his travels throughout the Continent, Russia and the United States, and also by his active participation in the Faith and Order movement of the World Council of Churches.

[80] Gillis Gerleman, *Ruth* (Neukirchen, Kreis Moers, Neukirchener Verlag, 1960).

Students from all over the world flock to Lund to study with him, many remaining for the long rigorous period preparing for the Doctor of Theology degree. Sweden has become a center for "the international history of ideas" (as Wingren calls it) and Wingren himself, as the Professor of Systematic Theology, must deal with such diverse dissertation topics as Ragnar Holte's, *Beatitude et sagesse; St. Augustine et le probleme de la fin de l'homme dans la philosophie ancienne* as well as my own, *Nature and the Supernatural in the Theology of Horace Bushnell.*[81]

Wingren's influence upon the Swedish theological scene and the life of the Swedish Church does not exclude others from creative works of scholarship and a similar impact upon the Church. In fact, one senses that Wingren's presence at Lund acts as a catalyst to provoke energetic and exciting theological scholarship throughout all of Sweden. Some mention must be made of these important developments.

A. *Special Scandinavian Theologico-historical Problems.*

As we have seen, there has been a long tradition in Sweden which interprets the task of Systematic Theology in an historical way: the "historising" of Systematic Theology, as some have called it. Although Wingren has been able to break out of this framework (but not until he wrote *The Living Word* and *Creation and Law*), much of the continued theological analysis in Sweden is directed back to some period in the past where "true Christianity" was expressed, or where a true interpreter of the Christian faith was found. For the Swedes (indeed for all Scandinavians), in order better to comprehend their own unique religious past, it becomes necessary to puzzle over the life and times of the Swedish reformers of the Sixteenth Century, the impact of the Middle Ages upon the Church of Sweden, and the Eighteenth Century and its relation to the Reformation. Swedish Church historians still deal with "periods" in their understanding of the development of the Church of Sweden. Pro-

---

[81] Ragnar Holte, *op. cit.*, Paris, Etudes augustiniennes; Worcester, Mass., Augustine Studies, Assumption College, 1962. William A. Johnson, *op. cit.*, Lund, Gleerup, 1963.

fessors Hilding Pleijel and Sven Kjöllerström have contributed significantly to an understanding of the developing life of the Swedish Church. The Swedish Reformers of the Sixteenth Century, Olavus Petri and his brother Laurentius Petri, the first Lutheran archbishop, have recently been made the subjects of a systematic theological analysis.[82]

The Danish "renaissance man" of the Nineteenth Century, N. F. S. Grundtvig, continues to be a subject of Scandinavian discussion. A young docent in Systematic Theology at Lund, Harry Aronson, has written one of the first comprehensive and systematic studies of Grundtvig.[83]

B. Continued Research on Luther.

No one will ever dissuade the Swedes from studying Luther, and the Swedes do not have to apologize for their reliance upon his faithful interpretation of the New Testament gospel. Swedish Lutheran studies, as we have indicated earlier, assume that a direct line can be drawn from the Bible to the Reformation. Luther has become the theologian for all of Christendom. Every Swedish dogmatician and church historian would agree to that. Luther, the Swedes assert, restored what was original in the Early Church, and he did so in the context of the deviationist Catholic theology of the Middle Ages.

Luther research in Sweden, and in Scandinavia, runs the gamut of problems that concern contemporary scholars of Luther. David Löfgren in his doctoral dissertation at Lund, *Die Theologie der Schöpfung bei Luther*, examined Luther's interpretation of the first article of the Creed.[84] Also at Lund, Docent Bengt Hägglund's book *De homine* studied the concept of man in the earlier Lutheran tradition.[85] Gunnar Hillerdal's doctoral dissertation *Gehorsam gegen Gott und Menschen* examines Luther's social ethic.[86]

---

[82] Sven Ingebrand, *Olavus Petris reformatiska åskådning*, (Lund, Gleerup, 1964).

[83] Harry Aronson, Mänskligt och kristet: En studie i Grundtvigs teologie (Stockholm, Bonniers, Svenska Bokförlaget, 1960).

[84] David Löfgren, *op. cit.* (Göttingen, Vanderhoeck & Ruprecht, 1960.) Many Swedish doctoral dissertations are now being written in German and published in Germany, in order to receive a broader readership.

[85] Bengt Hägglund, *op. cit.* (Lund, Gleerup, 1959).

[86] Gunnar Hillerdal, *op. cit.* (Göttingen, Vanderhoeck & Ruprecht, 1954.)

Luther research is definitely a Scandinavian love affair. A Norwegian, E. Thestrup Pedersen, wrote *Luther som skriftfortolker* (1959) (Luther as Interpreter of Scripture); a Dane, Regin Preter, *Der barmherzige Richter* (1961); a Norwegian, Ovar Asheim, *Glaube und Erziehung bei Luther* (1961). Luther is also studied in relation to other theological concerns. The Lund theologian, Bertil Werkström, dealt with "Confession and Absolution in the thought of Luther, Thurneysen and Buchman" in his book *Bekännelse och avlösning;* Gottfried Hornig dealt with Luther and Semler in *Die Anfänge der historisch-kritischen Theologie (Johann Salono Semlers Schriftverständnis und seine Stellung zu Luther)*; and Torsten Bergsten with the Reformation and the Anabaptist leader, Balthasar Hubmaier.[87]

C. Continued Trend toward Less Theological Parochialism.

Swedish theologians continue to demonstrate interest in, and familiarity with, the theological contributions of Continental and British thinkers. Barth and Brunner have long been discussed in Swedish circles, although usually in a critical manner. Barth's greatest influence can be seen in Denmark. Professor Regin Prenter's work on Dogmatic, *Skabelse og genløsning* (3d ed., 1963), and Professor N. H. Søe's work on Theological Ethics, *Kristelig etik* (5th ed., 1962), reveal a close dependence upon Barth.

Two studies of Emil Brunner's thought have appeared in Finland recently: Yrjo Salakka, *Person und Offenbarung in der Theologie Emil Brunners,* 1960; and Ivar H. Pöhl, *Das Problem des Naturrechtes bei Emil Brunner,* 1963.

Wingren has long quoted from Bonhoeffer's writings. Gustaf Aulén in his recent *Dramat och Syblolerna* discusses not only Bonhoeffer but alsJ Bishop John A. T. Robinson, Dag Hammarskjöld, and the Swedish authors Pär Lagerkvist, Harry Martinson, and Hjalmar Gullberg.[88]

---

[87] Bertil Werkström, *op. cit.,* Lund, Gleerup, 1963; Gottfried Hornig, *op. cit.* (Göttingen, Vanderhoeck & Ruprecht, 1961); Torsten Bergsten, *Balthasar Hubmaier; seine Stellung zu Reformation und Täufertum, 1521-1528* (Kassel, Oncken, 1961).
[88] Gustaf Aulén, *op. cit.,* (Stockholm, Diakonistyrelsens Bokförlag, 1965).

The influence of modern British and American analytical philosophy is evident in Swedish philosophy of religion. Professor Hampus Lyttkens, at Lund, is presently engaged in conversations across interdisciplinary lines. But there is no one at present who finds Heidegger (not even the later Heidegger) important for theological methodology or content.

D. *Roman Catholic–Lutheran Conversations.*

Per Erik Persson, the successor to Ragnar Bring in the chair of Dogmatic Theology at Lund, is currently engaged in a systematic analysis of Roman Catholic thought, especially as it engages Luther's theology. Persson serves to interpret Roman Catholicism to his colleagues, as well as to challenge its claims to theological absoluteness and ecclesiastical autonomy.[89] Persson possesses the scholarly abilities to provide a running evaluation of Roman Catholicism in the midst of the radical changes which that Church is effecting in the modern world. His starting point is always the theological one. He insists that the new spirit evidenced by the Roman Catholic Church *cannot* hide the basic theological differences which exist between that Church and Evangelical Protestantism.

But in addition to making his creative study of Roman Catholicism, Persson promises to be the scholar who may effect a bridge between the faculties of theology at Lund and Uppsala. His book *Kyrkans ämbete som Kristus representation* bodes well to stimulate discussion between the Biblical exegetes at Uppsala and the systematic theologians at Lund.[90]

E. *Greater Appreciation of the Role of Søren Kierkegaard in Scandinavian Theology and Church Life.*

Incredible as it may seem, Søren Kierkegaard has not been much discussed in Scandinavian theological circles. To Americans, whose contact with the North is often through the thought of "the melan-

[89] Cf. Per Erik Persson, *Romerskt och evangeliskt* (Lund, Gleerup, 1959); also *Sacra Doctrina* (Lund, Gleerup, 1957) in which St. Thomas' theology is analyzed.

[90] Persson, *Kyrkans ämbete som Kristus representation* (The Ministry as a Representation of Christ; A Critical Analysis of Recent Doctrines of the Ministry) (Lund, Gleerup, 1961).

choly Dane," the absence of Kierkegaard in the ongoing theological discussion would appear odd! [91]

But there is one haven for Kierkegaard studies, not in Sweden but more properly in Denmark. Niels Thulstrup, pastor of the Danish Church in Holbaeck, 60 miles west of Copenhagen, has championed the relevance of Kierkegaard to the modern world, and has written many monographs and articles on the important nineteenth-century philosopher and theologian. He is also the moving force behind the Søren Kierkegaard Selskabet, an international society that attempts to provide an academic forum for scholars interested in pursuing Kierkegaard research. Thulstrup has edited *Kierkegaardiana*, the Society's publication, as well as Kierkegaard's *Letters* (*Breve og Aktstykker vedrørende Søren Kierkegaard*, (I–II,) and other selected works; in addition, he has provided an introductory commentary to the English translations of Kierkegaard's *Philosophical Fragments*. He also edited *A Kierkegaard Critique,* published in the United States in 1962.

F. *Renewed Discussion of Methodological Questions.*

Outside of Nels Ferré's book, *Swedish Contributions,* Nygren's earliest philosophical writings have scarcely been dealt with in the United States. For this reason, the philosophical methodology underlying motif research is not adequately comprehended, nor is there a full appreciation of the philosophical and theological context in which Nygren did his earliest work. As his theological interests shifted to Biblical theology, Nygren wrote more dealing specifically with New Testament exegesis (cf. his *Commentary on Romans* and *Christ and His Church*). The method of motif research remains implicit in these later works, but its place in the theological discipline was no longer explicitly stated.

But all of this is subject to change. Nygren is reported writing a

---

[91] Among the few books on Kierkegaard which have appeared in recent years, two important studies come from Sweden. Valter Lindstrom, now Dean of the Cathedral in Karlstad, has written *Stadiernas teologie* (Lund, Gleerup and Copenhagen, G. E. C. Gad, 1943) and *Efterfölielsens teologi hos Sören Kierkegaard* (Stockholm, Diakonistyrelsens Bokförlag, 1956).

book on the philosophy of religion in which the influence of Wittgenstein for theological method promises to be important. This work was projected in an article "From Atomism to Context of Meaning in Philosophy," which appeared in a *Festschrift* (1963) to the Professor of Theoretical Philosophy at Lund, Gunnar Aspelin.

As a result of Nygren's new book, the whole area of the relation between philosophy and theology will become again an important topic for Swedish theologians. Ragnar Bring, too, continues his interest in methodological questions, and an article dealing with theological method in *Svensk teologisk kvartalskrift* is forthcoming.

Axel Gyllenkrok, at Uppsala, wrote an important book in Swedish entitled *Systematisk teologi och vetenskaplig metod* (Systematic Theology and Scientific Method [1959]), in which he discussed the whole nature of the claim that "theology is a science." Gyllenkrok is essentially critical of such an attempt because he cannot find methods to establish the "unity of the New Testament."

Gustaf Aulén, in a pair of recent books, *Eucharist and Sacrifice* (1956) and *Reformation and Catholicity* (1959), demonstrates again that he is an important theological figure on the Swedish scene. He has attempted to rework traditional Lundensian concerns into the most contemporary of theological problems, especially those prompted by the ecumenical movement and Protestant-Roman Catholic conversations. In *Reformation and Catholicity* he asserts the Lutheran doctrines of the primacy of the work of redemption, and of God's direct relation to man in Jesus Christ through the forgiveness of sins. The Roman Catholic theologian Yves Congar challenges him, in his work *Vrai et fausse dans l'eglise,* and asserts that Reformation theology (and especially the Lutheran confession) has narrowed the Gospel to the perspective *in loco iustificationis.* By so doing, theology cannot deal adequately with the "total work of God in creation," that is, with God as he has revealed himself in nature and history.[92]

One anticipates soon a new confrontation between Wingren and

[92] See Nels F. S. Ferré's trenchant and suggestive article "The Theology of Gustaf Aulén," *The Expository Times,* August 1963, pp. 324–327.

Nygren just on the matter of theological methodology. When Nygren answers Wingren a la Wittgenstein as to the place of the philosophy of religion with regard to Christian theology, the theological sparks are sure to fly. But the confrontation is sure to make evident the critical issues within Swedish theology of the Twentieth Century. I believe they will become evident in polar fashion: Nygren asserting the role of the philosophy of religion in the designation of the theological task, Wingren firmly resisting every attempt to permit an alien discipline to describe the nature and structure of the Gospel; Nygren insisting that religion is a human experience *sui generis,* Wingren rejecting the entire enterprise which characterizes religion as a phenomenon of culture; Nygren employing theology as a descriptive discipline, Wingren insisting that we hear again the Gospel, the Christian message of God as forgiving *agape,* which comes to man who stands already under the claim of God and who is *guilty* . . .

The stage is set for a new confrontation. The issues Nygren and Wingren will be debating are crucial ones for Christian theology; the exchange between the two men (and their hosts of disciples) will be sharp and creative. The Swedish theological scene has once again come profoundly alive.

BIBLIOGRAPHY

Andrae, Tor. *Det osynligas värld*. Uppsala: Lindblad, 1933.
———. *Nathan Söderblom*, 3rd edition. Uppsala: Lindblad, 1931.
———. "Nathan Söderblom som religiös historiker," in *Nathan Söderblom in memoriam* (cf. Söderblom).
Aulén, Gustaf. "Billing," in *Svenskt biografiskt lexicon*, Vol. IV. Stockholm: Bonnier, 1924.
———. *Den allmänneliga kristna tron*, 3rd edition. Stockholm: S.K.D., 1931.
———. *Den kristna försoningstanken, huvudtyper och brytningar*. Olaus Petri lectures given at the University of Uppsala, 1930. Stockholm: S.K.D., 1930.
———. *Den kristna gudsbilden genom seklerna och i nutiden, En konturteckning*. Stockholm: S.K.D., 1927.
———. "Den teologiska gärningen," in *Nathan Söderblom in memoriam* (cf. Söderblom).
———. "Det inkarnerade Ordet," in *Ordet och tron* (cf. Billing).
———. *Die Dogmengeschichte im Lichte der Lutherforschung*. Studien der Luther-Akademie (three lectures). Bertelsmann in Gütersloh, 1932.
———. "Die schwedische Theologie des 19. Jahrhunderts," *Ekklesia* II; *Die Kirche in Schweden*. Gotha: Klotz, 1935.
———. *Dogmhistoria, Den kristna lärobildningens utvecklingsgång från den efterapostoliska tiden till våra dager*, 3rd edition. Stockholm: Norstedt & Söner, 1933.
———. *Herdabrev till Strängnäs stift*, 2nd edition. Stockholm: S.K.D., 1935.
———. *I vilken riktning går nutidens teologiska tänkande?* Stockholm: S.K.S. skriftserie No. 133, 1921.
———. "Kristendom och idealism," in *Svensk teologisk kvartalskrift*, 1932.

Aulén, Gustaf. "Kristendomen och det nutida kulturläget," *Svenska Dagbladet*, Stockholm, March 31, 1935.
———. *Kristendomen och kulturkrisen*. Stockholm: S.K.D., 1936.
———. *Kristendomens etiska åskådning*. Stockholm: S.K.D., 1925.
———. *Kristendomens själ, Tillika ett ord om gammal och ny teologi*. Stockholm: S.K.S. skriftserie No. 148, 1922.
———. "Motiv och föreställning inom teologien," in *Svensk teologisk kvartalskrift*, 1930.
———. *Syndernas förlåtelse*. Uppsala: S.K.S., 1915.
———. *Teologiska studier*, Volumes II, III, and IV. (Private collection and binding)
Aulén, Gustaf, and Rosén, Hugo. *Den kristna tros-och livsåskådningen*. Stockholm: S.K.D., 1924.
Baillie, John, and Martin, Hugh. *Revelation*. London: Faber and Faber, 1937.
Billing, Einar. *De etiska tankarna i urkristendomen i deras samband med dess religiösa tro*, 2nd edition. Stockholm: S.K.D., 1932.
———. *Den svenska folkkyrkan*. Stockholm: S.K.S., 1930.
———. *Försoningen*, 2nd edition. Stockholm: S.K.S., 1921.
———. *Herdabref till prästerskapet i Wästerås stift*. Stockholm: S.K.S., 1920.
———. *Nathan Söderblom in memoriam*, Introduction (cf. Söderblom).
———. *Ordet och tron, till Einar Billing på hans sextioårsdag, den 6 oktober, 1931*. Stockholm: S.K.D., 1931.
Bohlin, Torsten. "Den systematiska teologiens metodfråga," in *Svensk teologisk kvartalskrift*, 1936.
Bring, Ragnar. "Coram deo-coram hominibus," in *Svensk teologisk kvartalskrift*, 1930.
———. "Den svenska Lutherforskningen under de sista tre decennierna i dess samband med den systematiska teologien," Tammerfors (Finland), *Teologiska tidskrift*, 1931.
———. *Dualismen hos Luther*. Stockholm: S.K.D., 1929.

Bring, Ragnar. "Förhållandet mellan tro och gärningar inom Luthersk teologi," Åbo, 1934, in *Acta Academica Aboensis Humaniora*, IX.
———. "Lag och evangelium," in *Svensk teologisk kvartalskrift*, 1936.
———. "Några synpunkter på problemet om nåden och den fria viljan," in *Från skilda tider*, S.K.D., 1937.
———. "Ordet, samvetet och den inre människan," in *Ordet och tron* (cf. Billing).
———. "Paradoxtanken i teologien," in *Svensk teologisk kvartalskrift*, 1934.
———. *Teologi och Religion*. Lund: Gleerup, 1937.
———. *Till frågan om den systematiska teologiens uppgift, Med särskild hänsyn till inom svensk teologi föreliggande problemställningar*. Lund: Ohlsson, 1933.
Eklund, J. A. *Människan och Gud, tankar om religionen*. Stockholm: S.K.S. Vol. I, 1918; Vol. II, 1936.
Engeström (von), Sigfrid. "Tro och erfarenhet," in *Ordet och tron* (cf. Billing).
Göransson, N. J. *Den kristna trons idealitet*. Stockholm: S.K.D., 1934.
Hägerström, Axel. *Die Philosophie der Gegenwart in Selbstdarstellungen*. Leipzig: Merner, 1929.
———. *Festskrift tillägnad Axel Hägerström*. Uppsala and Stockholm: Almqvist & Wiksell, 1928.
———. *Om moraliska föreställningars sanning*. Stockholm: Bonnier, 1911.
Harrie, Ivar. *Tjugotalet in memoriam*. Stockholm: Geber, 1936.
Hök, Gösta. *Värdeetik, rättsetik, kristen kärleksetik, tre alternativ*. Stockholm: Fritze, 1933.
Holmström, Folke. *Det eskatologiska motivet i nutida teologi. Tre etapper i 1900-talets teologiska tankeutveckling*. Stockholm: S.K.D., 1933.
———. *Eskatologisk nyorientering, en komparativ kritisk studie*. Lund: Gleerup, 1937.
———. "Eskatologiska slutperspektiv," in *Svensk teologisk kvartalskrift*, 1936.

Holmström, Folke. "Tre utkast till en eskatologisk totalsyn," in *Svensk teologisk kvartalskrift,* 1935.
Krook, Oscar. *Uppenbarelsebegreppet.* Stockholm: Norstedt, 1936.
Larsson, Hans. *Festskrift tillägnad Hans Larsson den 18 februari,* 1927.
Linderholm, Emanuel. *Från dogmat till evangeliet,* 5th edition: Stockholm: Wahlström & Widstrand, 1926.
Lindroth, A. Hjalmar J. "Diastas och syntes i teologien," in *Svensk teologisk kvartalskrift,* 1936.
————. "Om teologien såsom positiv vetenskap," in *Festskrift tillägnad Axel Hägerström* (cf. Hägerström).
————. *Tron och vetandets gräns. Kritiska synpunkter på den moderna Upsala-filosofien.* Uppsala: Lindblad, 1933.
————. *Verkligheten och vetenskapen. En inblick i Axel Hägerströms filosofi.* Uppsala: Lindblad, 1929.
Lindström, Martin. *Philipp Nicolais kristendomstolkning.* Stockholm: S.K.D., 1937.
Ljunggren, Gustaf. "Den 'aktiva' och den 'kontemplativa' livsformen, Några idehistoriska konturer," in *Teologiska studier* (cf. Stave).
————. "Luthers nattvardslära," in *Ordet och tron* (cf. Billing).
————. "Paradoxen som teologiskt uttrycksmedel," in *Svensk teologisk kvartalskrift,* 1928.
————. *Synd och skuld i Luthers teologi.* Stockholm: S.K.D., 1928.
Niebuhr, Reinhold. *An Interpretation of Christian Ethics.* New York: Harper and Brothers, 1935.
Nygren, Anders. *Agape and Eros. A Study of the Christian Idea of Love.* Vol. I. Authorized translation by A. G. Hebert, London: S.P.C.K., 1932.
————. *Den kristna kärlekstanken genom tiderna. Eros och agape.* Stockholm: S.K.D. Vol. I, 1930; Vol. II, 1936.
————. "Det religionsfilosofiska grundproblemet," *Bibelforskaren,* 1919.
————. *Dogmatikens vetenskapliga grundläggning, med särskild hänsyn till den Kant-Schleiermacherska problemställningen.* Stockholm: S.K.D., 1935.

Nygren, Anders. *Etiska grundfrågor.* Stockholm: S.K.S., 1926.
———. *Filosofisk och kristen etik,* 2nd edition. Stockholm: S.K.D., 1932.
———. *Försoningen, en gudsgärning.* Stockholm: S.K.D., 1932.
———. "Hur är filosofi som vetenskap möjlig?" in *Festskrift tillägnad Axel Hägerström* (cf. Hägerström).
———. "Motivforskning som filosofiskt och historiskt problem" in *Svensk teologisk kvartalskrift,* 1939.
———. *Religiositet och kristendom.* Uppsala: Lindblad, 1926.
———. *Religiöst apriori, dess filosofiska förutsättningar och teologiska konsekvenser.* Lund: Gleerup, 1921.
———. "Söka och finna," in *Festskrift tillägnad Hans Larsson* (cf. Larsson).
———. "Till frågan om teologiens objektivitet," in *Teologiska studier* (cf. Stave).
———. *Urkristendom och reformation, skisser till kristendomens idehistoria.* Lund: Gleerup, 1932.
Nystedt, Olle. *Från studentkorståget till Sigtunastiftelsen: ungkyrkorörelsens genombrottsår.* Stockholm: S.K.S., 1936.
Rodhe, Edvard. *Svenska kyrkan omkring sekelskiftet.* Stockholm: S.K.D., 1930.
Rosendal, Gunnar. *Kyrklig förnyelse.* Pro ecclesia, Osby, 1935.
Runestam, Arvid. "Etikens kristlighet," in *Teologiska studier* (cf. Stave).
———. "Gudstro och självkännedom," in *Ordet och tron* (cf. Billing).
———. *Kärlek, tro, efterföljd; om moralens anpassning efter verkligheten.* Stockholm: S.K.S., 1931.
Siegmund-Schultze, F. (editor). *Ekklesia* II. *Die Skandinavischen Länder; Die Kirche in Schweden.* Gotha: Klotz, 1935.
Söderblom, Nathan. *Den levande Guden. Grundformer av personlig religion,* 2nd edition. Stockholm: S.K.D., 1931.
———. *Nathan Söderblom in memoriam,* edited by Nils Karlström. Stockholm: S.K.D., 1931.

Söderblom, Nathan. *Religionsproblemet inom katolicism och protestantism.* Stockholm: Geber, 1910.

———. *Uppenbarelsereligion; några synpunkter i anledning av Bibeldiskussionen,* 2nd edition. Stockholm: S.K.D., 1930.

Stave, Erik. *Teologiska studier, tillägnade Erik Stave på 65 årsdagen, den 10 Juni, 1922.* Uppsala.

INDEX

Actualization, 59, 210
Agape, 33, 54, 104, 119, 123, 184, 219, 229
Alogical content, 74, 102
Althaus, 166
Andrae, 3, 19
Anglican Church, 2
Aquinas, 127
Aristotle, 113, 115, 118
Athanasius, 125
Atonement, The, 61, 65, 153
Augustine, 106, 125, 238
Aulén, 3, 26; *Agape*, 106; Atonement, 65, 102; Church, 189; Eschatology, 166; Holiness, 130; Resurrection, 172; Revelation, 98

Barth, 27, 48, 228
Bergson, 9
Billing, 3, 6, 8, 11
Björkquist, 18
Bohlin, 3, 19
Boström, 5
Bousset, 7, 167
Bowman, 238
Bring, 33, 150; Knowledge, 69; Law, 151; Man, 145; Paradox, 103; Theological methodology, 48
Brunner, 27, 49
Buddhism, 61, 206, 223

Church, 189
Confucius, 224
Coram deo, 142, 153, 176, 185
Coram hominibus, 142, 176, 178, 185, 197
Culture, 10, 43, 191

Dahlquist, 11

Eklund, J. A., 6 n., 18
Eklund, P., 8
Eros, 62, 108, 119, 123, 237
Eschatology, 24, 28, 165

Eternity, Category of, 44, 202
Ethics, 20, 30, 53, 75, 175
Eucken, 7, 8
Evil, 132

Faith, 21, 23, 103, 146, 159, 202, 214, 237; ——'s dynamic synthesis, 138
Fehr, 8
Fridricksen, 30
Fries, 8

Geijer, 6
Gnostics, 124
Gogarten, 27
Göransson, 6, 18
Gregory of Nyssa, 125

Hägerström, 6, 31, 79, 80
Harnack, 7, 65, 111
Harrie, 22 n.
Herrmann, 7, 8, 41, 77
Hinduism, 61, 223
Hirsch, 26
History, 12, 54, 136, 210
Hjärne, 7
Hocking, 238
Hök, 179
Holiness, 130, 234
Holl, 26
Holmström, 164
Husserl, 30

Idealism, 5, 18, 49, 98, 144

Jen, 224
Jülicher, 110

Kähler, 29
Kant, 26, 30, 36, 84, 199
Karma, 61
Knowledge, 69, 153
Krook, 98

303

Lao-tse, 224
Law, 150, 232
Lessing, 12
Liberalism, 5, 16, 49
Linderholm, 4, 16
Lindroth, 31, 193
Ljunggren, 139, 142
Luther, 24, 26, 53, 88, 107, 128
Lutherforschung, 24, 26, 142, 155

Man, 141, 235
Mandel, 77
Marcion, 106, 124, 133
Mayer, 77
Melanchthon, 27
Metaphysics, 12, 35, 48, 80, 107
Methodius of Olympia, 125
Mohammedanism, 22
Mysticism, 9

Nature, 136, 144
Naumann, 77, 196
Neo-Platonism, 115, 116
Niebuhr, 239
Nietzsche, 87, 89
Nirvana, 60, 206
Normative, 31, 49, 80, 215
Norström, 8
Nygren, 30, 36; *Agape*, 108; Atonement, 160; Culture, 192; Ethics, 76, 178; History, 60; Transcendental deduction, 41
Nystedt, 6 n.

Plato, 113
Psychology, 20, 32, 51, 144, 162

Qua homo, 155

Realization, 59, 210
Reason, 10, 15, 23, 209
Reitzenstein, 111
Resurrection, 21, 172
Revelation, 98, 203, 222, 235

Ritschl, 7, 8
Roman Catholic Church, 56
Rosén, 78
Rosendal, 23
Runestam, 3, 19
Rydberg, 7

Sahlin, 5
Scheler, 20
Schleiermacher, 31, 52, 59, 78
Schweitzer, 167
Science, 21, 209, 217
Scientific method, 5, 7, 34, 46, 79, 90
Segerstedt, 4
Sigtuna Foundation, 19
Simul iustus et peccator, 162, 178, 190
Söderblom, 4, 6, 8, 9
Sola gratia, sola fides, 31, 50, 155, 163
Stange, 26
Stave, 7
Stoicism, 29, 226
Sui generis, 41, 44, 84, 201
Süskind, 77

Tertullian, 125
Transcendental, 30, 38, 52, 85
Troeltsch, 7, 30, 77
Typological, 10, 16

Value judgment, 31, 50, 204

Weiss, J., 167
Wellhausen, 6, 7, 12
Wendt, 78
Westman, 11
Wikner, 5

Young Church Movement, 18

Zagreus myth, 113, 115
Zeller, 117

Selected titles: revised December, 1967

harper ⚜ torchbooks

HUMANITIES AND SOCIAL SCIENCES

American Studies: General

LOUIS D. BRANDEIS: Other People's Money, *and How the Bankers Use It* ‡ TB/3081
HENRY STEELE COMMAGER, Ed.: The Struggle for Racial Equality TB/1300
CARL N. DEGLER, Ed.: Pivotal Interpretations of American History Vol. I TB/1240; Vol. II TB/1241
A. S. EISENSTADT, Ed.: The Craft of American History: *Recent Essays in American Historical Writing* Vol. I TB/1255; Vol. II TB/1256
CHARLOTTE P. GILMAN: Women and Economics. ‡ *Ed. by Carl N. Degler with an Introduction* TB/3073
MARCUS LEE HANSEN: The Atlantic Migration: 1607-1860. TB/1052
JOHN HIGHAM, Ed.: The Reconstruction of American History△ TB/1068
ROBERT H. JACKSON: The Supreme Court in the American System of Government TB/1106
LEONARD W. LEVY, Ed.: American Constitutional Law TB/1285
LEONARD W. LEVY, Ed.: Judicial Review and the Supreme Court TB/1296
LEONARD W. LEVY: The Law of the Commonwealth and Chief Justice Shaw TB/1309
HENRY F. MAY: Protestant Churches and Industrial America TB/1334
RICHARD B. MORRIS: Fair Trial: *Fourteen Who Stood Accused, from Anne Hutchinson to Alger Hiss. New Preface by the Author* TB/1335
RALPH BARTON PERRY: Puritanism and Democracy TB/1138

American Studies: Colonial

BERNARD BAILYN: The New England Merchants in the Seventeenth Century TB/1149
JOSEPH CHARLES: The Origins of the American Party System TB/1049
HENRY STEELE COMMAGER & ELMO GIORDANETTI, Eds.: Was America a Mistake? *An Eighteenth Century Controversy* TB/1329
CHARLES GIBSON: Spain in America † TB/3077
LAWRENCE HENRY GIPSON: The Coming of the Revolution: 1763-1775. † *Illus.* TB/3007
PERRY MILLER & T. H. JOHNSON, Eds.: The Puritans: *A Sourcebook* Vol. I TB/1093; Vol. II TB/1094
EDMUND S. MORGAN, Ed.: The Diary of Michael Wigglesworth, 1653-1657 TB/1228
EDMUND S. MORGAN: The Puritan Family TB/1227
RICHARD B. MORRIS: Government and Labor in Early America TB/1244
WALLACE NOTESTEIN: The English People on the Eve of Colonization: 1603-1630. † *Illus.* TB/3006
JOHN P. ROCHE: Origins of American Political Thought: *Selected Readings* TB/1301

JOHN SMITH: Captain John Smith's America: *Selections from His Writings* TB/3078

American Studies: From the Revolution to 1860

MAX BELOFF: The Debate on the American Revolution: 1761-1783 TB/1225
RAY A. BILLINGTON: The Far Western Frontier: 1830-1860. † *Illus.* TB/3012
GEORGE DANGERFIELD: The Awakening of American Nationalism: 1815-1828. † *Illus.* TB/3061
WILLIAM W. FREEHLING, Ed.: The Nullification Era: *A Documentary Record* ‡ TB/3079
JOHN C. MILLER: Alexander Hamilton and the Growth of the New Nation TB/3057
RICHARD B. MORRIS, Ed.: The Era of the American Revolution TB/1180
R. B. NYE: The Cultural Life of the New Nation: 1776-1801. † *Illus.* TB/3026
A. F. TYLER: Freedom's Ferment TB/1074
LOUIS B. WRIGHT: Culture on the Moving Frontier TB/1053

American Studies: Since the Civil War

MAX BELOFF, Ed.: The Debate on the American Revolution, 1761-1783: *A Sourcebook* TB/1225
W. R. BROCK: An American Crisis: *Congress and Reconstruction, 1865-67* ○ △ TB/1283
A. RUSSELL BUCHANAN: The United States and World War II. † *Illus.* Vol. I TB/3044; Vol. II TB/3045
EDMUND BURKE: On the American Revolution. † *Edited by Elliot Robert Barkan* TB/3068
THOMAS C. COCHRAN & WILLIAM MILLER: The Age of Enterprise: *A Social History of Industrial America* TB/1054
WHITNEY R. CROSS: The Burned-Over District: *The Social and Intellectual History of Enthusiastic Religion in Western New York, 1800-1850* TB/1242
FOSTER RHEA DULLES: America's Rise to World Power: 1898-1954. † *Illus.* TB/3021
W. A. DUNNING: Reconstruction, Political and Economic: 1865-1877 TB/1073
HAROLD U. FAULKNER: Politics, Reform and Expansion: 1890-1900. † *Illus.* TB/3020
FRANCIS GRIERSON: The Valley of Shadows TB/1246
SIDNEY HOOK: Reason, Social Myths, and Democracy TB/1237
WILLIAM E. LEUCHTENBURG: Franklin D. Roosevelt and the New Deal: 1932-1940. † *Illus.* TB/3025
JAMES MADISON: The Forging of American Federalism. *Edited by Saul K. Padover* TB/1226
ARTHUR MANN: Yankee Reformers in the Urban Age TB/1247
GEORGE E. MOWRY: The Era of Theodore Roosevelt and the Birth of Modern America: 1900-1912 † TB/3022
R. B. NYE: Midwestern Progressive Politics TB/1202
JAMES PARTON: The Presidency of Andrew Jackson, *From Vol. III of the Life of Andrew Jackson* ‡ TB/3080

† The New American Nation Series, edited by Henry Steele Commager and Richard B. Morris.
‡ American Perspectives series, edited by Bernard Wishy and William E. Leuchtenburg.
* The Rise of Modern Europe series, edited by William L. Langer.
** History of Europe series, edited by J. H. Plumb.
¶ Researches in the Social, Cultural and Behavioral Sciences, edited by Benjamin Nelson.
§ The Library of Religion and Culture, edited by Benjamin Nelson.
Σ Harper Modern Science Series, edited by James R. Newman.
○ Not for sale in Canada.
△ Not for sale in the U. K.

1

FRANCIS S. PHILBRICK: The Rise of the West, 1754-1830. †
Illus.   TB/3067
WILLIAM PRESTON, JR.: Aliens and Dissenters: Federal Suppression of Radicals, 1903-1933   TB/1287
JACOB RIIS: The Making of an American ‡   TB/3070
PHILIP SELZNICK: TVA and the Grass Roots   TB/1230
TIMOTHY L. SMITH: Revivalism and Social Reform: American Protestantism on the Eve of the Civil War △   TB/1229
IDA M. TARBELL: The History of the Standard Oil Company. Briefer Version. ‡ Edited by David M. Chalmers   TB/3071
ALBION W. TOURGÉE: A Fool's Errand. ‡ Ed. by George Fredrickson   TB/3074
GEORGE B. TINDALL, Ed.: A Populist Reader ‡   TB/3069
VERNON LANE WHARTON: The Negro in Mississippi: 1865-1890   TB/1178

Anthropology

JACQUES BARZUN: Race: A Study in Superstition. Revised Edition   TB/1172
JOSEPH B. CASAGRANDE, Ed.: In the Company of Man: Portraits of Anthropological Informants   TB/3047
W. E. LE GROS CLARK: The Antecedents of Man: Intro. to Evolution of the Primates. ᴼᐃ Illus.   TB/559
CORA DU BOIS: The People of Alor. New Preface by the author. Illus.   Vol. I TB/1042; Vol. II TB/1043
DAVID LANDY: Tropical Childhood: Cultural Transmission and Learning in a Puerto Rican Village ¶ TB/1235
EDWARD BURNETT TYLOR: Religion in Primitive Culture. Part II of "Primitive Culture." § Intro. by Paul Radin   TB/34
W. LLOYD WARNER: A Black Civilization: A Study of an Australian Tribe. ¶ Illus.   TB/3056

Art and Art History

EMILE MÂLE: The Gothic Image. § △ 190 illus.   TB/44
MILLARD MEISS: Painting in Florence and Siena after the Black Death. 169 illus.   TB/1148
ERICH NEUMANN: The Archetypal World of Henry Moore. △ 107 illus.   TB/2020
DORA & ERWIN PANOFSKY: Pandora's Box: The Changing Aspects of a Mythical Symbol   TB/2021
ERWIN PANOFSKY: Studies in Iconology: Humanistic Themes in the Art of the Renaissance △   TB/1077
ALEXANDRE PIANKOFF: The Shrines of Tut-Ankh-Amon. Edited by N. Rambova. 117 illus.   TB/2011
OTTO VON SIMSON: The Gothic Cathderal △   TB/2018
HEINRICH ZIMMER: Myths and Symbols in Indian Art and Civilization. 70 illustrations   TB/2005

Business, Economics & Economic History

REINHARD BENDIX: Work and Authority in Industry   TB/3035
GILBERT BURCK & EDITORS OF FORTUNE: The Computer Age: And Its Potential for Management   TB/1179
THOMAS C. COCHRAN: The American Business System: A Historical Perspective, 1900-1955   TB/1080
ROBERT DAHL & CHARLES E. LINDBLOM: Politics, Economics, and Welfare   TB/3037
PETER F. DRUCKER: The New Society △   TB/1082
ROBERT L. HEILBRONER: The Limits of American Capitalism   TB/1305
FRANK H. KNIGHT: The Economic Organization   TB/1214
FRANK H. KNIGHT: Risk, Uncertainty and Profit   TB/1215
ABBA P. LERNER: Everybody's Business   TB/3051
HERBERT SIMON: The Shape of Automation: For Men and Management   TB/1245

Education

JACQUES BARZUN: The House of Intellect △   TB/1051
RICHARD M. JONES, Ed.: Contemporary Educational Psychology: Selected Readings   TB/1292
CLARK KERR: The Uses of the University   TB/1264

JOHN U. NEF: Cultural Foundations of Industrial Civilization △   TB/1024

Historiography & Philosophy of History

JACOB BURCKHARDT: On History and Historians. △ Intro. by H. R. Trevor-Roper   TB/1216
J. H. HEXTER: Reappraisals in History: New Views on History & Society in Early Modern Europe   TB/1100
H. STUART HUGHES: History as Art and as Science: Twin Vistas on the Past   TB/1207
ARNALDO MOMIGLIANO: Studies in Historiography ᴼ △   TB/1288
GEORGE H. NADEL, Ed.: Studies in the Philosophy of History: Essays from History and Theory   TB/1208
KARL R. POPPER: The Open Society and Its Enemies △
    Vol. I TB/1101; Vol. II TB/1102
KARL R. POPPER: The Poverty of Historicism ᴼᐃ TB/1126
G. J. RENIER: History: Its Purpose and Method △   TB/1209
W. H. WALSH: Philosophy of History △   TB/1020

History: General

WOLFGANG FRANKE: China and the West   TB/1326
L. CARRINGTON GOODRICH: A Short History of the Chinese People. △ Illus.   TB/3015
DAN N. JACOBS & HANS H. BAERWALD: Chinese Communism: Selected Documents   TB/3031
BERNARD LEWIS: The Arabs in History △   TB/1029
BERNARD LEWIS: The Middle East and the West ᴼ △   TB/1274

History: Ancient and Medieval

A. ANDREWES: The Greek Tyrants △   TB/1103
P. BOISSONNADE: Life and Work in Medieval Europe ᴼ △   TB/1141
HELEN CAM: England before Elizabeth △   TB/1026
NORMAN COHN: The Pursuit of the Millennium △ TB/1037
CHRISTOPHER DAWSON, Ed.: Mission to Asia △   TB/315
ADOLF ERMAN, Ed.: The Ancient Egyptians   TB/1233
HEINRICH FICHTENAU: The Carolingian Empire: The Age of Charlemagne △   TB/1142
GALBERT OF BRUGES: The Murder of Charles the Good. Trans. with Intro. by James Bruce Ross   TB/1311
F. L. GANSHOF: Feudalism △   TB/1058
DENO GEANAKOPLOS: Byzantine East and Latin West △   TB/1265
MICHAEL GRANT: Ancient History ᴼ △   TB/1190
W. O. HASSALL, Ed.: Medieval England: As Viewed by Contemporaries △   TB/1205
DENYS HAY: Europe: The Emergence of an Idea   TB/1275
DENYS HAY: The Medieval Centuries ᴼ △   TB/1192
J. M. HUSSEY: The Byzantine World △   TB/1057
SAMUEL NOAH KRAMER: Sumerian Mythology   TB/1055
ROBERT LATOUCHE: The Birth of Western Economy: Economic Aspects of the Dark Ages ᴼ △   TB/1290
NAPHTALI LEWIS & MEYER REINHOLD, Eds.: Roman Civilization   Vol. I TB/1231; Vol. II TB/1232
FERDINAND LOT: The End of the Ancient World and the Beginnings of the Middle Ages   TB/1044
ACHILLE LUCHAIRE: Social France at the Time of Philip Augustus   TB/1314
MARSILIUS OF PADUA: The Defender of the Peace. Trans. with Intro. by Alan Gewirth   TB/1310
G. MOLLAT: The Popes at Avignon: 1305-1378 △ TB/308
CHARLES PETIT-DUTAILLIS: The Feudal Monarchy in France and England ᴼ △   TB/1165
HENRI PIRENNE: Early Democracies in the Low Countries   TB/1110
STEVEN RUNCIMAN: A History of the Crusades △
    Vol. I TB/1143; Vol. II TB/1243; Vol. III TB/1298
J. M. WALLACE-HADRILL: The Barbarian West △ TB/1061

History: Renaissance & Reformation

JACOB BURCKHARDT: The Civilization of the Renaissance in Italy △   Vol. I TB/40; Vol. II TB/41

JOHN CALVIN & JACOPO SADOLETO: A Reformation Debate. Edited by John C. Olin TB/1239
G. CONSTANT: The Reformation in England △ TB/314
G. R. ELTON: Reformation Europe, 1517-1559 ** ○ △ TB/1270
WALLACE K. FERGUSON et al.: The Renaissance: Six Essays. Illus. TB/1084
JOHN NEVILLE FIGGIS: Divine Right of Kings TB/1191
FRANCESCO GUICCIARDINI: Maxims and Reflections of a Renaissance Statesman (Ricordi) TB/1160
J. H. HEXTER: More's Utopia TB/1195
HAJO HOLBORN: Ulrich von Hutten and the German Reformation TB/1238
JOHAN HUIZINGA: Erasmus and the Age of Reformation.△ Illus. TB/19
JOEL HURSTFIELD: The Elizabethan Nation △ TB/1312
JOEL HURSTFIELD, Ed.; The Reformation Crisis △ TB/1267
ULRICH VON HUTTEN et al.: On the Eve of the Reformation: "Letters of Obscure Men" TB/1124
ROBERT LATOUCHE: The Birth of Western Economy. ○ △ Trans. by Philip Grierson TB/1290
NICCOLÒ MACHIAVELLI: History of Florence and of the Affairs of Italy TB/1027
GARRETT MATTINGLY et al.: Renaissance Profiles. △ Edited by J. H. Plumb TB/1162
J E. NEALE: The Age of Catherine de Medici ○ △ TB/1085
ERWIN PANOFSKY: Studies in Iconology △ TB/1077
J. H. PARRY: The Establishment of the European Hegemony: 1415-1715 △ TB/1045
BUONACCORSO PITTI & GREGORIO DATI: Two Memoirs of Renaissance Florence: The Diaries of Buonaccorso Pitti and Gregorio Dati TB/1333
J. H. PLUMB: The Italian Renaissance △ TB/1161
A. F. POLLARD: Henry VIII ○△ TB/1249
A. F. POLLARD: Wolsey: Church and State in 16th Century England ○ △ TB/1248
CECIL ROTH: The Jews in the Renaissance. Illus. TB/834
A. L. ROWSE: The Expansion of Elizabethan England. ○△ Illus. TB/1220
GORDON RUPP: Luther's Progress to the Diet of Worms ○△ TB/120
FERDINAND SCHEVILL: Medieval and Renaissance Florence. Illus. Vol. I TB/1090; Vol. II TB/1091
R. H. TAWNEY: The Agrarian Problem in the Sixteenth Century TB/1315
G. M. TREVELYAN: England in the Age of Wycliffe, 1368-1520 ○△ TB/1112
VESPASIANO: Renaissance Princes, Popes, and Prelates: The Vespasiano Memoirs TB/1111

History: Modern European

MAX BELOFF: The Age of Absolutism, 1660-1815 △ TB/1062
EUGENE C. BLACK, Ed.: European Political History, 1815-1870: Aspects of Liberalism TB/1331
ASA BRIGGS: The Making of Modern England, 1784-1867: The Age of Improvement ○△ TB/1203
CRANE BRINTON: A Decade of Revolution, 1789-1799. * Illus. TB/3018
D. W. BROGAN: The Development of Modern France. ○△ Vol. I TB/1184; Vol. II TB/1185
ALAN BULLOCK: Hitler, A Study in Tyranny ○ △ TB/1123
E. H. CARR: German-Soviet Relations Between the Two World Wars, 1919-1939 TB/1278
E. H. CARR: International Relations Between the Two World Wars, 1919-1939 ○ △ TB/1279
E. H. CARR: The Twenty Years' Crisis, 1919-1939 ○△ TB/1122
GORDON A. CRAIG: From Bismarck to Adenauer: Aspects of German Statecraft. Revised Edition TB/1171
DENIS DIDEROT: The Encyclopedia: Selections. Ed. and trans. by Stephen Gendzier TB/1299
FRANKLIN L. FORD: Robe and Sword: The Regrouping of the French Aristocracy after Louis XIV TB/1217

RENÉ FUELOEP-MILLER: The Mind and Face of Bolshevism TB/1188
ALBERT GOODWIN, Ed.: The European Nobility in the Eighteenth Century △ TB/1313
ALBERT GUÉRARD: France in the Classical Age △ TB/1183
CARLTON J. H. HAYES: A Generation of Materialism, 1871-1900. * Illus. TB/3039
STANLEY HOFFMANN et al.: In Search of France TB/1219
LIONEL KOCHAN: The Struggle for Germany: 1914-45 TB/1304
HANS KOHN: The Mind of Germany △ TB/1204
HANS KOHN, Ed.: The Mind of Modern Russia TB/1065
WALTER LAQUEUR & GEORGE L. MOSSE, Eds.: Education and Social Structure in the 20th Century ○ △ TB/1339
WALTER LAQUEUR & GEORGE L. MOSSE, Eds.: International Fascism, 1920-1945 ○ △ TB/1276
WALTER LAQUEUR & GEORGE L. MOSSE, Eds.: The Left-Wing Intellectuals between the Wars, 1919-1939 ○ △ TB/1286
WALTER LAQUEUR & GEORGE L. MOSSE, Eds.: Literature and Politics in the 20th Century ○ △ TB/1328
WALTER LAQUEUR & GEORGE L. MOSSE, Eds.: The New History: Trends in Historical Research and Writing since World War II ○ △ TB/1327
WALTER LAQUEUR & GEORGE L. MOSSE, Eds.: 1914: The Coming of the First World War ○ △ TB/1306
FRANK E. MANUEL: The Prophets of Paris: Turgot, Condorcet, Saint-Simon, Fourier, and Comte TB/1218
KINGSLEY MARTIN: French Liberal Thought in the Eighteenth Century TB/1114
ROBERT K. MERTON: Science, Technology and Society in Seventeenth Century England ¶ TB/1324
L. B. NAMIER: Facing East: Essays on Germany, the Balkans, and Russia in the 20th Century △ TB/1280
L. B. NAMIER: Personalities and Powers △ TB/1186
NAPOLEON III: Napoleonic Ideas: Des Idées Napoléoniennes, par le Prince Napoléon-Louis Bonaparte TB/1336
FRANZ NEUMANN: Behemoth: The Structure and Practice of National Socialism 1933-1944 △ TB/1289
DAVID OGG: Europe of the Ancien Régime, 1715-1783 ** ○ △ TB/1271
JOHN PLAMENATZ: German Marxism and Russian Communism. ○△ New Preface by the Author TB/1189
PENFIELD ROBERTS: The Quest for Security, 1715-1740. * Illus. TB/3016
GEORGE RUDÉ: Revolutionary Europe, 1783-1815 ** ○ △ TB/1272
LOUIS, DUC DE SAINT-SIMON: Versailles, The Court, and Louis XIV △ TB/1250
HUGH SETON-WATSON: Eastern Europe Between the Wars, 1918-1941 TB/1330
A. J. P. TAYLOR: From Napoleon to Lenin: Historical Essays ○ △ TB/1268
A. J. P. TAYLOR: The Habsburg Monarchy, 1809-1918 ○ △ TB/1187
G. M. TREVELYAN: British History in the Nineteenth Century and After: 1782-1919 △ TB/1251
H. R. TREVOR-ROPER: Historical Essays ○△ TB/1269
ELIZABETH WISKEMANN: Europe of the Dictators, 1919-1945 ** ○ △ TB/1273
JOHN B. WOLF: France: 1814-1919 TB/3019

Intellectual History & History of Ideas

HERSCHEL BAKER: The Image of Man TB/1047
R. R. BOLGAR: The Classical Heritage and Its Beneficiaries △ TB/1125
J. BRONOWSKI & BRUCE MAZLISH: The Western Intellectual Tradition: From Leonardo to Hegel TB/3001
NORMAN COHN: Pursuit of the Millennium △ TB/1037
C. C. GILLISPIE: Genesis and Geology: The Decades before Darwin § TB/51
FRANK E. MANUEL: The Prophets of Paris: Turgot, Condorcet, Saint-Simon, Fourier, and Comte TB/1218
BRUNO SNELL: The Discovery of the Mind: The Greek Origins of European Thought △ TB/1018

3

w. warren wagar, Ed.: European Intellectual History since Darwin and Marx — TB/1297
philip p. wiener: Evolution and the Founders of Pragmatism. △ Foreword by John Dewey — TB/1212

Literature, Poetry, The Novel & Criticism

jacques barzun: The House of Intellect △ — TB/1051
james boswell: The Life of Dr. Johnson & The Journal of a Tour to the Hebrides with Samuel Johnson LL.D. º △ — TB/1254
ernst r. curtius: European Literature and the Latin Middle Ages △ — TB/2015
a. r. humphreys: The Augustan World: Society in 18th Century England º△ — TB/1105
richmond lattimore: The Poetry of Greek Tragedy △ — TB/1257
j. b. leishman: The Monarch of Wit: An Analytical and Comparative Study of the Poetry of John Donne º △ — TB/1258
j. b. leishman: Themes and Variations in Shakespeare's Sonnets º△ — TB/1259
samuel pepys: The Diary of Samuel Pepys. º Edited by O. F. Morshead. Illus. by Ernest Shepard — TB/1007
v. de s. pinto: Crisis in English Poetry, 1880-1940 º△ — TB/1260
robert preyer, Ed.: Victorian Literature — TB/1302
c. k. stead: The New Poetic: Yeats to Eliot º △ — TB/1263
paget toynbee: Dante Alighieri: His Life and Works. Edited with Intro. by Charles S. Singleton. — TB/1206
dorothy van ghent: The English Novel — TB/1050
basil willey: Nineteenth Century Studies: Coleridge to Matthew Arnold º△ — TB/1261
basil willey: More Nineteenth Century Studies: A Group of Honest Doubters º △ — TB/1262
raymond williams: Culture and Society, 1780-1950 º △ — TB/1252
raymond williams: The Long Revolution º△ — TB/1253

Myth, Symbol & Folklore

mircea eliade: Cosmos and History § △ — TB/2050
mircea eliade: Rites and Symbols of Initiation: The Mysteries of Birth and Rebirth § △ — TB/1236
theodor h. gaster: Thespis: Ritual, Myth & Drama in the Ancient Near East º △ — TB/1281
dora & erwin panofsky: Pandora's Box △ — TB/2021

Philosophy

g. e. m. anscombe: An Introduction to Wittgenstein's Tractatus. º △ Second edition, Revised — TB/1210
henri bergson: Time and Free Will º△ — TB/1021
h. j. blackham: Six Existentialist Thinkers º △ — TB/1002
crane brinton: Nietzsche — TB/1197
ernst cassirer: The Individual and the Cosmos in Renaissance Philosophy △ — TB/1097
frederick copleston: Medieval Philosophy º △ — TB/376
f. m. cornford: Principium Sapientiae: A Study of the Origins of Greek Philosophical Thought — TB/1213
f. m. cornford: From Religion to Philosophy § — TB/20
a. p. d'entrèves: Natural Law △ — TB/1223
marvin farber: The Aims of Phenomenology — TB/1291
paul friedländer: Plato: An Introduction △ — TB/2017
j. glenn gray: The Warriors: Reflections on Men in Battle. Intro. by Hannah Arendt — TB/1294
w. k. c. guthrie: The Greek Philosophers: From Thales to Aristotle º △ — TB/1008
g. w. f. hegel: The Phenomenology of Mind º △ — TB/1303
f. h. heinemann: Existentialism and the Modern Predicament △ — TB/28
edmund husserl: Phenomenology and the Crisis of Philosophy — TB/1170
immanuel kant: The Doctrine of Virtue, being Part II of the Metaphysic of Morals — TB/110
immanuel kant: Groundwork of the Metaphysic of Morals. Trans. & analyzed by H. J. Paton — TB/1159
immanuel kant: Lectures on Ethics §△ — TB/105

immanuel kant: Religion Within the Limits of Reason Alone. § Intro. by T. M. Greene & J. Silber — TB/67
quentin lauer: Phenomenology — TB/1169
maurice mandelbaum: The Problem of Historical Knowledge: An Answer to Relativism — TB/1338
gabriel marcel: Being and Having △ — TB/310
george a. morgan: What Nietzsche Means — TB/1198
h. j. paton: The Categorical Imperative: A Study in Kant's Moral Philosophy △ — TB/1325
michael polanyi: Personal Knowledge △ — TB/1158
willard van orman quine: Elementary Logic. Revised Edition — TB/577
willard van orman quine: from a Logical Point of View: Logico-Philosophical Essays — TB/566
bertrand russell et al.: The Philosophy of Bertrand Russell Vol. I TB/1095; Vol. II TB/1096
l. s. stebbing: A Modern Introduction to Logic △ TB/538
alfred north whitehead: Process and Reality: An Essay in Cosmology △ — TB/1033
philip p. wiener: Evolution and the Founders of Pragmatism. Foreword by John Dewey — TB/1212
ludwig wittgenstein: The Blue and Brown Books º — TB/1211

Political Science & Government

jeremy bentham: The Handbook of Political Fallacies. Introduction by Crane Brinton — TB/1069
c. e. black: The Dynamics of Modernization: A Study in Comparative History — TB/1321
kenneth e. boulding: Conflict and Defense — TB/3024
crane brinton: English Political Thought in the Nineteenth Century — TB/1071
robert conquest: Power and Policy in the USSR: The Study of Soviet Dynastics △ — TB/1307
robert dahl & charles e. lindblom: Politics, Economics, and Welfare — TB/3037
f. l. ganshof: Feudalism △ — TB/1058
g. p. gooch: English Democratic Ideas in Seventeenth Century — TB/1006
sidney hook: Reason, Social Myths and Democracy △ — TB/1237
dan n. jacobs, Ed.: The New Communist Manifesto & Related Documents. Third edition, Revised — TB/1078
hans kohn: Political Ideologies of the 20th Century — TB/1277
roy c. macridis, Ed.: Political Parties: Contemporary Trends and Ideas — TB/1322
kingsley martin: French Liberal Thought in the Eighteenth Century △ — TB/1114
barrington moore, Jr.: Political Power and Social Theory: Seven Studies ¶ — TB/1221
barrington moore, jr.: Soviet Politics—The Dilemma of Power ¶ — TB/1222
john b. morrall: Political Thought in Medieval Times △ — TB/1076
karl r. popper: The Open Society and Its Enemies △ Vol. I TB/1101; Vol. II TB/1102
john p. roche, Ed.: American Political Thought: From Jefferson to Progressivism — TB/1332
charles i. schottland, Ed.: The Welfare State — TB/1323
benjamin i. schwartz: Chinese Communism and the Rise of Mao — TB/1308
peter woll, Ed.: Public Administration and Policy — TB/1284

Psychology

alfred adler: The Individual Psychology of Alfred Adler △ — TB/1154
arthur burton & robert e. harris, Editors: Clinical Studies of Personality Vol. I TB/3075; Vol. II TB/3076
hadley cantril: The Invasion from Mars: A Study in the Psychology of Panic — TB/1282
herbert fingarette: The Self in Transformation ¶ — TB/1177
sigmund freud: On Creativity and the Unconscious §△ — TB/45

WILLIAM JAMES: Psychology: *Briefer Course* TB/1034
C. G. JUNG: Psychological Reflections △ TB/2001
KARL MENNINGER: Theory of Psychoanalytic Technique TB/1144
ERICH NEUMANN: Amor and Psyche △ TB/2012
MUZAFER SHERIF: The Psychology of Social Norms TB/3072

Sociology

JACQUES BARZUN: Race: *A Study in Superstition.* Revised Edition TB/1172
BERNARD BERELSON, Ed.: The Behavioral Sciences Today TB/1127
KENNETH B. CLARK: Dark Ghetto: *Dilemmas of Social Power.* Foreword by Gunnar Myrdal TB/1317
LEWIS A. COSER, Ed.: Political Sociology TB/1293
ALLISON DAVIS & JOHN DOLLARD: Children of Bondage ¶ TB/3049
ST. CLAIR DRAKE & HORACE R. CAYTON: Black Metropolis △ Vol. I TB/1086; Vol. II TB/1087
ALVIN W. GOULDNER: Wildcat Strike ¶ TB/1176
CÉSAR GRAÑA: Modernity and Its Discontents: *French Society and the French Man of Letters in the Nineteenth Century* ¶ TB/1318
R. M. MACIVER: Social Causation TB/1153
ROBERT K. MERTON, LEONARD BROOM, LEONARD S. COTTRELL, JR., Editors: Sociology Today: *Problems and Prospects* ¶ Vol. I TB/1173; Vol. II TB/1174
TALCOTT PARSONS & EDWARD A. SHILS, Editors: Toward a General Theory of Action TB/1083
ARNOLD ROSE: The Negro in America TB/3048
GEORGE ROSEN: Madness in Society: *Chapters in the Historical Sociology of Mental Illness* ¶ TB/1337
PHILIP SELZNICK: TVA and the Grass Roots TB/1230
HERBERT SIMON: The Shape of Automation △ TB/1245
PITIRIM A. SOROKIN: Contemporary Sociological Theories: *Through the first quarter of the 20th Century* TB/3046
WILLIAM I. THOMAS: The Unadjusted Girl: *With Cases and Standpoint for Behavior Analysis* ¶ TB/1319
EDWARD A. TIRYAKIAN, Ed.: Sociological Theory, Values and Sociocultural Change: *Essays in Honor of Pitirim A. Sorokin* ¶ ○ △ TB/1316
W. LLOYD WARNER & Associates: Democracy in Jonesville: *A Study in Quality and Inequality* TB/1129
W. LLOYD WARNER: Social Class in America TB/1013

RELIGION

Ancient & Classical

J. H. BREASTED: Development of Religion and Thought in Ancient Egypt TB/57
HENRI FRANKFORT: Ancient Egyptian Religion TB/77
G. RACHEL LEVY: Religious Conceptions of the Stone Age and their Influence on European Thought △ TB/106
MARTIN P. NILSSON: Greek Folk Religion △ TB/78
ERWIN ROHDE: Psyche △ § Vol. I TB/140; Vol. II TB/141
H. J. ROSE: Religion in Greece and Rome △ TB/55

Biblical Thought & Literature

W. F. ALBRIGHT: The Biblical Period from Abraham to Ezra TB/102
C. K. BARRETT, Ed.: The New Testament Background: *Selected Documents* △ TB/86
C. H. DODD: The Authority of the Bible △ TB/43
M. S. ENSLIN: Christian Beginnings △ TB/5
JOHN GRAY: Archaeology and the Old Testament World. △ Illus. TB/127
JAMES MUILENBURG: The Way of Israel △ TB/133
H. H. ROWLEY: Growth of the Old Testament △ TB/107
GEORGE ADAM SMITH: Historical Geography of Holy Land. ○ △ *Revised and reset* TB/138
WALTHER ZIMMERLI: The Law and the Prophets: *A Study of the Meaning of the Old Testament* △ TB/144

The Judaic Tradition

MARTIN BUBER: Eclipse of God △ TB/12
MARTIN BUBER: Hasidism and Modern Man. △ *Edited and Trans. by Maurice Friedman* TB/839
MARTIN BUBER: The Knowledge of Man △ TB/135
MARTIN BUBER: Moses △ TB/837
MARTIN BUBER: Pointing the Way △ TB/103
MARTIN BUBER: The Prophetic Faith TB/73
GENESIS: *The NJV Translation* TB/836

Christianity: General

ROLAND H. BAINTON: Christendom: *A Short History of Christianity and its Impact on Western Civilization.* △ Illus. Vol. I TB/131; Vol. II TB/132

Christianity: Origins & Early Development

AUGUSTINE: An Augustine Synthesis. △ *Edited by Erich Przywara* TB/335
W. D. DAVIES: Paul and Rabbinic Judaism: *Some Rabbinic Elements in Pauline Theology* ○ △ TB/146
ADOLF DEISSMANN: Paul: *A Study in Social and Religious History* TB/15
EDWARD GIBBON: The Triumph of Christendom in the Roman Empire. § △ Illus. TB/46
EDGAR J. GOODSPEED: A Life of Jesus TB/1
ADOLF HARNACK: The Mission and Expansion of Christianity in the First Three Centuries TB/92
R. K. HARRISON: The Dead Sea Scrolls ○ △ TB/84
EDWIN HATCH: The Influence of Greek Ideas on Christianity § △ TB/18
GERHART B. LADNER: The Idea of Reform: *Its Impact on Christian Thought and Action in the Age of the Fathers* TB/149
ARTHUR DARBY NOCK: St. Paul ○ △ TB/104
ORIGEN: On First Principles △ TB/311
SULPICIUS SEVERUS et al.: The Western Fathers △ TB/309
JOHANNES WEISS: Earliest Christianity Vol. I TB/53; Vol. II TB/54

Christianity: The Middle Ages and The Reformation

ANSELM OF CANTERBURY: Truth, Freedom and Evil: *Three Philosophical Dialogues* TB/317
JOHN CALVIN & JACOPO SADOLETO: A Reformation Debate. *Edited by John C. Olin* TB/1239
G. CONSTANT: The Reformation in England △ TB/314
JOHANNES ECKHART: Meister Eckhart: *A Modern Translation by R. B. Blakney* TB/8
DESIDERIUS ERASMUS: Christian Humanism and the Reformation TB/1166

Christianity: The Protestant Tradition

KARL BARTH: Church Dogmatics: *A Selection* △ TB/95
KARL BARTH: Dogmatics in Outline △ TB/56
KARL BARTH: The Word of God and the Word of Man TB/13
RUDOLF BULTMANN et al.: Translating Theology into the Modern Age TB/252
NELS F. S. FERRÉ: Swedish Contributions to Modern Theology. *New chapter by William A. Johnson* TB/147
ERNST KÄSEMANN, et al.: Distinctive Protestant and Catholic Themes Reconsidered TB/253
SOREN KIERKEGAARD: On Authority and Revelation TB/139
SOREN KIERKEGAARD: Crisis in the Life of an Actress *and Other Essays on Drama* △ TB/145
SOREN KIERKEGAARD: Edifying Discourses △ TB/32
SOREN KIERKEGAARD: The Journals of Kierkegaard ○ TB/52
SOREN KIERKEGAARD: The Point of View for My Work as an Author § TB/88
SOREN KIERKEGAARD: The Present Age § △ TB/94

SOREN KIERKEGAARD: Purity of Heart △ TB/4
SOREN KIERKEGAARD: Repetition △ TB/117
SOREN KIERKEGAARD: Works of Love △ TB/122
WALTER LOWRIE: Kierkegaard Vol. I TB/89
Vol. II TB/90
JOHN MACQUARRIE: The Scope of Demythologizing: Bultmann and his Critics △ TB/134
WOLFHART PANNENBERG, et al.: History and Hermeneutic TB/254
JAMES M. ROBINSON et al.: The Bultmann School of Biblical Interpretation: New Directions? TB/251
F. SCHLEIERMACHER: The Christian Faith. △ Introduction by Richard R. Niebuhr
Vol. I TB/108; Vol. II TB/109
PAUL TILLICH: Dynamics of Faith △ TB/42
EVELYN UNDERHILL: Worship △ TB/10

Christianity: The Roman and Eastern Traditions

DOM CUTHBERT BUTLER: Western Mysticism § o △ TB/312
A. ROBERT CAPONIGRI, Ed.: Modern Catholic Thinkers △
Vol. I TB/306; Vol. II TB/307
THOMAS CORBISHLEY, S. J.: Roman Catholicism TB/112
G. P. FEDOTOV: The Russian Religious Mind: Kievan Christianity, the 10th to the 13th Centuries TB/370
ÉTIENNE GILSON: The Spirit of Thomism TB/313
GABRIEL MARCEL: Being and Having TB/310
GABRIEL MARCEL: Homo Viator TB/397
FRANCIS DE SALES: Introduction to the Devout Life TB/316
GUSTAVE WEIGEL, S. J.: Catholic Theology in Dialogue TB/301

Oriental Religions: Far Eastern, Near Eastern

TOR ANDRAE: Mohammed § △ TB/62
EDWARD CONZE: Buddhism o △ TB/58
ANANDA COOMARASWAMY: Buddha and the Gospel of Buddhism. △ Illus. TB/119
H. G. CREEL: Confucius and the Chinese Way TB/63
FRANKLIN EDGERTON, Trans. & Ed.: The Bhagavad Gita TB/115
SWAMI NIKHILANANDA, Trans. & Ed.: The Upanishads: A One-Volume Abridgment △ TB/114

Philosophy of Religion

NICOLAS BERDYAEV: The Beginning and the End § △ TB/14
NICOLAS BERDYAEV: Christian Existentialism △ TB/130
NICOLAS BERDYAEV: The Destiny of Man △ TB/61
RUDOLF BULTMANN: History and Eschatology o TB/91
RUDOLF BULTMANN AND FIVE CRITICS: Kerygma and Myth: A Theological Debate △ TB/80
RUDOLF BULTMANN AND KARL KUNDSIN: Form Criticism: Two Essays on New Testament Research △ TB/96
MIRCEA ELIADE: Myths, Dreams, and Mysteries: The Encounter between Contemporary Faiths and Archaic Realities § o △ TB/1320
MIRCEA ELIADE: The Sacred and the Profane TB/81
LUDWIG FEUERBACH: The Essence of Christianity § TB/11
ÉTIENNE GILSON: The Spirit of Thomism TB/313
ADOLF HARNACK: What is Christianity? § △ TB/17
FRIEDRICH HEGEL: On Christianity TB/79
KARL HEIM: Christian Faith and Natural Science △ TB/16
IMMANUEL KANT: Religion Within the Limits of Reason Alone. § Intro. by T. M. Greene & J. Silber TB/67
K. E. KIRK: The Vision of God △ TB/137
JOHN MACQUARRIE: An Existentialist Theology: A Comparison of Heidegger and Bultmann o △ TB/125
EUGEN ROSENSTOCK-HUESSY: The Christian Future or the Modern Mind Outrun. Intro. by Harold Stahmer TB/143
PIERRE TEILHARD DE CHARDIN: The Divine Milieu o △ TB/384
PIERRE TEILHARD DE CHARDIN: The Phenomenon of Man o △ TB/383
PAUL TILLICH: Morality and Beyond TB/142

Religion, Culture & Society

WILLIAM A. CLEBSCH & CHARLES R. JAEKLE: Pastoral Care in Historical Perspective: An Essay with Exhibits. New Preface by the Authors TB/148
C. C. GILLISPIE: Genesis and Geology: The Decades before Darwin § TB/51
KYLE HASELDEN: The Racial Problem in Christian Perspective TB/116
WALTER KAUFMANN, Ed.: Religion from Tolstoy to Camus TB/123
H. RICHARD NIEBUHR: Christ and Culture △ TB/3
H. RICHARD NIEBUHR: The Kingdom of God in America TB/49
TIMOTHY L. SMITH: Revivalism and Social Reform: American Protestantism on the Eve of the Civil War △ TB/1229

NATURAL SCIENCES AND MATHEMATICS

Biological Sciences

CHARLOTTE AUERBACH: The Science of Genetics Σ △ TB/568
W. E. LE GROS CLARK: The Antecedents of Man o △ TB/559
W. H. DOWDESWELL: Animal Ecology. △ Illus. TB/543
R. W. GERARD: Unresting Cells. Illus. TB/541
EDMUND W. SINNOTT: Cell and Psyche: The Biology of Purpose TB/546
C. H. WADDINGTON: The Nature of Life △ TB/580

History of Science

MARIE BOAS: The Scientific Renaissance, 1450-1630 o △ TB/583
W. DAMPIER, Ed.: Readings in the Literature of Science. Illus. TB/512
A. HUNTER DUPREE: Science in the Federal Government: A History of Policies and Activities to 1940 △ TB/573
ALEXANDRE KOYRÉ: From the Closed World to the Infinite Universe △ TB/31
A. G. VAN MELSEN: From Atomos to Atom: A History of the Concept Atom TB/517
STEPHEN TOULMIN & JUNE GOODFIELD: The Architecture of Matter o △ TB/584
STEPHEN TOULMIN & JUNE GOODFIELD: The Discovery of Time o △ TB/585

Mathematics

E. W. BETH: The Foundations of Mathematics △ TB/581
S. KÖRNER: The Philosophy of Mathematics △ TB/547
WILLARD VAN ORMAN QUINE: Mathematical Logic TB/558
FREDERICK WAISMANN: Introduction to Mathematical Thinking. Foreword by Karl Menger TB/511

Philosophy of Science

R. B. BRAITHWAITE: Scientific Explanation TB/515
J. BRONOWSKI: Science and Human Values △ TB/505
ALBERT EINSTEIN et al.: Albert Einstein: Philosopher-Scientist Vol. I TB/502; Vol. II TB/503
WERNER HEISENBERG: Physics and Philosophy △ TB/549
KARL R. POPPER: Logic of Scientific Discovery △ TB/576
STEPHEN TOULMIN: Foresight and Understanding △ TB/564
STEPHEN TOULMIN: The Philosophy of Science △ TB/513

Physics and Cosmology

JOHN E. ALLEN: Aerodynamics △ TB/582
P. W. BRIDGMAN: Nature of Thermodynamics TB/537
C. V. DURELL: Readable Relativity △ TB/530
ARTHUR EDDINGTON: Space, Time and Gravitation: An Outline of the General Relativity Theory TB/510
GEORGE GAMOW: Biography of Physics Σ △ TB/567
STEPHEN TOULMIN & JUNE GOODFIELD: The Fabric of the Heavens: The Development of Astronomy and Dynamics. △ Illus. TB/579